DATE DUE

JY 1 3 '99			
JE 1 ø '00			

DEMCO 38-296

David Brierley has been with the Professional Association of Teachers since 1984, as a full-time solicitor. He has written numerous articles on legal and safety matters affecting schools.

To Rita and the boys

HEALTH AND
SAFETY
IN SCHOOLS

DAVID BRIERLEY

P·C·P
Paul Chapman
Publishing Ltd

While every effort has been made to ensure the accuracy of the material in this book, the author and publishers accept no liability for any errors contained in it.

British Library Cataloguing in Publication Data
Brierley, David 1954
  Health and safety in schools.
  1. Great Britain. Schools. Health & Safety
  I. Title
  371.70941

  ISBN 1−85396−130−2

Typeset by Setrite Typesetters Ltd
Printed and bound by Butler & Tanner Ltd, Frome, Somerset

A B C D E F 6 5 4 3 2 1

CONTENTS

FOREWORD

In recent years, the issue of health and safety in schools has been at the forefront of public debate. Media reports of incidents in and out of school, when children have been placed at risk, have highlighted the duties and responsibilities of teachers to safeguard children in their care.

At the same time, parents have become increasingly litigious in their attitude to what happens to children when they are with their teachers. When accidents occur, the teacher is far more likely today than was once the case to face legal action. The need for professional educators to be well advised cannot be exaggerated.

For the past six years, David Brierley has provided an outstanding service by way of legal advice to the 40,000 members of the Professional Association of Teachers, which is one of the nationally recognized teachers' unions in the United Kingdom. There is a regular stream of letters to the headquarters of the Association, testifying to the teachers' great appreciation of his work.

Anyone who wants to know what the legal position is with regard to health and safety legislation relating to schools will not find a better adviser than David Brierley. This book contains the distillation of his thinking, and constitutes an invaluable source of information and advice for all who have any kind of interest in the subject.

Peter Dawson OBE BSc(Econ)
Derby 1991

PREFACE

Since I joined the Professional Association of Teachers in 1984, I have come across hundreds of teachers who have been injured in school. This came as an enormous shock, as I had assumed that schools were relatively safe places. There have also been many cases of injuries to pupils and there have been pupil fatalities. The most recent accident figures for the education sector have been produced by the Health and Safety Commission in its 1990 Annual Report for the period April 1988 to April 1989. These show that 2 employees were killed, there were 1,061 non-fatal major injuries involving employees and 4,444 injuries to employees lasting more than 3 days. There were 7,791 non-fatal major injuries and 5 fatalities to pupils and other non-employees in education. These figures have been released as provisional figures, and as the Annual Report draws attention to the problem under–reporting, it is likely that in reality there are considerably more serious accidents than are recorded.

It seems to me that writing a book on health and safety at school is worthwhile. I have attempted to show that it is an area of the law which teachers should not forget at a time when they are being bombarded with new legislation, impinging upon many aspects of their day–to–day work. But this book is not primarily a legal work and it should certainly not be regarded as a comprehensive health and safety manual. It is a commentary on health and safety in schools, containing some background information and discussion on a number of safety issues, as well as some illustrations of practical safety measures. The book makes constant reference to expert advice, which is available both at local education authority level and from national bodies, expert in their own field. I make no apology for this because in the health and safety area, there is an enormous amount of expert advice available.

Safety is not simply a matter of rules and regulations; a positive and responsible attitude to safety is all-important for those involved in the care of school children. Schools are exciting places for children, where they can explore, investigate, learn new experiences and test their own initiative, strength and physical attributes. There are many different materials for children to use in school as well as various types of equipment and apparatus. So children will be involved in hazardous processes, dangerous experiments and challenging exercises. It is impossible to eliminate any possibility of accidents in an environment like this, and to attempt to do so would inhibit experimental learning and the children's development of initiative and self confidence. But children should not be exposed to unnecessary risks, and this book attempts to illustrate ways of identifying and eliminating those risks.

It is ironic that, at a time when teachers are confronted with major new education law, this book illustrates that there is very little legislation dealing with health and safety in schools. In three areas in particular, school buildings, first aid in schools and fire safety in schools, legal protection is virtually non-existent. Readers of this book will be surprised and no doubt very concerned that the law overlooks the safety of children in this way.

David Brierley
Derby, 1991

to ensure that every child under his or her control is not exposed to unacceptable risks. The risk must be foreseeable, that is a risk that can be anticipated.

If a pupil is injured at school and there is subsequent legal action in which it is claimed that a member of staff was negligent, then except in very unusual circumstances, the legal action will be against the employer. This will be the LEA in the case of maintained schools (including schools operating under a delegated budget), the governors in aided schools and the school proprietors, whoever they may be in the case of independent schools and grant maintained schools. At law, the employer is vicariously responsible for the consequences of an employee's negligence in the course of his or her employment. Any compensation will normally be paid by the employer, although in exceptional circumstances the law does allow an employer to require a negligent employee to contribute to, or even to pay all, of the compensation. All employers must by law be insured against their vicarious liability.

It is not inevitable that an employer has to accept vicarious responsibility for an employee's negligence simply because an accident happened at the workplace. The accident must also have happened during the course of the employee's duties. If an employee happens to be at work, but for private reasons rather than for work, the employer will not be responsible for the consequences of any negligence. In a 1987 case called *Stenner v Taff-Ely Borough Council*, an instructor at a Council leisure centre invited some friends to use the facilities on a Sunday morning when there were no other members of the public there. While one of the friends was using the trampoline he had an accident and severely damaged his spine. The Council successfully argued that it was not vicariously liable for the instructor's negligence, because even though he had permission to use the leisure centre on a Sunday, he was not there in the course of his employment, but purely for private recreation. Teachers must bear this in mind if they arrange private events in school. The teachers' unions provide contingency liability insurance in the event of a teacher not being covered by the employer's liability insurance and having to accept personal liability.

Legal proceedings must be started within three years of the date of the accident, but most claims are either withdrawn or settled before they get to court. If there is a hearing, which will be in the County Court or in the High Court, depending on the size of the claim, it could be many years after the accident before the case is heard. A teacher directly involved in the incident giving rise to a claim will be called upon to give evidence.

The court will look into all the relevant circumstances to determine whether there has been negligence in a particular case. The duty of care is not owed to the notional child and certainly not to 'the reasonable child', but to each individual child, with his or her own particular characteristics and personality. One of the most important factors to take into account is the child's age, and a far greater degree of care needs to be taken to look after pupils in an infant class than in the case of pupils at the top of a secondary school. This is because older pupils can normally be expected to respond to instructions and warnings, to exercise their own discretion and to look after themselves. This is not the case with young children. The age of the children is particularly important if supervision arrangements are being examined. The legal test here is again whether or not appropriate precautions have been taken to prevent foreseeable accidents.

Supervision

Assistant teachers are contractually required under their conditions of employment to maintain good order and discipline among pupils, and to safeguard their health and safety whenever they are legitimately on school premises, or alternatively involved in authorized activities out of school. Teachers are required to be available for a maximum of 1,265 working hours a year, although the duty of care applies not just within contractual hours, but also where a teacher voluntarily takes an activity which includes pupils. Governors have a general responsibility for the conduct of the school, and this includes responsibility for seeing that there is an adequate system of supervision at all times when the pupils are on the school premises. The head is responsible for setting up and maintaining such a system. The system will have to take into account, among other things: the number and ages of the children, the number of teachers available and the school premises, particularly any potential danger spots.

It is physically impossible, as well as educationally and socially undesirable, for teachers to supervise all the children all of the time. One judge said that it is all about striking a balance between 'the meticulous supervision of children every moment they are under care of their school master and the very desirable object of encouraging the sturdy independence of children as they grow up'. There was another interesting judicial observation by Mr Justice Kilner-Brown in the 1970 case of *Pettican v London Borough of Enfield*. He said that supervision 'is the implanting of the feeling that there is authority about, that is that there is some control and sanction'.

Mr Justice Hilberg gave judgement in the case of *Hudson v the Governors of Rotherham Grammar School and Selby Johnson* in 1937, and gave his considered view of the school's obligation to pupils:

If boys were kept in cotton wool, some of them would choke themselves with it. They would manage to have accidents: we always did ... we did not always have action at law afterwards. You have to consider whether or not you would expect a Headmaster to exercise such a degree of care that boys could never get into mischief. Has any reasonable parent yet succeeded in such care as to prevent a boy getting into mischief and if he did, what sort of boys would we produce? (Yorkshire Post, March 24 and 25, 1938: LCT303)

So far as general playground supervision is concerned, the law says that pupils do not have to be under constant supervision at all times when they are not in class contact with a teacher. Many schools discharge the duty of care for playground supervision by using nonteaching staff, and this will be perfectly satisfactory, provided that the school can show that there is an adequate system of surveillance and supervision, so that if children approach potential danger spots, they will be seen by those supervising them. That is not to say that playground supervisors have to be watching all of the premises all of the time, but there must be a thought out supervision system which operates effectively.

In Scotland, there is legislation on playground supervision. The Schools (Safety and Supervision of Pupils) (Scotland) Regulations 1990, which came into force on 1 April 1990, say that every education authority has a statutory duty to take reasonable care for the safety of pupils, and that every primary school with at least fifty pupils and every special school must provide at least one adult supervisor in the playground during any break time. 'Adult' means a person who has reached the age of eighteen; 'break time' means any break between classes in the school day and; 'playground' means an outdoor area for recreational play by pupils attending the school. The Regulations give no indication of the number of supervisors required for pupils, and so it will be for the school to decide what supervision is necessary in order to discharge the duty of care.

Teachers often ask for advice about the school's obligation to supervise children before and after school. Pupils cannot be expected to arrive at school all at the same time when parents will themselves be leaving for work at different times. In addition, school transport arrangements mean that there are early arrivals in the morning and children waiting for buses after school. While the school's duty of care exists so long as the pupils are on the school premises with the school's consent, it is unreasonable for the school to have to take responsibility for children arriving at school before supervision could reasonably be expected. For a number of years, it has been generally accepted that teachers can reasonably be asked to be available to supervise children at school up to 10 minutes before school starts and for the same period after school ends, and any such supervision time needs to be included in a teacher's Directed Time. The relevant section of the teachers' Conditions of Employment requires teachers to supervise pupils 'whether ... before, during or after school sessions'. Communication with parents in these situations is particularly important. The school prospectus should say when the school will take responsibility for children before school opens and remind parents that before then, there will be nobody to supervise the pupils. If for any reason arrangements have to be changed, then the parents should be told in advance. This is particularly important at schools where for many years teachers have arrived at school in time to supervise any early arrivals. Parents may well have come to regard this as a permanent and reliable arrangement and so they would need as much advance warning as possible of any alteration, so that they could adjust their own arrangements.

Children who arrive at school knowing that supervision arrangements are not in operation are there at their own risk. However, should a teacher be present and a dangerous situation develop, then legally as well as professionally and morally, the teacher should attempt to intervene or to seek assistance, as the situation requires.

There should be similar procedures for supervising children at the end of the school day and, again, reasonable arrangements must be brought to the parents' attention. Teachers are not contractually obliged to supervise children waiting outside school for the school bus, and the school should make sure that parents are familiar with arrangements.

Teachers are not contractually required to undertake supervision during the midday break, unless they arrange to do so under a separate contract with the LEA. If they supervise the children on a voluntary basis or are involved in any lunchtime activity, then they have to exercise the normal duty of care. The head is responsible for seeing that adequate arrangements are in operation, and if the head choses to leave school at lunch then he or she has to delegate this responsibility to a responsible person.

One case called *Blasdale v Coventry City Council* considered in 1981 whether or not extra supervision could be needed during a wet dinner break, when children were kept in their classrooms. In that case, there were two second year junior classes in adjoining classrooms during a lunch break because it was raining. There were thirty-two children in one room and thirty-five in the other. An ancillary kept an eye on both classrooms by moving from room to room, looking into each of the classroom doors. As she moved from one classroom to the other, a child in the classroom she had just left, flicked a paper clip and hit another child in the eye. The judge in that case decided that the supervision arrangements were not adequate and that the authority was negligent.

The judge decided that although it was possible to see into both classrooms from the same point, it was necessary to go into each classroom to properly supervise the class. He decided that it was too much to ask the ancillary to supervise two classrooms at the same time, because the system was such that she had to move from one classroom to another and this inevitably left one room without supervision. According to the head's evidence 'the only safe system is to have one person in each classroom'.

If a child is let out of school early, then the school will be legally vulnerable if that puts the child at unnecessary risk. In a 1969 case called *Barnes v Hampshire County Council*, the LEA was liable where a five year old was let out of school five minutes before her mother arrived to collect her at the school gates. The girl wandered off on to the main road, where she was knocked down. The risk arising from such a young child being free to wander alone on a main road was so great that even a relatively short period, such as five minutes, created an unacceptable risk. This case is not saying that schools are responsible for seeing that every child is individually collected, but it emphasizes that there must be a satisfactory arrangement with parents for collecting children and, with young children in particular, the school should not release children at a time when a parent cannot be guaranteed to be at the school gates.

The school is not legally responsible if a child is injured on the way to school or on the way home. This is the case even if the child is travelling on a school bus. But if a child is injured while off school premises during the school day, the school may be responsible. This can happen when a child runs out of school. In a well-known case in 1953 called *Lewis v Camarthenshire County Council*, the following circumstances resulted in the County Council's liability. A four-year-old boy in a nursery school escaped from the classroom while the teacher was away attending to an injured child. The boy then escaped from the school playground through an unlocked gate and ran into a busy road. Sadly a driver who swerved to avoid him was killed when his lorry hit a telegraph post. The House of Lords decided that the school should have foreseen the possibility of a child of this age trying to escape from school and putting himself and others at risk. Reasonable precautions could have been taken, such as locking the gate, or in some other way making the gate child proof. The teacher who had left the class unsupervised was not negligent, because she was simply doing the best she could in very difficult circumstances. She could not be expected to be in two places at once or to have eyes in the back of her head.

The age of the child was a very significant factor in this case, and it is recognized that it is impossible to guarantee that all the pupils who come to school in the morning stay there for the whole of each session. Schools need to show that they have recognized the problem of absconding children and taken reasonable precautions to prevent it. Nevertheless, schools are not security zones and teachers are not jailers, but because of the risk of harm befalling pupils if they wander out of school unnoticed, the school should take precautions to stop this happening. There also needs to be an efficient procedure to set in motion where a child does abscond.

Gaps in perimeter fences and hedges can be tempting, particularly for younger children, and so these should be repaired as quickly as possible, especially where the school is on a busy road or close to dangerous open ground. Teaching staff and ancillaries should know where the known 'escape routes' are, and it will help those who supervise the pupils if exits from the school can be restricted to just one or two places.

Sometimes children can run out of class without warning. The teacher will have to decide whether to chase after the absconder leaving the class unattended, or to stay with the class and report the absconder. The school should have a procedure to deal with this difficult situation. If not, then the teacher, who is not expected to be in two places at once, must make a reasonable decision.

In secondary schools, there will be procedures that pupils must follow before being allowed out of school, and this will involve seeking permission from a senior member of staff. An up-to-date record must be kept of children who are off the premises, and the school office is usually the best place to keep this. Rules about leaving school should be made known to pupils and also to parents through the school prospectus and, perhaps, reminders issued at regular intervals. If a teacher sends a child out of school on a personal errand and the child is injured, the teacher could well be legally vulnerable. The age of the child and to where he or she was being sent would be important factors.

Children often have to leave school during the day for perfectly acceptable reasons, such as medical appointments, and the school should be satisfied that reasonably adequate arrangements have been made for the child to be taken by a parent, or by a teacher, or some other responsible person. Again, the child's age will be important.

A teacher is not responsible for seeing children across the road as a road crossing patrolman does. Indeed, a teacher has no authority to control traffic in this way. Where a school crossing patrol is necessary, it should be provided by the LEA, and in local management schemes the cost of school crossing patrols is normally retained by the LEA. Should a school crossing patrol not be available or should the patrol man or woman be absent, then teachers are still not expected to assume school crossing responsibilities. But the school will need to do all it can to warn the children and parents that there is no patrol so that parents can, if they feel it necessary, arrange for the child to be accompanied to school and collected after school.

If a teacher agrees to exercise general oversight of a crossing area on a voluntary basis, then he or she would be well advised to make sure that the extent of this commitment was well understood. At all times that the teacher was exercising general oversight, he or she would be obliged to discharge the duty of care in the normal way.

Classroom supervision

Teachers are entirely responsible for children in the classroom and they are accountable for their own supervision and also for seeing that the children are safe in the hands of others who may be in the classroom, such as student teachers or parents. As a general rule, neither parent helpers nor student teachers should be left in sole charge of a class, unless the teacher can be absolutely certain that they are able to deal competently with pupils and take proper care over their safety.

Teachers must see that lessons are organized in an ordered, controlled way, that equipment is safe and used safely, and that general class discipline is conducive to good order among the pupils. (There is further information about classroom safety on pp. 31–2.)

Two recent cases, one in 1969 called *Butt v Cambridgeshire and Isle of Ely County Council*, and another in 1983, called *Black v Kent County Council*, dealt with accidents caused by sharp-pointed scissors in class. The earlier case concerned a nine-year-old girl in a class of thirty-seven pupils, all of whom were given scissors during a geography lesson to cut out pictures and stick them in scrapbooks. The class was told by the teacher to put the scissors down when they were not being used. The accident happened when one of the girls, who had scissors in her hand, talked to another girl, who turned and caught the point of the scissors in her eye. The court looked closely at the classroom arrangements and decided that the teacher was conducting the class properly and, in particular, that supervision was adequate. There was no liability.

In the other case, a seven-year-old, boy who was using a pair of scissors in an art class, was nudged as he sat on his chair and the sharp end of the scissors went into his eye. The teacher had allowed the class to choose between blunt-ended or sharp-ended scissors, and this boy chose a pair of sharp scissors. The court decided that with young children, there was a far greater risk of injury with sharp-ended scissors, and that risk should not have been allowed in the absence of a compelling educational reason for using them. Consequently, it was negligent to let the boy use sharp-ended scissors.

Particular care is needed where children are working with dangerous equipment or substances. Here, discipline and good order are particularly important so that the children are in no doubt about the serious consequences of misbehaving. In one case in 1966, *Crouch v Essex County Council*, horseplay between pupils led to one child being seriously injured. During a chemistry class, the pupils were carrying out an experiment involving oxides, alkali and caustic soda. Some pupils used a weak solution of caustic soda for the experiment, but others used a more concentrated solution. The teacher explained the theory of the experiment and told the class how it should be carried out. He warned the pupils that the strong solution of caustic soda was dangerous. There was an unlabelled beaker of the strong solution on the teacher's demonstration bench, and the pupils were given pipettes to draw the solution from the beaker. Shortly afterwards, a fifteen-year-old boy had some of the strong solution squirted into his eyes by a girl who thought that the solution was water. She had not been listening to the teacher. The court did not find negligence in this case and decided that in the circumstances, it was proper for the teacher to allow fifteen year old pupils who were experienced in chemistry theory and practice to draw off caustic soda without being directly supervised, so long as they had been given adequate warning about the dangers involved. The irresponsible action of the girl which caused the accident was not reasonably foreseeable by the teacher, and the court felt that he had maintained a sufficient standard of discipline from the point of view of safety.

The important point is that the court accepted that the fifteen-year-old pupils in this particular class could reasonably be expected to listen to the teacher's instructions and to act on his warnings. In these circumstances, he could not foresee that one of then would act so irresponsibly as to squirt caustic soda on another pupil.

Many science and practical departments have drawn up their own internal safety rules, which are drawn to the pupils' attention. A growing number of LEAs are offering schools detailed guidance on safety rules and procedures in particular departments, and any such rules and procedures must from necessity be communicated to the children and observed by both staff and pupils (see p. 33).

The courts have had to consider a number of cases resulting from accidents to children during PE and games and, in these cases, they look to see if a generally-approved practice has been adopted by the teacher in charge.

If a teacher can show that he or she has followed a well established and approved practice of conducting a particular lesson, whether it is a PE lesson, a practical lesson, or part of normal classroom teaching, then he or she will be well placed to defend any allegation of negligence. If normal practice has not been followed, then that does not mean that the teacher will be unable to establish that the duty of care had been discharged, but it would be that much more difficult to demonstrate this. As one judge said

> if a teacher can say "in all that I did, I followed the approved practice generally adopted throughout the land" . . . he is in a position of considerable strength to answer the charge of negligence. It is a truism to say that each case depends on its own particular facts, but certainly it is of inestimable assistance for those who are preparing the defence of a teacher who is alleged to have acted negligently to be able to show that the teacher followed the well worn paths that his professional colleagues had trodden before him. (*Meeham v Derby County Council*).

It is the teacher's responsibility to make reasonable checks to see that all equipment and apparatus are safe and suitable for the particular children that are using them. If the teacher does decide that a piece of apparatus is defective, then it should be reported to the head or to the head of department as appropriate without delay and, of course, not used until it is repaired. If there is a defect which the teacher does not detect by normal inspection, then if there was an accident caused by the defect, the teacher would not be liable, unless in the circumstances, something more than a normal inspection was required. If there was a latent defect, then it could be the manufacturer that was legally responsible. (See pp. 49–65 for a detailed discussion of safety issues in school sport and PE.)

Supervision arrangements in schools are becoming more difficult for heads to maintain, because teacher numbers are dropping. In September 1989, a survey of all maintained schools in England and Wales commissioned by all the teachers' unions found that 1.9 per cent of all permanent teaching posts in ordinary schools were vacant.

Special schools had 3.9 per cent vacant posts, and had the highest proportion of vacant posts left unfilled for at least one term (44 per cent). Fifty-nine per cent of special schools who responded to the survey considered that their supply cover was inadequate or bad. Two responses to the teachers' shortage survey show how special schools are particularly badly hit by teacher shortages. A teacher from a special school in Birmingham said, 'we find it increasingly difficult to find staff who are willing to work with children with severe learning difficulties. Classroom assistants frequently find themselves running the class. Obvious resentment is felt'. Another special school teacher, this time from Buckinghamshire, said 'because we find it difficult to fill vacancies we are getting more and more part-time teachers. This does not help either the children or communication within the school.'

A second survey was carried out in 1990. This showed that more than one school in four had a vacancy and in primary schools, 3% of posts were vacant across the country. Special schools again had an above average number of vacancies.

There have in recent years been calls for maximum class sizes and in its 1990 report, the Interim Advisory Committee on School Teachers Pay and Conditions considered proposals for statutory class sizes. It decided that statutory requirements on class size would unduly fetter managerial discretion. However, the Committee recommended that the issue should be given full and proper consideration by LEAs and governors when establishing policies and priorities.

In Scotland, teachers' national conditions of service stipulate that the number of pupils to a classroom should not exceed:

(1) Thirty-three pupils in primary schools and the first two years of secondary school (but with an upper limit of thirty-nine pupils).
(2) Thirty pupils in the third to sixth years of secondary school (but with an upper limit of thirty-four pupils in the third and fourth years).
(3) Twenty pupils in secondary school practical classes, as in home economics and technical and science subjects, etc. (the upper limit is the same).

Allocation of health and safety responsibilities in schools

Apart from teachers, there are others who have health and safety responsibilities for children at school.

An LEA retains overall responsibility as an employer under the Health and Safety at Work etc Act 1974; it has a statutory duty of care under the Occupiers' Liability Act 1957; and it also has a common law duty of care for both staff and pupils. Governors have similar health and safety responsibilities in schools where the governing body is the employer, and governors also have responsibilities in schools with a delegated budget. The position in these schools is discussed in detail later.

Within the school, those with health and safety responsibilities include:

Headteachers

Heads are responsible for the internal organization and management of the school and so they will have day-to-day responsibility for safety matters. They must also see that health and safety legislation, regulations, LEA rules and school rules are being implemented and that staff and pupils are operating safe working practices. The head can also give personal leadership so far as safety attitudes are concerned. One way in which the head's attitude to safety can be demonstrated, is by ensuring that prompt action is taken if any dangerous situation, dangerous equipment or machinery or dangerous work area is reported. The head's health and safety responsibilities can be delegated either to a deputy or to some other senior member of staff reasonably capable of carrying those responsibilities, and properly briefed about the nature of those delegated responsibilities.

Head of department

The head of department must be reasonably sure that all equipment and any machinery or apparatus in the department is in good condition and can be used safely. In practical departments, the head of department may, if suitably qualified, be the person nominated to carry out an assessment under the Control of Substances Hazardous to Health Regulations 1988. Details of these regulations appear later in this book, but it will be noted that assessments must set out steps that can be taken to minimize or eliminate the risks presented by hazardous substances. Heads of department will be involved in implementing these steps and will in any event be responsible for seeing that all hazardous substances are correctly used, handled, stored, transported and disposed of (see p. 24). Where protective clothing and equipment are necessary, they should be readily available, and safety equipment, such as first aid kits and fire appliances, should be kept in operational condition.

Heads of department need to keep abreast of relevant safety legislation, regulations and guidelines produced by the LEA so as to be sure that these requirements are known within the department and complied with.

Ancillary assistants

In primary and special schools, ancillary assistants have an important role to play in the classroom. In addition to clerical and administrative work, many of the ancillary's duties will involve contact with children: an ancillary will be expected to supervise the class when the teacher has no alternative but to leave the pupils, and there may also be supervising responsibilities alongside the teacher or supervisor for specific activities or areas in the teacher's presence. Many schools also take ancillary staff on school trips to assist with supervision.

There needs to be a clear understanding between the teacher and the ancillary about how the ancillary's duties are carried out so that there is no misunderstanding about where particular responsibilities fall.

Nursery nurses

The National Nursery Examination Board (NNEB) Certificate in Nursery Nursing covers the physical, social and emotional development of children from birth to the age of seven years and the skills needed to care for them.

Qualified nursery nurses are employed at nursery schools or nursery classes and also at special schools. The nursery nurse will work in the classroom alongside the teacher and will be involved in supervising the children, providing general care and welfare and seeing that the classroom environment is safe for the pupils. The supervision duties could include supervising activities and practical areas/corners, supervising children in outdoor play areas and looking after children awaiting collection by parents. Other specific responsibilities could include caring for sick children and assisting with the development of the children's social skills, such as toileting, washing and dressing.

Nursery nurses employed in special schools can work with children of all ages. Once again, the nursery nurse will be part of the classroom team and will have supervisory duties, usually in the presence of the classroom teacher.

School cooks

The cook in charge has overall responsibility for the preparation and cooking of school meals in safe and hygienic conditions. Responsibilities will include ensuring that the correct hygiene and health and safety practices are observed in the kitchen, reporting any faults in equipment and requesting routine maintenance of the kitchen premises as necessary. The kitchen must be run in accordance with LEA guidelines and procedures, and the cook in charge will need to be aware of these matters and ensure that other kitchen workers have the necessary information to follow all safety and hygiene rules in the kitchen.

Caretaker

The school caretaker is responsible for among other things, security, heating, lighting and cleaning. He or she will carry out routine checks and maintenance on heating boilers and be responsible for seeing that proper safety precautions are observed in the boiler house (see p. 99). There will be a wide range of caretaking and cleaning equipment to maintain and keep in a safe condition, and any defective or unsafe furniture, fittings or apparatus should be reported to the head. The caretaker is normally responsible for the cleaning staff and this will include ensuring that they are wearing appropriate clothing and footwear.

Cleaners

Cleaners are responsible for cleaning, sweeping, polishing, sweeping and mopping in the school. It is important that all equipment, particularly mechanical equipment, is used properly and that cleaners use the protective clothing provided for them and wear correct footwear. Safety precautions are particularly important when cleaners are working above floor level and any defect in steps or any other equipment should be reported immediately. Similarly, the caretaker should be told about any unsafe furniture or apparatus, or any other defect that any of the cleaners may have noticed.

Cleaning staff have an important role to play in preventing accidents and the Education Service Advisory Committee of the Health and Safety Commission lays down some simple rules that cleaners can follow to help take care of themselves and to prevent accidents. The rules are set out in a check-card, called *Guidance to Cleaning Staff in Educational Establishments* — reproduced here with the Commission's permission:

(1) Do check equipment before use and report defects to the supervisor.
(2) Do not use defective equipment — always report it and do not work unless wearing the correct protective clothing.
(3) Leave unattended equipment in a safe place.
(4) Beware of wet floors and report wet floors and also any trailing leads.
(5) Do take special care when handling or moving equipment or furniture.
(6) Do not mix cleaning materials unless permitted by instructions.
(7) Do not block any exit from the building.
(8) Do not smoke unless you are in a designated smoking area.

Cleaners working in laboratories should wear the protective clothing provided for them, and to be particularly careful emptying waste bins as there can be glass or very sharp objects and contaminated towels and papers. Cleaners should not touch any laboratory equipment or apparatus and should not attempt to mop up any spillages but, instead, report the spillage to the person responsible for the laboratory.

In 1988, the Health and Safety Executive in conjunction with Health and Safety Services Ltd produced a video for all those who have responsibility for health and safety in schools. The video deals with legal issues arising from the legislation and the common law duty of care, and also deals with practical arrangements for a safe system of work, health and safety organization and arrangements. The video illustrates common hazards on school premises and also shows good safety practice. The video is called *Managing Safety* and is available from Health and Safety Services Ltd, Silbury Business Centre, Silbury Court, Milton Keynes MK9 2LR. Telephone 0908 666642.

2
HEALTH AND SAFETY LAW

Health and safety legislation

The Robens Committee was set up in 1970 to look into health and safety at work and, as expected, it concluded that the law protecting the health, safety and welfare of employees at work was a shambles. The principal outcome of the Committee's recommendations was the Health and Safety at Work etc Act 1974, which lays down general duties for safety at work on employers, the self-employed and employees.

The Robens Committee heard evidence about health and safety in educational establishments and in hospitals, and drew the following conclusion: 'We are not satisfied from the evidence that maintenance of standards of safety and health for employees in these establishments is so uniformly satisfactory that it is unnecessary to bring them within the ambit of new legislation.' The 1974 Act implemented that recommendation.

Health and Safety legislation is administered by the Health and Safety Commission which initiates safety legislation, provides information, advice and guidance to the public and carries out research into safety matters. The Health and Safety Executive is responsible for seeing that health and safety law is observed and this is carried out by Health and Safety Executive Inspectors, who systematically visit and review safety in separate work areas. There is no branch of the inspectorate specifically for education – educational establishments are covered by HM Factory Inspectorate. A list of local offices of the Health and Safety Executive and their applications are given in the Appendixes.

The Education Service Advisory Committee was appointed in 1981 to advise the Health and Safety Commission on health and safety at workplaces in the education service, and on the protection of pupils, students and others from directly-related hazards arising from work activities. The Committee has a membership which is representative of both employers and employees in education, and has produced a number of authoritative information and advice booklets, details of which appear in this book.

The general duties of employers are set down in Section 2 (1) of the 1974 Act, which says that it is the duty of every employer to ensure so far as reasonably practicable the health, safety and welfare at work of his employees. In addition to these general duties, Section 2 (2) lays down specific obligations, all of which use the test of reasonable practicability. These specific duties are:

(1) To provide and maintain plant and systems at work which are safe and without risk to health. In this context 'plant' includes any machinery, equipment or appliance at the workplace.

(2) To ensure the safety and absence of risks to health in connection with the use, handling, storage and transport of articles and services at the workplace.

(3) To provide such information, instruction, training and supervision as is necessary to ensure the health and safety at work of employees.

In other words, the employee has the right to know about safety matters. This particular obligation has been reinforced by the Health and Safety (Information to Employees) Regulations 1989, which require employers to either display a poster or distribute leaflets to employees, giving them health and safety information. Leaflets and posters are available from the Health and Safety Executive.

(4) To provide and maintain means of access to and egress from the workplace which are safe and without risk to health.

This is an acknowledgement that most injuries at work are caused by employees slipping or tripping on staircases or floors.

(5) To provide a working environment for employees which is safe, without risk to health and adequate so far as facilities and welfare arrangements are concerned.

In other words, employees are entitled to proper amenities at work. Employers must be especially aware of the position of a pregnant woman at work. The Health and Safety Executive has produced a leaflet giving advice to both employers and expectant mothers. *Pregnancy and Work – Guidance for Women and their Employers* emphasizes that although pregnancy is not an illness, it does put extra strain on the mother to be.

Expectant mothers should not be exposed to dangerous working environments, or required to undertake any manual work; and by virtue of the Control of Subtances Hazardous to Health Regulations 1988 (see pp. 24–5), the employer must identify and attempt to reduce or eliminate the risks presented by potentially hazardous substances.

The Health and Safety Executive booklet, *Protecting Your Health at Work*, advises that as the baby is very sensitive in the first three months of its life, the working mother should take particular care with excessive lifting and/or prolonged standing, and if she is working with chemicals, including pesticides and solvents (see p. 27).

The key phrase is 'so far as is reasonably practicable'. This means that faced with any potential hazard, the employer must weigh up the seriousness of the risk to employees' health, safety and welfare at work that the hazard presents against the practical problems and costs of attempting to remove it. If a particular risk is shown to be so insignificant that it is not a safety threat, the employer need take no action; and in some cases where the risk is more significant, it may be that practical difficulties and the costs involved in attempting to remove the risk are prohibitive. But there may be some cases where there are simply no alternatives to getting things done, because the risk of a serious accident is so great.

There are obligations to protect nonemployees under the Act. Section 3 says that employers must conduct their undertakings in such a way as to ensure that those who are not in their employment but who are nevertheless at the workplace, should not be exposed to risks to their health and safety. This follows recommendations from the Robens Committee, which considered the safety at workplaces of members of the public. But this was in relation to industrial and commercial premises and building sites, and did not include schools.

The Act imposes duties not just on the employer but also on those who actually have day-to-day control of premises, and the obligation is again to ensure as far as is reasonably practicable that premises are safe and without risk to health. As well as this there is a further 'reasonableness' condition in that the person in control must take such measures as is reasonable for a person in his or her position to take. This duty, set out in Section 4, will apply to heads who are in charge of the internal organization, management and control of the school, but whose authority to take decisions about health and safety matters is, in many cases, conditional upon the governors' agreement or the LEA's sanction.

Section 6 of the Act says that any person who designs, manufacturers, imports or supplies any article for use at work must ensure, so far as is reasonably practicable, that the article is so designed and constructed as to be safe and without risks to health when properly used. This person must carry out or arrange any necessary testing and also to ensure that any necessary safety instructions are made available. Designers and manufacturers must take responsibility for carrying out any necessary research to discover and, so far as is reasonably practicable, eliminate or minimize risks to health or safety from the design.

Section 7 of the Act requires employees to take reasonable care for their own safety, the safety of other workers and the safety of anyone else who may be affected by their actions. They must also co-operate with the employer on health and safety matters at work. A number of lorry drivers have been prosecuted under Section 7 for failing to observe traffic signs and road works, and for failing to properly secure their loads. There have been convictions against charge hands and foremen who have not reported faulty machine guards or for reporting that guards were safe, when, in fact, they were defective. A safety supervisor for a construction company, who was responsible for inspecting scaffoldings, was convicted for failing to report defective scaffolding.

In 1986, the Health and Safety Executive took out its first prosecution against a teacher for an offence under Section 7 of the Act. The teacher pleaded guilty to failing to take reasonable care to protect children during a science lesson. He was demonstrating an experiment which showed how metal oxide was reduced into pure metal, and this involved passing hydrogen gas over the oxide. The children gathered around the bench and as the teacher lit the bunsen burner, there was an explosion and fifteen of the twenty-three children in the second form class were taken to hospital after being spattered with sulphuric acid on their arms and bodies. One child was kept in hospital overnight, but there were no lasting injuries.

The Executive did not take out the prosecution simply because there had been an accident and children had been injured. It was the teacher's failure to use safety equipment that was available when he knew there was a risk that led to the conviction. The teacher was fined £500.

The Health and Safety Executive is a keen enforcement agency, but it rarely prosecutes in the education sector. Nevertheless, there was a case in the summer of 1989, when the Executive secured a conviction against the Polytechnic of Central London on account of its failure to maintain two lifts in the building. The polytechnic had its lifts examined at the end of 1988, and it was discovered that a goods lift needed immediate repair and a passenger lift needed new suspension ropes within two months. These maintenance works were not carried out and the polytechnic was found to have contravened the Act, even though there had not actually been an accident. The polytechnic was therefore prosecuted for failing to take preventative maintenance precautions. Also in 1989, a teacher and an LEA were both prosecuted because of unsafe wiring at a school. Some electrical alterations had been carried out by a sixteen-year-old pupil, but had not been checked.

The employer's health and safety policy statement

All employers who employ five or more people must have a written statement on health and safety at work. The policy statement should include three aspects:

(1) A statement of the employer's general policy with regard to the health and safety of employees at work. This will confirm the employer's commitment to discharge its statutory duties. It will stress the importance of staff co-operation and good communication at all levels.
(2) The system and procedures that the employer has established to carry out the policy. This will set out how health and safety matters are dealt with at LEA level and identify those officers with health and safety responsibilities.
(3) The steps that the employer has taken to make the policy effective. This will describe the systems and procedures for ensuring health and safety at work.

The Health and Safety Commission's Education Service Advisory Committee has produced a booklet *Safety Policies in the Education Sector*, which provides further information. So far as carrying out the health and safety policies is concerned, it says

> To achieve successful implementation of the safety policy, there should be clear lines of communication in health and safety matters throughout the organisation, be it a university, education authority, college, school or other education institution. The employer should establish the necessary systems for health and safety within the management structure and the levels of responsibility at which the function is described in the policy which are to be carried out should be defined (Safety Policies in the Education Sector, para. 11).

In addition to the employer's health and safety policy statement, schools should produce their own policy for health and safety. This will give details of the health and safety organization within the school and also details of the staff involved with health and safety responsibilities, so that each member of staff knows which colleague is responsible for specific work areas and specific activities. The policy could also include arrangements for a school health and safety committee for reporting and investigating accidents, for monitoring safety standards and procedures, and for briefing staff and consulting with staff on health and safety issues. One way of achieving this is to have health and safety as a fixed agenda item at each staff meeting.

It is important that health and safety policies are not simply written and then forgotten. There should be a system for carrying out a regular review of the policy, particularly to take into account new health and safety legislation, and also arrangements for ensuring that the policy and any amendments or alterations are brought to the attention of all staff.

Safety representatives

The Safety Representatives and Safety Committees' Regulations 1977 came into force on 1 October 1978 and, at the same time, the Health and Safety Commission drew up a code of practice on the rights and duties of safety representatives. The Commission has also issued two sets of guidance notes, the first dealing with the appointment and functions of safety representatives and the second covering safety committees.

The Regulations state that a recognized trade union may appoint representatives from among the employees in all cases where one or more employees are employed. A 'recognized trade union' is an independent trade union which the employer recognizes for the purpose of negotiation and collective bargaining related to one or more of the matters set out in S 29 (1) of the Trade Union and Labour Relations Act 1974. The governors of a school with a delegated budget can recognize any union at school level to represent the staff or a group of staff.

Neither the Act nor the Regulations set out the number of representatives in any particular place, although the Code of Practice does give some guidance. Among the criteria that it suggests should be considered are:

(1) The total number of employees.
(2) The variety of different occupations.
(3) The size of the workplace and variety of locations.
(4) The type of work activity and the degree and character of the inherent dangers.

In small schools one safety representative may suffice but in large schools more than one may well be necessary.

The Regulations say that representatives should have had, so far as is reasonably practicable, two years' previous employment with the employer, or at least two years' experience in similar employment. This is intended to ensure that the representative has the necessary understanding of the employer's undertaking. A teacher is not required to have spent those two years in the school he or she represents. The Regulations only require him or her to have taught for two years either within the LEA concerned or elsewhere.

The Regulations give safety representatives the following rights:

(1) To represent the interest of employees in health and safety matters.
(2) To receive health and safety information from the employer. These arrangements should be laid down by the employer in the written health and safety policy or elsewhere. The Code of Practice suggests that this information will include:
   (a) Information about the plans and performance of the employer's undertaking and any changes proposed in so far as they affect the health and safety of their employees at work.
   (b) Information of a technical nature about hazards to health and safety and precautions deemed necessary to eliminate or minimize them in respect of machinery, plant, equipment, processes, systems of work and substances in use at work.
   (c) Information which the employer keeps about any accident, dangerous occurrence or notifiable industrial disease and any statistical records relating to such matters.
   (d) Any other information specifically related to matters affecting the health and safety at work of his employees.
   The Code of Practice also states that the employer must pass on relevant information provided by consultants, manufacturers, importers, or suppliers of any article or substance used or to be used at work by their employees. This includes explanatory instruction manuals, labels and data sheets accompanying potentially hazardous machinery, articles and substances. The Control of Substances Hazardous to Health Regulations 1988 reiterate this obligation (see p. 24).
(3) To carry out inspections and investigations. In addition to routine inspections, there should also be ad hoc inspections following a notifiable accident or after substantial changes in conditions at work.
   Routine inspections will normally be on a quarterly basis, but in some situations, such as where there is a high risk activity or where circumstances are rapidly changing, it may be appropriate for more frequent inspections to be agreed.
   In large schools, it may not be practicable to conduct a formal inspection of the entire premises at a single session but, instead, the inspection could be carried out in stages, perhaps on a departmental basis.

Investigations take place when it is necessary for a safety representative to investigate potential hazards or dangerous occurrences at the work place, or to examine the cause of an accident. An investigation can also take place following a complaint by an employee about a health and safety matter, and the employer's health and safety policy should set out the procedure for such complaints.

(4) To have time off work. The Regulations state that 'an employer shall permit a safety representative to take such time off with pay during the employee's working hours as shall be necessary for the purposes of:

(a) Performing his or her functions under the Regulations.

(b) Undergoing such training in aspects of those functions as may be reasonable in all the circumstances, having regard to any relevant provisions of a Code of Practice relating to time off for training approved for the time being by the Health and Safety Commission.

This responsibility rests with the LEA whether or not the school concerned has its own delegated budget.

A safety representative like any other teacher is an employee, and has the same legal responsibilities of an employee under statute and common law. However, the Regulations state clearly that none of the functions given to safety representatives imposes any legal duty on them over and above these statutory and common law obligations.

Consequently, a safety representative who either accepts or does not object to any steps taken by the employer in a health and safety matter, does not incur any legal responsibility for those steps. The Inspectorate will not prosecute a representative for any act or omission in the performance of his or her statutory functions, unless there are exceptional circumstances.

Nevertheless, the Code of Practice states that representatives should take all reasonable steps to keep themselves aware of:

(1) The legal requirements as to health and safety of people at work in general and the group of people represented in particular.

(2) Any particular hazards in their work place and relevant hazard prevention measures.

(3) The employer's safety policy and the arrangements connected with it.

School safety representatives have an important role to play in school safety and they need to be prepared to take their role seriously. Similarly, the LEA and school management should understand that a safety representative should play an important and active part in the school's administration and organization.

The COSHH Regulations 1988

The Control of Substances Hazardous to Health (COSHH) Regulations 1988, which became law on 1 October 1989, make it a statutory obligation for employers to assess the risks created when a hazardous substance is used at work and to take appropriate action to prevent or control these risks.

The risk from a substance at work is the likelihood that it will harm an employee in the actual circumstances of use. The degree of risk will depend on:

(1) The hazard presented by the substance.
(2) How it is used.
(3) How it is controlled.
(4) How long any employee has been exposed to the substance and to how much.

Substances that are 'hazardous to health', and so fall within the Regulations, include substances that are dangerous, harmful, irritant, corrosive, toxic or very toxic. There are very few substances that are excluded from these Regulations, and they are intended to cover any material, mixture or compound, that can harm people's health. So substances hazardous to health can include harmful microorganisms and dust in sufficient quantity to harm people's health.

Where there are hazardous substances at work, the employer is required to take the following steps:

(1) Assess the risk to health arising from work and what precautions are needed.
(2) Introduce appropriate measures to prevent or control the risk and ensure that they are observed. Some preventative measures can be easily implemented. For example, a potentially dangerous solvent could be replaced by something safer. If any particular experiment poses risks then, as an alternative, the teacher can demonstrate the experiment.
(3) Monitor the exposure of workers and carry out an appropriate form of surveillance of their health.
(4) Inform, instruct and train employees about the risks and the precautions to be taken.

The Health and Safety Executive neatly sums up the rationale of the Regulations when it says that poor control can create a substantial risk even from a substance with a low hazard, but with proper precautions, the risk of harm by even the most hazardous substances can be satisfactorily controlled.

The obligations under COSHH lie primarily with the employer, but heads, deputies and all others who to any extent have control of the premises also bear responsibility to see that these steps are carried out. What action is needed in any particular school will depend upon the risks that are present, and the amount of action that has already been taken to control the risk. The person who is actually given responsibility for carrying out the assessment must have the necessary authority and ability to gather together all the necessary information and to make informed judgements about the degree of risk and controls and precautions that are necessary. The assessor will also need to know about the Regulations and what is required by them. The Health and Safety Executive suggests that an assessment should involve the following questions:

(1) What substances are present? In what form?
(2) What harmful effects are possible?
(3) Where and how are the substances actually used or handled?
(4) What harmful substances are given off, etc.?
(5) Who could be affected, to what extent and for how long?
(6) Under what circumstances?
(7) How likely is it that exposure will happen?
(8) What precautions need to be taken to comply with the rest of the COSHH Regulations?

The Health and Safety Education Service Advisory Committee in its booklet *COSHH – guidance for schools*, confirms that a number of general assessments have already been made for science departments by expert bodies such as the Association for Science Education, The Consortium of Local Education Authorities for the Provision of Science Services, and the Scottish Schools Equipment Research Centre.

In other areas such as art, design and technology, where general assessments are not so readily available, the Committee advises that the starting point should be to refer to information from manufacturers and suppliers which, by law must be provided.

The Professional Association of Teachers has produced a specimen assessment form for schools, which is reproduced with the Association's permission in Appendix II.

Noise at Work Regulations 1989

Exposure to high noise levels can cause hearing damage which can be serious and, in some cases, incurable. The important factors are the noise level and how long people are exposed to the noise both daily and over a number of years. There can be occasions when the pressure of a sound wave is so great that there is a risk of instantaneous damage.

The Noise at Work Regulations 1989 came into force on 1 January 1990 and require employers to take positive steps to reduce noise levels at work to the lowest level that is reasonably practicable.

The Health and Safety Executive has produced a brief guide to the new Regulations called *Introducing the Noise at Work Regulations*, which contains a useful summary of the Regulations.

Noise levels are measured in decibel units, which are represented as dB(A). The dB(A) level in a quiet library would be around 30, in a quiet office around 45 and during a normal conversation around 60. A loud radio would produce a dB(A) level of approximately 70, in a busy street it would be around 80 and a heavy lorry around 7 metres away would produce a level of about 100 dB(A).

Employers are required by the Regulations to carry out noise assessment exercises at regular intervals and any employees at risk must be given adequate information, instruction and training about the nature and extent of the risk, and what they can do to minimize it − by using personal ear protectors for example. The key levels of daily personal exposure to noise are 85 dB(A) and 90 dB(A). The Health and Safety Executive advises that if people have to shout or have difficulty being understood by somebody around 2 metres away, there could be a noise problem and the Regulations will apply.

If the noise level is measured at 90 dB(A) or above, then there is a legal duty for employees to wear ear protection. If the daily personal noise exposure is 85 dB(A) or above, then action must be taken (other than by providing personal ear protectors) to reduce that exposure. In other words, ear protectors should not be regarded as a substitute for noise reduction.

The Regulations impose duties on manufacturers, designers, importers and suppliers of machines which are likely to cause anybody at work to be exposed to noise reaching 85 dB(A) to provide adequate information about the noise the machines are likely to generate. This can include supplying data about noise tests that are being carried out on the machine and advice on safe use and installation.

Europe

The European Communities Act 1972 brought about the United Kingdom's accession to the European Community and enacted that EC treaties should have legal force in the United Kingdom, without further legislation. The most significant treaty is the Treaty of Rome, which has as one of its objectives, the harmonization of laws in the various member states in relation to a number of issues, including health and safety at work.

The institutional machinery of the European Community includes the European Commission, which initiates and implements European legislation; the Council of Ministers, which takes Executive decisions; and the European Parliament, which is elected by direct vote and has financial and supervisory powers. The Economic and Social Committee is another influential body, which represents economic and social interest groups in the member states and produces opinions on Community issues, including health and safety, referred to it by the Council or Commission. The United Kingdom has 24 seats on the Committee, one of which is held by the General Secretary of the Professional Association of Teachers.

Either the European Commission or the Council of Ministers may issue directives which are binding, with the member states deciding how the directives are applied.

The six new health and safety directives under Article 118A are firstly a framework directive dealing with health and safety at work generally and five specific directives dealing with the workplace, the use of work equipment, the use of personal protective equipment, use of display screen equipment (VDUs) and manual handling of loads.

The general directive is similar to the 1974 Act in that it lays down broad general duties for safety at work. The employers bear primary responsibility for protecting employees' health and safety at work and must:

(1) Develop a coherent overall policy on health and safety.
(2) Evaluate risks and introduce necessary preventive measures.
(3) Co-operate with other employers.
(4) Designate personnel to carry out health and safety activities, or enlist competent external services.
(5) Take necessary measures for first aid, fire fighting and evacuation of employees.
(6) Provide health and safety information and training for employees.
(7) Consult employees or their representatives.

A draft directive in 1990 on maternity leave contains provision for protecting pregnant women from physical, chemical or biological agents or processes which could damage their health.

3
INSURANCE

Many thousands of people are injured each year in all sorts of ways. Many are not aware of the possibility of claiming compensation, others are deterred by the prospect of a long and expensive battle with an insurance company and its solicitors to get compensation. If a case has to go to court, then even if it succeeds, there will have been many anxious and stressful years before any compensation is received. There are a number of insurance schemes available which offer payment for personal injuries without the need for litigation, because payment does not depend on the victim proving negligence.

Personal accident insurance for pupils

There are a number of personal accident insurance schemes for pupils which cover serious injury or permanent disability caused by accident during organized school sports and physical education. For example, the Central Council of Physical Recreation has set up, through the Commercial Union, insurance cover for all pupils in participating schools, at a cost of around thirty-five pence per annum for each child at the school. A school which takes out this cover will have sports personal accident insurance for all its pupils. The cover includes death, loss of limbs or permanent loss of use of limbs, loss of sight, loss of speech or hearing and any other permanent disablement which prevents the pupil from earning a proper living.

The premium covers pupils for £50,000 disablement, and for around sixty-two pence per pupil, the disablement cover is £100,000. So a fifteen-year-old who lost an eye in 1988 when he was struck in the face while playing hockey at school received £50,000 insurance compensation within weeks of the accident.

There is also a school accident plan arranged by Brown Shipley Insurance Services Ltd which, again, is a blanket policy for every pupil in a school. It is available to state schools, grant maintained schools, voluntary aided schools and city technology colleges.

The cover applies during term time, at school and on school trips and it also applies on school trips during holiday periods and weekends. There are payments in the event of death and disability the premium being around fifty pence per pupil per year.

A similar scheme has been arranged by the National Confederation of Parent Teacher Associations. The Confederation has arranged a pupil's personal accident plan, which covers children in full-time education and gives 24 hour, world-wide cover against permanent disability. There is cover for total paralysis and the loss of limbs. A premium can be paid for £100,000 of cover or a reduced premium for £50,000 of cover.

Many schools are taking up these insurance schemes even though there is no legal obligation to do so. As well as deciding this point, the Court of Appeal in the case of *Van-Oppen v Bedford School* (see p. 51) also held that the school did not have a legal duty to advise parents of the inherent danger of serious injury in rugby and of the need to take out personal accident cover for themselves.

Personal accident cover for teachers

LEAs have a voluntary personal accident insurance scheme for teachers, which is arranged through Municipal Mutual Insurance Ltd. Those teachers who take up the scheme and are not injured at work do not have to prove that the LEA has been negligent in order to claim, as benefits are paid out on the basis of medical evidence. A premium can be as little as six pence a week for up to £5,000 cover, and LEAs can arrange for any premium to be taken directly from a teacher's salary. The scheme is open to full-time, part-time permanent and temporary teachers.

Personal accident insurance is not based on the principle of indemnity; the payment depends upon the premiums paid and the extent of the injury. So any payments received under a personal accident policy do not have to be paid back to the insurers if the teacher subsequently receives compensation from the LEA for negligence.

Permanent health insurance

Permanent health insurance (PHI) is also referred to as replacement income insurance. This is insurance to provide financial protection to anybody who is disabled for a long period of time and, as a result, loses his or her earning capacity.

Like personal accident cover, PHI pays out on a non-negligence basis, but while benefits paid by a personal accident scheme to a claimant who is off work on account of an accident are limited (usually to two years), PHI pays out on a long-term basis. In most schemes there is a deferment period, which means that for a stated period when the claimant is first unable to work, no benefit will be paid. The deferment period could be six months and, in some schemes, it is a year. Thereafter there is a continuous monthly payment until the insured person can resume work, or until he or she reaches normal retirement age. What the payment is depends on the premium paid and deferment policies may have different limits on the maximum payment. In some cases it is 75 per cent of the claimant's total average earnings in the previous twelve months, and in other schemes it is 50 per cent. Again, subject to the particular policy and the level of premium paid, there will be an automatic increase every year which is known as an annual escalation.

4
SAFETY IN WORK AREAS

In schools, children are in many different types of environments, undertaking different tasks, using all sorts of equipment and materials. So different precautions and safety measures will be needed in different situations but, in all cases, there should be basic safety rules and proper order, so that the risk of anything untoward happening is kept to a minimum.

Classrooms

There are teaching areas in schools which are more potentially hazardous than classrooms but, nevertheless, there is a need to observe basic safety rules in classrooms to minimize the risk of accidents happening.

(1) The layout of the classroom is important, for if there has to be an emergency evacuation, it is important that there are clear, exact escape routes. In any event, pupils' bags should not be allowed to block aisles as they can be a dangerous obstruction.
(2) Where there is a fire door, it should be kept clear and nonflammable materials should be used for displays.
(3) Good discipline can prevent accidents occurring as a result of horseplay.
(4) Electrical equipment may be used in class and the normal safety precautions should be taken to guard against electric shock, fire or injuries caused by misuse of equipment (for more detailed information see pp. 106–9).

(5) Tables and chairs should be checked for any defects such as splinters or insecure legs.
(6) Teachers should be careful when they have to lift heavy loads or heavy equipment. Staff should be told how to lift equipment safely, using the correct grip, the correct foot position and keeping the back straight. A teacher who finds any item too heavy should seek assistance.

Pen tops

There is a danger that children, particularly children under secondary age, can be asphyxiated by accidentally swallowing detachable pen tops. For various reasons, for example, because they are concentrating intensely or because they are bored, children do tend to bite or chew the end of their pens, and the caps can accidentally become detached and then inhaled. In recent years, several pupils have died in this way.

Research carried out in 1986 by the Child Accident Prevention Trust showed that detachable tops with a clip that extends at least the full length of the top would avoid asphyxiation by allowing the necessary air flow until the top could be removed. The research pointed out that with retractable pens, there was virtually no risk of this type of accident.

In March 1988, the DES wrote to all chief education officers, pointing out the dangers of children accidentally swallowing a pen top and this contained three recommendations.

(1) That all pens and ballpoint instruments with detachable tops supplied for use in school should only be issued to pupils without the top.
(2) That a suitable warning should be given to all pupils, teachers and parents of the risks involved if pens are brought to school for pupils use or used at home with detachable tops fitted.
(3) That LEAs may wish to consider replacing pens with detachable tops with those with ventilated tops or those without a separate top.

A number of pen manufacturers have produced new safety designs and introduced measures to attempt to eliminate the risk of this type of accident. For example, there are now detachable tops with holes or vents, which allow a free flow of air and some pens have extra large caps which cannot be swallowed. As well as possible dangers from the pen top, there is the danger of swallowing the end plug in a pen, and some manufacturers have attempted to recess the end plug so as to make it virtually impossible to pull out with the teeth.

There is a new British Standard BS7272, 'Specification for safety caps for writing and marking instruments', which gives further guidance.

Science laboratories

Laboratory safety depends a great deal on good habits and practices, sound discipline, clear and consistently enforced laboratory rules, and the teacher's own knowledge and experience of the hazards involved. Booklet No. 2 in the DES safety series, 'Safety in Science Laboratories', was revised in 1988. It gives advice on various aspects of safety under the headings of laboratory design of furniture, electricity, fire, chemical hazards, biological experiments, disposal of waste, ionizing radiations, particular operations, lasers, plastics and polymerization and dangerous experiments. It also includes a laboratory safety check list. Advice is also available from the expert bodies, such as the Association for Science Education, which, in 1988, produced a ninth edition of its booklet *Safeguards in the School Laboratory*.

The Association sets out the respective roles of the teacher, student teacher, technician and head of department in managing safety. There is also specific advice about safety rules, safety equipment, first aid and fire precautions. A number of special hazards are discussed, including mechanical hazards, radiation hazards and biological hazards.

Rules

In all teaching environments where children are involved in inherently dangerous activities, safety rules are necessary. In science and practical areas, safety rules are vital and will include the following:

(1) Pupils should not be allowed into the teaching room without permission.
(2) Pupils should never run about or rush around the room.
(3) Pupils should never interfere with or fool around with equipment, with tools or with chemicals.
(4) There should be no throwing.
(5) Protective clothing, including eye protection, should be worn when necessary.
(6) Long hair should be tied back and ties, cardigans and loose-fitting pullovers should not be allowed to hang down over a bench.
(7) Bags and cases or coats should never be put on benches or tables or worktops; they should be put where they will not cause an accident. Bench tops and floors must be kept clear.
(8) Electrical equipment and fittings, gas fittings, taps and fire extinguishers should not be interfered with.

(9) Rubbish should be put in the waste bins, and not into sinks on the side of benches or tables or on the floor.

(10) There should be high standards of hygiene and children should always wash their hands after practical work with chemicals, radio-active materials, animals or plants. There should be no eating, drinking or smoking in laboratories.

(11) Fire precautions are important and examples are given on p. 123.

(12) There should be an established procedure for dealing with accidents and also for reporting other serious, or potentially serious, incidents.

There should also be a procedure to allow pupils to carry out experiments in an orderly, safe and efficient way. As a guideline, pupils should be told to:

(1) Make sure that all the instructions about the experiment, particularly those relating to safety precautions, are clearly understood and to ask the teacher anything that is unclear.

(2) Check any equipment or apparatus for obvious defects before the experiment gets underway.

(3) Wear any protective clothing or equipment that is necessary.

(4) After the experiment, put the equipment and apparatus away and clear up as the teacher instructs. The teacher will also give instructions about left over materials.

(5) Report any accidents or near misses without delay.

The Education Service Advisory Committee of the Health and Safety Commission has produced a check card, *Do you work with chemicals and other materials in educational establishments?*, which sets out simple safety rules. These rules, which are reproduced with the Commission's permission, are as follows:

(1) Do take all the recommended health and safety precautions.

(2) Do consult your head of department/supervision safety adviser/safety representative if you are not sure how to use the material.

(3) Do report all incidents involving materials in use to your head of department/supervisor/safety adviser.

(4) Do make sure you know what to do in case of an incident, spillage or fire involving a particular material.

(5) Do use the minimum quantity necessary and return the container to the store when finished with.

(6) Do be careful about personal hygiene and always wash before going to eat.

(7) Do not transfer the material from the original to unsuitable containers such as milk bottles or jam jars.

(8) Do not mix materials, such as cleaners, unless permitted by instructions.

(9) Do not leave containers open.

(10) Do not transfer the contents into other proprietary containers unless it is safe to do so and the old label is removed and replaced with a new one.

(11) Do not use materials from containers with indistinct, or no, labels.

(12) Do not be untidy – good housekeeping promotes health and safety and sets an example for others to follow.

(13) Always remember, if in doubt, find out.

A number of other matters should be considered:

(1) Section 2 (2)(b) of the Health and Safety at Work etc Act 1974 deals with the storage and handling of dangerous substances and the Control of Substances Hazardous to Health Regulations 1988 (see pp. 24–5) lay down further requirements in relation to any substance which is hazardous to health.

In *Safeguards for the School Laboratories*, the Association for Science Education offers practical advice on safe storage both generally and in special cases. The Association advises teachers not to buy any more chemicals than are necessary so far as inflammable liquids and solids are concerned. The DES advises that stocks should not be more than is necessary for one year's use. Any stock which shows any signs of deterioration should be disposed of.

(2) Chemicals must be stored in their proper containers, properly labelled, and they should never be stored in containers otherwise or previously used for foodstuffs.

(3) Poisons must be stored in locked cupboards.

(4) Poisonous substances, hot solutions, volatile organic solvents, corrosive and other harmful liquids, must not be pipetted by mouth. For dilution, strong acids should be added to water, not vice versa.

(5) Mopping-up cloths, mops or buckets, absorbent granules, neutralizing solutions or compounds must be available, and be used as appropriate for chemical spills.

(6) If goggles or protective spectacles are placed on a laboratory bench, care must be taken to ensure that they do not come into contact with acids or other harmful chemicals.

(7) Radioactive substances can cause cancer and the advice in DES

Administrative Memorandum 2/76, 'Use of ionising radiations in educational establishments', should be followed.

(8) The misuse of lasers can damage eyes and the advice of the DES in Administrative Memorandum 7/70, 'Use of Lasers in Schools and other Educational Establishments', should be followed.

Electrical fittings in science laboratories need to be treated with respect and care. For example:

(1) Before making any adjustments to equipment, the apparatus should be completely disconnected from the mains supply. The same applies if the apparatus is being inspected or repaired.

(2) The cause of a fuse failure should always be ascertained and rectified before replacement.

(3) Cable and plug connections must be examined regularly for wear and displacement, and regular inspection and maintenance, particularly of portable equipment, is essential.

(4) Electrical apparatus must not be connected to a light fitting.

For more detailed advice about electrical safety, see pp. 106–9.

Safety equipment

It is most important that appropriate safety equipment is available and used when necessary. Failure by a teacher to use reasonable safety precautions has led to a criminal prosecution by the Health and Safety Executive.

(1) Protective spectacles, goggles or face shields must be worn where there is a risk attached to any particular experiment. Ordinary spectacles do not generally give sufficient protection, and so pupils who wear spectacles should be given goggles. Eye protection should always be worn when heating chemicals, handling corrosives or irritants, such as acids, alkalais, and methanol solution (formalin), or when carrying out potentially exothermic reactions. British Standard BS2092, 'Specification for Industrial Eye Protectors', is the relevant safety standard.

(2) Protective clothing, such as laboratory coats and aprons (except those made from synthetic materials), should be encouraged. They can provide some degree of protection against, for example, splashing and corrosive liquids.

(3) Protective gloves should be worn when handling apparatus that may be contaminated with chemicals or microorganisms, and when handling

dangerous chemicals or chemicals known to sensitize the skin or cause allergic reactions. Gloves should also be worn when handling hot apparatus, although care does need to be taken with objects being held, particularly glassware, that they do not slip.

(4) Whenever an experiment is being demonstrated, where there is a known or suspected risk of explosion or implosion, a safety screen should be used. A screen should be made of thick plastic or special glass and fixed securely in position. As far as possible, apparatus being used should be enclosed by screens.

(5) Fume cupboards are needed in rooms where toxic or irritant gasses and vapours, and particles of irritant solids, are being handled. Almost all laboratories will need a fume cupboard. DES Design Note No 29, 'Fume cupboards in schools', offers further advice, and British Standard DD80 includes minimum safety requirements for fume cupboards and recommendations about their use and maintenance.

There will be occasions when experimental apparatus has to be left unattended during school hours, and the Education Service Advisory Committee of the Health and Safety Commission has produced guidance on the safety aspects of such arrangements. It is recommended that an authorization document is used in which the member of staff responsible for setting up the experiment gives written information about the location of the apparatus, the services that are being used for the experiment, and where they can be safely isolated. There should also be instructions on what to do in an emergency and who to contact.

High Risk Activities

The Association for Science Education in *Safeguards in the School Laboratory* lists seven activities which are described as high risk activities and where particular care is needed.

(1) Demonstrations. Demonstrations by the teacher tend to involve more hazardous tasks than pupils are allowed to carry out themselves and while carrying out the demonstration, the teacher also has to keep an eye on the pupils. During demonstrations, the pupils should sit at a safe distance (the Association recommends two or three metres) and, if necessary, they should wear eye protection and safety screens should be used. The prosecution by the Health and Safety Executive of a science head of department in 1986 illustrates this point (see p. 19).

(2) Ethanol (alcohol) fires. The Association points out that pupils have

been badly burned using ethanol (alcohol, methylated spirits) as a fuel for model steam engines. Solid fuel should be used instead. It is particularly dangerous to decant hot ethanol too close to a lighted bunsen burner, or to attempt to fill a thermometer bulb with ethanol by repeated heating and cooling of the bulb, where the heating comes from a naked flame.

(3) Hydrogen explosions. Hydrogen and air mixture is explosive at the range of 4 per cent to 75 per cent hydrogen. This can be ignited not just by a naked flame, but also by catalysts, such as transition metals or their oxides at temperatures of 500°C. So if hydrogen is being used to reduce copper oxide, the oxide must not be heated until all the air has been flushed out of the apparatus. The Association gives practical advice on how to minimize the volume of air in the apparatus, and also on a fail-safe way of testing if all the air has been flushed out.

(4) Chlorine preparation. Chlorine is made by dripping concentrated hydrochloric acid in potassium manganate (vii) (permanganate) crystals. If concentrated sulphuric acid is mistaken for hydrochloric acid, the result can be disastrous and this has often happened, even to experienced chemists, because sulphuric acid was on the bench to use as a drying agent and was used by mistake.

Chlorine should only be prepared in a fume cupboard, because even small amounts are capable of causing lung damage.

(5) The alkali metals and phosphorus. Alkali metals (lithium, sodium potassium) react very vigorously with water, and phosphorus can react the same way with air. Phosphorus is easily ignited by heat generated by the friction of a knife cutting it. Only small pieces (the size of rice grains) of alkaline metals should be used. Also, lithium may explode if heated on pieces of porcelain or pottery.

(6) The thermite reaction. This reaction, says the Association, is very vigorous and can shower sparks over a wide area. So safety screens must be used and the pupils kept a safe distance away (the Association recommends three or four metres). The Association gives practical advice on how to set off the reaction safely.

(7) Blood sampling and cheek cell scrapes. The Association draws attention to the risk of AIDS, and the DES recommends that blood samples or cheek cell samples should not be taken either by a teacher or pupils. For further information about AIDS, see pp. 150−3.

The Educational Service National Industry Group of the Health and Safety Executive has collated a number of accident summaries prepared by HM Inspectorate of factories as a result of school science accidents from April 1986 to June 1987. Included in this summary, which was produced as a simple aid to training sessions, are the following injuries to pupils (IP means Injured Person).

Pupil injured by explosion in chemistry laboratory when concentrated acid was mistakenly added to potassium permanganate in place of hydrochloric acid, during an attempt to generate chlorine gas.

Pupil got solution of dilute sulphuric acid in his face whilst heating the solution in a test tube as part of an experiment. Solution overheated and went up into his face. The class was supervised and goggles were issued on an individual basis but IP was not wearing them. IP attended to quickly, no lasting injuries. Sufficient goggles were provided and were in a reasonable condition.

Pupil sustained hot chemical splash whilst carrying out distillation of i-bromo-butane during chemistry lesson. Cause of accident unexplained, possibly due to over-heating of reaction vessel causing stopper to be expelled along with the ejection of hot liquid. Experiment involves reaction of sulphuric acid, sodium bromide and butane-i-ol as described in standard *Nuffield Advanced Science Textbook*. IP wearing goggles, splash to face only, no injuries.

During chemistry experiment child, under direct supervision of teacher, tried smelling chlorine gas from bottle. Instead of taking sniff as instructed by teacher child inhaled fully causing gasping and coughing. Only small quantity of chlorine estimated to be in bottle, but child taken to hospital as precaution (appeared distressed). No injuries – returned to school following day. Standard teaching experiment.

These examples indicate the variety of risks that are present in laboratories, the real value of protective equipment and the need for the teacher to be constantly alert. However, accidents can happen despite proper precautions, and children can act in a totally unpredictable way, even when directly in the sight of the teacher.

Biology

The main risks present in biology laboratories include infection, allergic reaction and poisoning. So good laboratory routine and practices are important in keeping these risks to a minimum, and hygiene must be of the highest standard.

For example, children should be warned not to eat or drink anything when they are in the laboratory, or to suck pencils, because this could cause an infection.

The DES advises that no British wild mammals or birds, whether they are dead or alive, should be brought into schools, because they are invariably verminous and many species carry diseases which are transmittable to man.

With animals, high standards of hygiene and cleanliness are essential. Animal faeces and soiled bedding should be put in plastic bags before being put in the waste bin and incinerated. Protective gloves and protective clothing should be worn when touching animals, excreta or cages.

Animals can carry a variety of different diseases and these are as follows:

Budgerigar	Psittacosis (ornithosis), salmonella
Cat	Ringworm, bite infections, cat scratch fever
Cattle	Brucellosis, Q fever, ringworm
Dog	Ringworm, bite infections, toxocariasis
Fowl	Salmonella, Newcastle disease
Goat	Orf
Guinea pig	Listeriosis, brucellous pneumonia, lymphocytic chorio-meningitis
Mice	Lymphocytic choriomeningitis, ringworm
Monkey	B virus, rabies, hookworm
Pig	Ringworm
Pigeon/dove	Psittacosis
Rabbit	Pasteurella, listeriosis
Rat	Leptospirosis, rat-bite fever, ringworm, bite infections
Sheep	Orf, ringworm
Snake	Salmonella
Terrapin	Salmonella
Tortoise	Salmonella

Teachers should also be vigilant for those pupils who may be allergic to animal skin, hair or feathers and those who may be vulnerable to asthma, hay fever or dermatitis.

Plastic, stainless steel or galvanized cages are best because they can be sterilized far better than other types of cages. All cages should be thoroughly cleaned and sterilized on a regular basis with a disinfectant solution. There should be regular checks to see that the cages are secure, so that there is no risk of animals escaping, especially small rodents, such as gerbils, that can knaw through wood and plastic. Advice on housing and feeding animals can be obtained from the Medical Research Council, The Laboratory Animals Centre, Woodmansterne Road, Carshalton, Surrey SM5 4EF. The local vet can also be consulted on queries about the health, feeding and management of animals, and the British Veterinary Association is also able to offer advice at 7 Mansfield Street, London W1M 0AT.

DES Administrative Memorandum 3/90, 'Animals and plants in schools: legal aspects', draws attention to the responsibilities of those who bring animals and plants into educational establishments. The introduction confirms the value of bringing animals into schools where it says 'There are many excellent reasons for introducing live animals into the school environment. Animals are not found in schools as often as they could be and there are sound educational advantages to be gained from pupils having immediate experience of animals right from early years.' The Memorandum then explains in detail the effect of a number of pieces of legislation that affect this situation.

A number of basic safety and hygiene rules should be applied in biology laboratories. For example:

(1) All cages should be regularly cleaned and sterilized, preferably with steam, but if not, then with disinfectant solution.
(2) Pupils should not be allowed to take animals home unless the teacher can be sure that conditions are adequate and there will be proper supervision.
(3) The teacher and pupils must always wash their hands immediately after handling animals, excreta, cages and cleaning utensils, or water containing fish or reptiles.
(4) Food for human consumption must not be stored in laboratory refrigerators.
(5) Preserved material needs to be handled carefully, because it contains formaldehyde, which can cause irritation to the nose, throat, eyes and skin.
(6) Bacteriological or fungal cultures must be destroyed before disposal.
(7) A biological safety cabinet (a transfer cabinet) should always be used when cultures, bacteria, fungi and viruses are transferred from one container to another. The inside of the cabinet should be sterilized or disinfected regularly.

The DES booklet, *Microbiology, an HMI guide for schools and non-advanced further education*, contains advice to teachers working with micro-organisms on how to reduce the risk of infection or other illness. It contains a list of suitable species for culture. Also DES pamphlet No 61, *The use of micro-organisms in schools*, contains advice on the safe use and disposal of biological materials. Both the DES and the Association for Science Education give advice about safeguards when pupils examine cultures in petri dishes.

Technology

Craft, design and technology (CDT)

There are an ever increasing number of materials and equipment being used in practical departments in schools, and these present a wide range of hazards. In some cases, for example, in school workshops, the pupils will be working in conditions close to the work environment, and they must learn how to work safely and with due regard to the importance of eliminating unnecessary risks. The teacher's role is important both by way of setting an example to the pupils and also through the teacher's knowledge and experience of the hazards involved. Observations in this book about staff not specifically trained to teach a subject, which are made in relation to sports and PE (see p. 52), apply equally to the teaching of practical subjects.

Many schools have their own workshop facilities, which will have a variety of tools, equipment and machinery as well as potentially dangerous substances.

Workshops give pupils a foretaste of conditions that some of them may find in full-time employment. Again, good routine, good discipline and sensible procedures are the basis of safety. For example:

(1) Specialist equipment should only be used by children when supervised by appropriately trained staff.
(2) Neckties and long hair should be restrained to avoid them becoming entangled in machinery.
(3) Food or drink should not be brought into craft areas.
(4) Hands must be washed after practical activities.
(5) Fire extinguishers, buckets and blankets must be ready to hand.
(6) Electrical equipment and apparatus must be checked regularly (see p. 107).

DES Building Bulletin No. 31, 'Secondary school design: workshop crafts', gives advice about the layout of school workshops and how to arrange things so that working conditions are as safe as possible. Another source of information is British Standard BS 4163; 'Recommendations for health and safety in workshops in schools and colleges'. This makes recommendations about planning, environmental factors, workshops management, equipment and tools, handling of materials, personal protection and safety precautions.

It is essential that all tools and equipment are in good working condition and that the pupils are trained in how to use them correctly. Where protective clothing and/or eye protection are needed, they should be available and pupils instructed to wear them. Safety guards on electric drills, saws and other equipment should always be used.

The Education Service National Industry Group of the Health and Safety Executive has collated brief accident summaries by HM Inspector of factories as a result of investigations into woodwork machine accidents in schools from July 1984 to May 1986. These summaries, which are used as training aids, include the following accidents (IP means 'injured person'):

IP was injured on blade of Startrite bandsaw whilst brushing material off bandsaw table. Machine was switched off but blade still in motion. Injury involved cut to tip of index finger. No breaches of Woodworking Machine Regulations. Warning signs concerning rundown time of blade now displayed.

IP cutting timber with circular saw using push stick and also pushing timber with left hand. Left hand touched the blade removing top of thumb. IP experienced and trained.

IP cut three right fingers whilst pushing 18″ × 19.5″ × 3″ wood against circular saw; push stick not used. Adequate guarding provided but not properly adjusted.

Secondary school technical department technician sustained laceration to fleshy area between thumb and forefinger left hand whilst cleaning blade of circular sawing machine with wire brush. Forgot to check that machine was isolated. Start button is shrouded.

Fourteen year old pupil lost tip of thumb on Startrite bandsaw in school worskhop. Dowel being cut in jig with guard correctly adjusted. Pupil under direct supervision of teacher.

These details illustrate the importance of routine safety precautions, but nevertheless as the final example shows, accidents can happen with no explanation and despite all proper precautions.

There can be some highly flammable materials in craft rooms, such as foamed plastics like polystyrene or polyurethane, which can ignite easily and give off dense, toxic fumes. Only foam that is to be used should be stored in the workroom and their use must be kept under strict control. There may also be highly flammable paints, solvents, resins, and catalysts, and their use must similarly be controlled.

Information technology

Information technology (IT) is defined by the DES in 'Information Technology from 5 to 16' as 'the technology associated with the handling of information: its storage processing and transmission in a variety of forms by electronic means and its use in controlling the operation of machines and other devices'. The DES adds that through the use of IT in the curriculum, pupils can become knowledgeable about the nature of information, comfortable with new technology and able to exploit its potential. As pupils will be using electrical equipment, care has to be taken with plugs, flex and sockets (see p. 106), and there should be no trailing wires of any nature that could cause someone to trip or fall over. There are potential risks from visual display screens, and this subject is dealt with elsewhere in this book (see pp. 112–14).

Home economics

The aim of teaching home economics is to prepare children for some of the important aspects of everyday living and home economics matters. Courses will include food nutrition and textiles. As well as looking at these subjects in theory, there will also be practical work.

At all times when a practical session is in progress, there should be high standards of discipline and an adequate safety routine. Rules about dress, protective clothing and hygiene must be observed, and special care will be needed with cookers, microwaves, pans, deep-fat fryers, refrigerators, freezers and other electrical equipment. Pupils will be using sharp instruments and working with hot liquids. Everything should have its proper place and the organization of the class and the positioning of furnishings and fittings is most important (see p. 31).

In the fashion and textile areas, there will be sewing machines, irons and ironing boards, as well as scissors and other sharp implements. Many safety measures are very simple. For example:

(1) Electric irons should have proper pilot lights and stands, which are efficiently insulated against heat should the iron be left on. Metal stands can be used so long as air can circulate underneath them.
(2) Irons should always be allowed to cool down before they are put away and there should be regular maintenance checks.
(3) The supply to all electrical appliances should be turned off when they are not being used. Any damaged electrical equipment should be taken out of use immediately. There is more information about electrical safety on pp. 106–9.
(4) Surplus off cuts from sewing and dress making should be cleared away and put in a safe place at the end of each day.

Art

A large variety of materials are used in art departments, and a wide range of equipment is available to children of all ages who are involved in a number of different art activities. Safety is, therefore, an integral part of an art teacher's responsibilities.

(1) Advice already given in relation to classroom organization and furnishing is relevant (see p. 31). The art room design should be such that there is enough space for the children to move about safely, and for the teacher to be able to supervise pupils effectively. There must be sufficient storage space so that floors and passageways are not cluttered up with materials and equipment.

(2) Care must be taken with the way that children dress, and protective clothing and protective equipment must be worn or used where either appears necessary. Using aprons or overalls to protect pupils' clothes from paint, plaster or glue is not a pressing safety issue, whereas the use of goggles to protect the eyes, or respirators when dust is being created, are pertinent safety matters.

(3) Many art rooms have electrical equipment and advice either from the manufacturer, the installer or the LEA, given about the equipment's installations and upkeep must be followed. Further advice on electrical safety is given on pp. 106−9.

(4) There will be a large variety of cutting facilities in an art room including sharp knives, guillotines and cutting machinery. In all cases, the equipment must be in good condition, safely stored away or shut down when not being used, and only used by children under clear instruction and subject to whatever supervision is necessary.

(5) Where pupils are allowed to use kilns for pottery work, they should be fully briefed about how the kiln works and is operated. There needs to be proper space around the kiln so that pupils are not working in cramped conditions, and kilns which are placed in working areas should be caged. The Institute of Ceramics has produced an advisory booklet, *Health and Safety in Ceramics*, which gives detailed advice.

(6) Many of the tools in art rooms are potentially dangerous and need to be handled with care. DES Administrative Memorandum 2/65, 'Poisonous Substances in Pencils and other Allied Materials used in Schools', gives advice on the potential danger of paints, crayons and other materials containing poisonous substances. Plastics are highly flammable and therefore need to be used and stored with great care. Pupils using glues and adhesives must be warned that they can set quickly and that there can be serious problems if glues or adhesives come into contact with the skin. There may be corrosive substances in the art room such as acids used for etchings and these need to be treated with care.

Nursery classes

Children of preschool age are small and unpredictable in their action's. Potential hazards at low level which would not present a problem to older children and adults could be dangerous for very young children, and this, together with the erratic behaviour of some small children, can mean that they can become exposed to a wide range of risks.

Nursery teachers seek to encourage children to want to learn and find out about things by investigating and exploring, and by doing so develop a sense of independence. While this is an exciting time for children, they must be protected from harming themselves while being taught to recognize the dangers and so to avoid them in the future.

Hygiene is particularly important in nurseries, and the toilet area must be kept clean and disinfected: all spillages must be cleaned up immediately and disinfected if necessary. Sand and water need to be checked for germs.

The basic safety precautions already mentioned are necessary to ensure safety in the nursery and, in addition, the following points need to be considered.

(1) The teacher needs to be particularly vigilant for hazards near to ground level, and either remove them or take suitable precautions.

(2) There is a wide range of play equipment in nurseries, and these must be in a safe condition. Any defective equipment should be taken away immediately and not returned until it has been properly repaired. Knives and scissors must be stored away safely.

(3) Any materials that need to be kept away from the children should be beyond their reach and, if necessary, locked in a cupboard. Cleaning or cooking materials are the most obvious examples.

(4) To avoid children slipping over, all spillages should be cleaned up immediately. Drinks, water or paints will often be spilt, and sand or mud can be brought in from outside. Young children want to run about but they should not be allowed to do this in the nursery, especially if there is a wet area.

(5) Children should be told that although plants are attractive and interesting, they can be poisonous and the teacher should be vigilant to see that no child attempts to eat any plant or flower. There are a number of common plants which are poisonous, for example, hyacinths and poinsettia.

(6) Particular care is needed in cooking areas. The children must be closely supervised and guards fitted to equipment if necessary. Loose pan handles are dangerous and should be seen to immediately. When

saucepans are being used, the handle should be turned away from the front of the stove.

(7) Outdoor equipment should be checked regularly to see that there are no broken, cracked or splintered parts. Children can be harmed by cat or dog waste and outdoor sandpits should be covered when they are not being used, so as to prevent animals from fouling them.

Cleaning materials and any other dangerous or inflammable substances should be kept in a secure place, out of children's reach.

Children of nursery age can never be left unsupervised, and it will be the teacher's responsibility to see that there is always adequate supervision. There may be occasions when there is absolutely no alternative but to have only one person in charge of the children, but this situation should be avoided if at all possible, because if one child or a group of children need attention or emergency treatment, then the rest of the children are unsupervised. If the nursery is detached from the rest of the school with no quick way of summoning help, then this leaves a single supervisor in a very difficult situation, should any incident or emergency occur.

The teacher shortage survey in September 1989 indicated that nursery schools had the highest proportion of vacant posts at 5 per cent. One, a London nursery school head said, I am a head with two years' experience in the post, my deputy has one and a half years, one teacher has three years, and two only one year each. The staff is inexperienced round the school.[1] Another comment from an infant school in the south east was 'a teacher employed for four year olds has no experience or training for very young children. There is no nursery nurse available to assist her, so an inexperienced ancillary is employed.'

There has recently been a great deal of public concern about the safety of children's toys following a large number of accidents, some of which have been fatal. Toys used in schools must always be of an appropriate type, in good condition, used properly and stored safely.

So great was the concern about toy safety that the government has introduced legislation to enforce safety standards. The Toys (Safety) Regulations 1989 came into force on 1 January 1990, and any breach of these Regulations is a criminal offence with a maximum fine of £2,000 or a six-month jail sentence. In the Regulations, toys are defined as any 'product or material designed or clearly intended for use by children of less than fourteen years of age'. Toys must satisfy essential safety requirements set out relating to flammability, toxicity and other health hazards. The Regulations require toys to be safe, even if misused in a way that can be anticipated.

There is also a European Community directive on toy safety and for identification purposes, safe toys that comply with the directive carry the 'CE' mark (derived from the French acronym for the Community). All products will be tested by approved bodies and, if satisfactory, will be issued with certificates confirming that they meet the required standard. The relevant British Standard is BS5665.

The Lion Mark is the safety symbol for toys in the United Kingdom. Any toys bearing the Lion Mark, conform with BS5665. Only members of the British Toy and Hobby Manufacturers' Association are permitted to display the Lion Mark.

Toys with sharp edges can be particularly dangerous to young children. Some toys that are badly designed have sharp edges, while in other cases, toys may be damaged causing sharp edges. Small toys may also be dangerous if they can be swallowed or choked on by a child. The same applies to small, detachable parts of large toys. Some plastic toys present a risk of toxicity, but reputable manufacturers will have carried out specific safety tests for plastic toxicity in their products.

Any teacher who discovers a dangerous toy can report it to the local Trading Standards of Consumer Protection Departments, which can enforce product safety laws.

Many schools produce wooden toys, and it is important to see that these are safe for those who play with them. The British Standards Institution has produced a leaflet of guidelines for the amateur toy maker, giving advice about appropriate materials and proper construction. The leaflet is called *Playtime – wooden toys*, and its advice includes information about the safe construction of detachable parts, nondetachable parts, folding mechanisms, hinges and springs. Another BSI booklet, *Playtime – soft toys*, gives advice about materials and construction with particular reference to detachable parts and nondetachable parts, points and wires, cords and tubes or rigid parts. It also deals with the requirements of stuffing materials, including flammability tests.

5
SCHOOL SPORTS AND PHYSICAL EDUCATION

Physical education will always involve challenge and risk, which is part of the attraction of a subject that allows pupils to display their initiative, determination and courage. No list of safety precautions, however long, can remove all risks in physical education, but unnecessary dangers cannot be tolerated. A teacher who follows safe practice and promotes responsible behaviour, will enable pupils to benefit from exciting and challenging activities without exposing themselves to unnecessary risks.

There are a number of authoritative booklets and other publications dealing with safety in physical education. Number 4 in the DES safety series is *Safety in physical education*, which contains authoritative guidance and recommendations. More recently in 1990, the British Association of Advisers and Lecturers in Physical Education (BAALPE), produced the latest revision of its booklet *Safe practice in physical education*. This is an excellent booklet which has been approved by the DES and deals with general safety issues, as well as covering each sporting activity in detail. BAALPE has produced other helpful literature, which is listed in the bibliography, and a number of other sports bodies and school sports bodies have also produced their own written advice and information.

Physical education in schools seeks to nurture and encourage children's enthusiasm for physical activity and movement, and to give them the opportunity to develop body control and co-ordination, strength, stamina and special skills. One of the booklets in the HMI series, 'Curriculum Matters', is *Physical Education from 5 to 16*, and the objectives of physical education are set out as follows:

(1) To develop a range of psycho-motor skills.

(2) To maintain and increase physical mobility and flexibility.

(3) To develop stamina and strength.

(4) To develop an understanding and appreciation of a selection of physical activities.

(5) To develop the capacity to express ideas in dance form.

(6) To develop the appreciation of fair play, honest competition and good sportsmanship.

(7) To develop the ability to appreciate the aesthetic qualities of movement.

(8) To develop the capacity to maintain interest and to persevere to achieve success.

(9) To foster self esteem by the acquisition of physical competence and poise.

(10) To develop self confidence through understanding the capabilities and limitations of oneself and others.

(11) To develop an understanding of exercise for a healthy life.

General safety issues

There are three basic safety issues that apply in all aspects of school sports, in some more than others. First there is the question of the leader's specialist sport qualifications. Secondly, there is the issue of supervision by nonspecialist teachers and, finally, the extent to which a teacher can participate in competitive sports.

Sports qualifications

In an ideal word, all PE lessons would be taken by properly qualified PE teachers. But we are not in an ideal world. In November 1988 a Parliamentary Question was put in the House of Commons asking how many teachers taking school sports had a specialist qualification. The Education Minister replied that in January 1984 (the latest date for which figures where then available for maintained secondary schools in England), there were around 40,500 full- and part-time teachers who taught PE (including sport). Of these, 42 per cent did not hold a post A level qualification in the subject, and that these 42 per cent were responsible for 12 per cent of PE tuition. In response to a further Question about the encouragement that could be given to teachers to take up training schemes with the various national sporting bodies, the Minister replied that it is for the LEAs and schools to consider the in-service training of their staff in relation to their own resources, using the LEA training grant scheme where appropriate.

There are some sports where there simply must be somebody with suitable training on hand. For example, whenever children are in a swimming pool, there must be an adult present who is able to effect a rescue and carry out resuscitation in an emergency. Teaching certificates from the Swimming Teachers' Association or Amateur Swimming Association are suitable qualifications. Similarly, in body contacts sports such as rugby union, skilled teaching is essential, not only to provide terms of expert coaching about safe techniques, but also to ensure correct refereeing and enforcement of rules of the game, which are vital for safety.

In 1983, proceedings were commenced against Devon County Council by a former pupil of Exeter College, Brian Quinn, who seriously injured his back during one of the Devon Cup semi-finals in 1981 when he was playing for the college. He was seventeen years old at the time, and had been selected for an England under nineteen trial.

The college team had been coached in the manoeuvre of 'making the ball available', that is driving on into the opposition with the ball and then making the ball available between the legs for team mates coming up from behind to form a loose scrum. It was alleged that this technique was dangerous because the player's head could be pinned to the ground and his neck broken.

On match day, the college team did not have a warm up and had to wait for about thirty minutes until the other team were ready to start. Brian Quinn was injured right at the start of the game when he charged into the opposition and attempted to make the ball available. He fell to the ground with an opponent on top of him, and as his team mates piled in he was pushed forward and his head was pushed into the ground.

It was claimed that the team coach was negligent in failing to coach this particular technique safely and in failing to tell Brian Quinn not to drop his head too low and that impact with an opposing player should always be with the shoulder and not the head. It was also alleged that it was negligent to allow Brian to play without a proper warm up, and not instructing him to keep warm while waiting for the opposition to arrive.

The court case started in January 1988 and a settlement was agreed between the parties after the first week.

Another case in 1988, *Van-Oppen v Bedford School Trustees*, dealt with an injury to a pupil on the rugby field − the boy was injured as he attempted to tackle another player. The basis of the claim in this case was that the school had failed to take reasonable care for his safety, by failing to provide adequate coaching and instruction in proper tackling techniques.

The High Court examined the school's coaching and playing arrangements in detail and decided that the standard of supervision was high, the refereeing was vigilant and strict, and that the school had provided proper coaching and instruction, together with an emphasis on discipline, which meant playing the game correctly. The court also rejected the arguments that the boy's father should have been advised of the inherent risk of serious injury in the game of rugby, and also the need to take out personal accident insurance to cover this risk. The Court of Appeal confirmed that view in 1989.

A qualification from a national sporting body will include first aid training, and this is most desirable in many PE situations. All teachers in charge of PE should be prepared for some injury which could be a bruise, a graze, a cut, a break, a dislocation or an emergency requiring resuscitation.

Nonspecialist supervisors

This issue follows on from the last one. In many schools, nonsports teachers cover for PE teachers, and sometimes supply teachers find themselves in charge of a PE class. In some cases, a colleague from another department will come in to help during a particular PE lesson or during a large event such as a school sports day.

It is the head's ultimate responsibility to be satisfied that supervision arrangements are satisfactory. It will not be acceptable for any teacher to supervise a PE or games lesson unless he or she is able to organize events so that the children can play safely. In the case of PE activities, this means being familiar with the activities that the children are attempting, what the inherent dangers are, what the safe procedures are, and how able or otherwise the children are to attempt these activities. In the case of competitive games, a teacher must be able to control and referee the game and enforce the rules. Any teacher who feels that he or she is placed in a situation where the duty of care cannot be satisfactorily discharged, should put this concern in writing to the head before the event so that there is an opportunity to resolve the problem.

On sports day, it is perfectly acceptable for teachers to help with the general organization of the event, and to carry out tasks such as time keeping and measuring, but special experience is needed to deal with throwing and jumping events, and it would be unreasonable to put untrained teachers in charge of these activities unless they have been adequately briefed.

Teacher participation

There is case law on this subject. In 1984, the case of *Affutu-Nartoy v Clarke* discussed the teacher's duty of care during a game of rugby. The facts were that a rugby teacher taking a group of fifteen-year-old pupils for a practice game included himself in one of the sides, and when he got the ball, he put up a high kick, chased after it and high tackled the boy who caught the ball. The tackle, which was illegal according to the rules of the game, seriously injured the boy's back. The court decided that the teacher, who was a local rugby club player, was negligent. His mistake was to involve himself in the physical contact element of the game, because it was likely that this would put a pupil at risk, bearing in mind the teacher's advantage of height, weight, strength, skill and experience of the game. The court did not say that it was wrong for the teacher to have picked himself in one of the teams, because being involved in the game to demonstrate the noncontact skills such as catching, passing and kicking, was perfectly acceptable.

This principle applies in football, hockey and cricket, or any other competitive sport where a teacher can foresee the possible consequences of active participation. Following this case, many schools have experienced doubts about staff versus pupils matches, or matches between the school and former school players. The law is not banning such matches, but careful thought is required where players of different physical size and experience could be matched against each other and any player with these superior qualities should be made to understand the potential risks.

There are a wide range of sporting and physical activities available to children of all ages at school and, in each case, safety measures should be established and operated.

Gymnastics

Gymnastics has developed considerably in recent years, and now involves a number of exciting and challenging but potentially dangerous routines and exercises. There is likely to be a wide range of abilities in any class of children learning gymnastics, and the teacher will need to make suitable choices of exercise for each of the pupils and to keep a close watch on the class, to see that no child is doing anything that he or she is not able to do safely, or is attempting something in unsafe conditions.

Young children should first of all be taught control and co-ordination of basic movements such as running, jumping, skipping, rolling and climbing.

They should also be given experience of apparatus so as to know how to get on the apparatus, perform the exercise, and then get off it. By the time children reach secondary school age, they should have been given an opportunity of building on the basic actions they have already learnt and producing sequences of movements. They will also have participated in team games and learnt the importance of rules and the need to conform to them. As pupils progress through secondary school, they will develop physically, intellectually and emotionally at different rates, so there will be differences in height, weight, strength and commitment. By the age of sixteen, pupils should have had experiences which enable them to invent and improvise sequences of movement, and they will have the ability to devise their own practice and routines. They will also have developed a knowledge of the effect of different types of physical exercise and exertion, and the need for appropriate relaxation and rest when the body is tired.

Initially, young children will react to short, simple instructions, but gradually the instructions can become more complicated, and so they are able to respond to an idea by improvisation, arranging their own activity and chosing their own apparatus.

Safe routines and practices are essential and they should take account of the following points:

(1) Proper discipline is vital, so that the risk of horseplay or a breakdown of good order is kept to a minimum.

(2) All gymnastic apparatus should conform to the relevant British Standards and, where necessary, apparatus should be adjusted according to manufacturers' instructions, to accommodate the needs of a particular group of pupils. All apparatus should be inspected regularly.

(3) Apparatus should be put together according to manufacturers' instructions, and it should be checked carefully before any activity begins.

(4) Staff and pupils should know how to handle apparatus carefully if they are involved in erecting or dismantling it, and pupils should be told that it is important to do this correctly and safely. They should be encouraged to keep a watch for any defects or potential dangers, and told to report any defects straight away.

(5) Care should be taken when positioning the apparatus. There are obvious dangers if apparatus is put too near to walls, windows or other pieces of apparatus. The teacher should also arrange groups and apparatus, so that there is no danger of gymnasts colliding with each other.

(6) The floor of the gymnastics area should be clean, clear of anything that someone could fall over, and it should be smooth and nonslip.
(7) Mats should be used whenever a child has to jump over, or jump down from, apparatus and the landing needs to be cushioned. The mats should be placed carefully and not thrown down indiscriminately on the floor. It is very important that mats are kept in good condition and old mats, in particular, should be checked for wear and tear. Thin and worn mats can cause accidents.
(8) Appropriate dress should be worn, and footwear should be suited to the activity and the conditions. On no account should pupils work indoors in stockinged feet.
(9) Watches and jewellery should not be worn.

One of the necessary skills of a teacher in charge of gymnastics is to assess the children's own capabilities: what they can safely attempt, what they cannot attempt, what they can attempt only with support, and what can be attempted without support. Children should not be allowed to attempt any exercise for which they do not have the necessary physical strength or flexibility. It may be that a particular child has a physical problem which makes it unsafe for that child to be involved in physical exercise. Any information provided by parents should be taken into account, as the 1982 case of *Moore v Hampshire County Council* illustrates. A twelve-year-old girl with a congenital hip defect told her PE teacher that her doctor had said she was now allowed to do PE, even though her mother had earlier told the school that she was not fit to join in. The Head had, in fact, made a special note to say that the girl should not do PE. The teacher accepted the girl's word and let her attempt to do a handstand, assisted by another girl in the class. The girl was injured and successfully sued for negligence. The court decided that the teacher had been careless in allowing the girl to take part in the PE lesson without first checking that she was allowed to do so, and also that the teacher had failed to properly supervise the girl's handstand as her special condition required.

A different problem arises if a pupil does not bring a note to excuse him or her from PE, but nevertheless claims to be unfit or unwell. It can be a risk to insist that a pupil participates in these circumstances, and the school should write to the parent for clarification if there is any doubt.

The decision whether or not a child should be allowed to attempt an exercise unassisted must always be a matter of judgement. The teacher should be reasonably satisfied that the child is sufficiently prepared, motivated and has been properly trained to take on an activity alone. In any event, the child must have successfully completed the preliminary stages leading up to any new exercise, before attempting the exercise itself.

There may be circumstances when children cannot be left to look after themselves on account of the inherent danger of the exercise. In a 1982 case, *Kershaw v Hampshire County Council*, the children were using a trampette to vault over a box, and although the teacher did organize two catchers, there was an accident when one pupil jumped and bounced too high for the catchers and fell, injuring herself. Although the pupils had already practised this exercise without mishap, the court decided that because a trampette was more dangerous than a normal springboard, the teacher should have been present to supervise the exercises, whereas in fact she left the gymnasium to go to the office just before the accident occurred.

In a 1952 case, *Wright v Cheshire County Council*, a twelve-year-old boy was injured as he vaulted over an exercise buck. He was one of ten boys who were vaulting one after each other, and the instruction from the teacher was that the boy who had just vaulted over would wait to assist the next boy to come over. As one boy was vaulting over the buck, the school bell rang for playtime and the boy who should have been receiving him ran off. The teacher was elsewhere in the gymnasium and the boy who was vaulting over fell and injured himself. The court was told that all the ten boys had done this particular exercise before, and that it was normal practice to allow boys with experience to do the exercise themselves in this way. There was no proof of negligence. It was not necessary to have an adult at the receiving end of the buck, and the accident was caused by something that could not have been foreseen, which was the pupil who had just vaulted, running away at the crucial moment.

Many schools have trampolines and these have been the cause of a number of accidents.

The Leisure Service Department of the Metropolitan Borough of Bolton has produced a video on how to improve trampoline safety, which explains how to safely erect and dismantle a trampoline, and describes safety techniques when the pupils start to use the trampoline. Both the British Trampolining Federation and the Institution of Occupational Safety and Health have endorsed the video, and RoSPA and the Sports Council have also approved it. The video lasts for twenty minutes and costs £45 from the Department of Leisure Services, Bolton Metropolitan Borough Council, 2nd floor, The Wellsprings, Bolton, Lancs BL1 1US. Telephone 0204 22311.

Football

Football is a physical contact sport, which is played competitively. There will inevitably be a risk of injury. Cuts, grazes, bruises, sprains and strains are commonplace, but more serious injuries can happen and the teacher in charge should be able to recognize the symptoms of any such serious injury.

Football is played indoors and outdoors, and in each case it is essential that both the playing surfaces and the surrounding areas are safe. A football field should be clear of glass, wire or any other dangerous debris, and if a game is being played indoors, the floor area should be free of any other equipment or apparatus. Moveable apparatus should be moved away, and any fixed apparatus should be covered, so that no player is injured if there is a collision. Halls with unprotected windows or glass should never be used for a game of football. Light bulbs should be protected.

It is normally safe to play football outdoors, whatever the weather conditions are, with the exception of very cold weather, when there could be frozen ridges over the field. If a game is allowed in these conditions, then the players should be told to wear tracksuit trousers to prevent them from grazing their legs if they fall over and, in any event, goalkeepers should wear tracksuit trousers when the ground is hard.

It is important for safety's sake that the rules of the game and the code of conduct are explained to the players, so that they know what the rules are and why they are imposed. Some examples of those rules are given in the next section. Few stipulations are necessary about clothing and equipment, other than that boots should be checked regularly for any worn or sharp edges, and to see that they are properly studded.

Violent foul tackles can cause serious injuries, and pupils should be strongly discouraged from any excessive play.

Rugby union

Rugby is a vigorous, physical contact game, and a number of safety precautions should be taken to prevent injury.

(1) Equipment should be checked. Boots should be firm fitting with ankle support and the studs must be in good condition. It is recommended that shin guards made of light material and strapped on to the leg are worn by all forwards.

(2) Mouth guards are also recommended, but they should be checked to see that they are fitted correctly.

(3) Players should not be allowed to eat sweets or chew gum during a game or training, because this could cause an obstruction in the air passage.

(4) Rings or jewellery should not be worn.

(5) The playing area should be regularly inspected to ensure that there are no stones or holes, or anything dangerous like glass. The perimeter of the field should be clear of obstructions and the corner flag should be flexible. Wherever possible, the base of the uprights on rugby posts should be padded.

(6) Rules must be laid down and enforced so that injuries are not caused by anyone breaking the laws of the game.

The Rugby Football Union has produced a series of leaflets under the general title of injury prevention. Each leaflet deals with a particular topic and these are 'The spirit of rugby', 'The role of the teacher/coach', 'Play hard, play safe' 'Keep your head up', 'Be prepared', 'What to do, . . . concussion, neck injuries, kiss of life', 'What to do, . . . fractures, dislocations, bleeding, infections' and 'Physical conditioning exercises for young players'.

The leaflets stress the importance of learning proper techniques and of players continually having refreshers on those techniques. It is pointed out that three-quarters of the injuries arising from tackles in rugby happen to the tackler, which is a clear example of the importance of proper technique. There is advice on warm-ups, why they are needed and what they should include, and technical advice on rucking, scrummaging, mauling and tackling.

Hockey

Hockey is a fast-running game and played with a hard ball and hard sticks. Therefore it inevitably contains an element of danger. Safety precautions that should be taken include:

(1) The hockey pitch should be checked to see that it is flat and well maintained, as an uneven bounce can cause a hockey ball to kick up. On an artificial surface, players should be advised to wear tracksuit trousers, to stop the legs being burnt when they fall down. Hockey goals should be kept in good condition and, if they are portable, they should be properly secured to prevent them from tipping up.

(2) All equipment should be kept in good condition, and sticks should be

checked for rough wood or splinters.

(3) Footwear should be kept in good condition and players should be encouraged to wear mouthguards and shinpads. The goalkeeper needs to be particularly well protected, and should always wear adequate pads, gloves and abdominal protection. It is strongly recommended that a goalkeeper is given a full helmet/mask which protects the head.

(4) The rules of the game must be clearly understood and strictly observed. In particular, players should be told about dangerous stick play.

(5) No dangerous jewellery should be worn.

Cricket

Cricket is a competitive team game, played with a hard ball, and so safety considerations do need to be taken into account. For example:

(1) Discipline is essential on the cricket field, and pupils should be told that the highest standards of sportsmanship and conduct are expected of them. Good order and discipline is just as important when pupils are practising in cricket nets.

(2) Protective equipment is particularly important in cricket. Teachers should make sure that there is a sufficient stock of the right size of equipment and that it is kept in good condition. The laws of cricket lay down dimensions for equipment, such as the ball, bat and pitch, but these do not fully cover school cricket. The National Cricket Association's recommendations are listed in Table 5.1. Up until under fourteen level, the stumps should be 27 × 8 in. and thereafter 28 × 9 in. Batsmen should be instructed to wear pads, batting gloves and a

Table 5.1 Recommended cricket equipment for use in schools

Age group	Size of ball	Size of bat	Length of pitch
Under 7	4¾ oz	3	16 yards
Under 9	4¾ oz	4	17 yards
Under 10	4¾ oz	4/5	18 yards
Under 11	4¾ oz	5/6	19 yards
Under 12	4¾ oz	6/Harrow	20 yards
Under 13	4¾ oz	6/Harrow	21 yards
Under 14	5½ oz	6/Harrow	22 yards
Under 15	5½ oz	Harrow/full size	22 yards

protector and the wicket keeper should wear pads, gloves and a protector.

(3) The Association also recommends that no fielder who is under fifteen years of age, except the wicket keeper, should be allowed to field nearer than 8 yards measured from the middle stump, except behind the wickets and on the off-side. At under thirteen level and below this, the distance should be 11 yards. In addition, the Association recommends that should any fielder come within that distance, the umpire should stop the game immediately and instruct the fielder to move back. The English Schools' Cricket Association has a similar rule. It adds that where it proves helpful, umpires should have a mark laid down so that there is no doubt about what the respective distances are.

In an unreported case in 1939, East Sussex County Council was held vicariously liable for the negligence of a teacher in charge of a game of cricket at school, during which a fielder was hit by the ball. Although there was a dispute about where exactly the boy had originally been placed by the teacher, the court did decide that when the accident occurred, he was considerably less than 10 yards from the wicket on the leg side and that this was a dangerous position. The teacher had not noticed that the boy was close to the wicket before allowing the bowler to start his run, and the court said this was negligent.

(4) The playing surface should be flat and clear of bumps or holes. If an artificial wicket is used, then it should be kept in good repair and matting should be fastened securely so that there are no bumps or uneven parts.

Swimming

In primary schools, the emphasis in swimming lessons is to develop safety and confidence in the water, as well as the pupils' ability to master the fundamentals of some of the recognized strokes. At secondary level, the teacher should be able to concentrate on improving pupils' technique with strokes they already know, increasing the number of strokes they can use and adding lifesaving and survival skills.

There can be a danger of complacency creeping into swimming arrangements, and it must never be forgotten that swimming is an activity where, even for experienced swimmers, safety precautions must be clear and rigorously enforced.

Many LEAs now have their own regulations about swimming in school pools and elsewhere, and these must be complied with. They will deal with supervision requirements, and may also lay down stipulations about qualifications for supervisors. A number of other points should be borne in mind:

(1) Pool rules and procedures must be spelt out clearly to the children and understood by them.
(2) There should be a competent life-saver present, who knows how to carry out resuscitation, and is capable of entering the water and going to the rescue of any child in difficulty.
(3) When the children are in the pool, the teacher at the poolside must be able to see the whole class all the time. The teacher should be able to carry out any rescue procedure from the poolside, but should not get in the water unless there is an emergency, if that would leave no adult on the poolside to keep an eye on the children in the water.
(4) There needs to be a clear and simple communication system between the teacher and the children in the water. The children must know how to tell the teacher if something is wrong.
(5) There should be a simple signalling system for the teacher to use in an emergency. This will normally be a whistle.
(6) Children should always be counted before and after they go into the water.
(7) There should be adequate life saving equipment and first aid equipment at the poolside, and there should be a telephone connection for use in an emergency.
(8) Safety rules must be properly enforced. For example, children should not be allowed to eat anything in the water, to wear jewellery, or to misbehave, either in the water or on the poolside.
(9) The children need to be familiar with any sharp change of depth in the pool, and a rope across the water dividing shallow from deep water is particularly helpful. Young children who may have learnt to swim in a teaching pool with a flat bottom may not appreciate that a large pool has different depths.
(10) Staff should check that the floors of showers and other wet areas are safe. Smooth floor tiles can become dangerously slippery, and tiles should ideally be grooved or ridged.

Athletics

Athletics is a sport where safe practices and sound techniques must be taught from the beginning. Children involved in athletics are learning new skills, some involving dangerous equipment, and so there must be sound instruction. During competitions, there will be many children running, jumping and throwing, and teaching staff may be preoccupied with judging, measuring or time keeping. Proper order and a respect for safety considerations are essential.

Dangerous situations are also likely to occur in a class teaching situation where a large group of children of differing abilities are being coached on a school playing field.

As well as the literature already referred to at the start of this section, the Schools' Consultative Committee of the Amateur Athletic Association in its leaflets, 'Safety Measures in Athletics', lays down a number of recommendations and guidelines for teachers. The leaflet gives advice on safety aspects of the throwing events, jumping and track events.

Throwing events

The throwing events are the javelin, shot, discus and hammer, and a number of safety measures are necessary.

(1) Equipment should be kept in good repair and stored safely, so that there can be no unauthorized use. Throwing implements should always be treated with respect and they should never be played around with or mishandled.

(2) Throwers should stand well behind the throwing circle or scratch line and stay there until they are called to make a throw.

(3) Before throwing, the thrower should watch out that there is no-one in the landing area or probable line of flight of the implement before making a throw. This responsibility rests with the thrower as well as with the teacher.

(4) After making a throw, the thrower should stay behind the circle or scratch line and should only attempt to retrieve the implement when all the other throwers in the group have thrown. A javelin, discus, shot or hammer should never be thrown back to the throwing circle or scratch line.

(5) Footwear has to be safe, in good condition and give the thrower a firm foothold.

(6) Extra care is needed in wet conditions, when the implements themselves will be wet and more likely to slide after landing. In any event, in wet conditions the runways and take-off areas should be checked, to see that they are not too slippery.

(7) The Association gives advice about training programmes and how to prepare and train children for throwing. It must be left to the

teacher's own judgement to decide when a pupil is able to make a throw safely. The pupil must have been sufficiently trained, must be familiar with the throwing rules, and relied upon to comply with those rules.

(8) All persons except the thrower must remain behind the circle or scratch line.

(9) The throwing implement must only be retrieved on instruction.

(10) Protective cages must be used for hammer throwing events.

Jumping events

(1) Sand pit landing areas can be used safely to train beginners for high jumps where the bar is at a low height and jumpers normally land on their feet. This includes the preliminary learning stages of pole vaulting. But for jumps where athletes land on their back and also for more advanced training and competition, a soft landing area made of manufactured foam is necessary.

(2) A number of safety checks should be carried out before jumping starts. If the edges of a sand pit landing area are lined with wood or concrete, the edges must be flush with the surrounding ground and safely covered so that there is no risk of a jumper hitting them. Any other hard surfaces should also be covered.

(3) The sand in the landing area should be 'sharp' sand that will not cake, and it should be deep enough to prevent any jarring on landing. The pit should be dug over before use and also at regular intervals during use. A fork used as a rake is only adequate for levelling.

(4) Nothing should be left in the landing area or near to it as this could injure a jumper. Teachers should check that spades, forks or rakes are not left there. The sand should be checked for any other dangerous objects, such as glass, metal or wire.

(5) The runway surface needs to be checked for holes or crumbling. Unless the pupils have spikes, grass should not be used as a take-off surface.

(6) Nobody should start a jump while there is somebody in the landing area.

Track events

Track events are relatively safe, but precautions are still necessary.

(1) There must be proper control at the start of races. The runners should be told that for safety's sake they should not bunch early in

the race, because there could be collisions or accidents with spikes. Where spikes are worn, then the number of athletes in a race will need to be kept to a safe limit.

(2) Starting blocks should be removed from the track after they have been used and not left lying around. Hurdles must be kept in good condition and checked for any dangerous edges, before any competitive or practice sessions. The Amateur Athletic Association lays down rules for the weight and resistance of hurdles.

(3) The finishing tape should be a length of worsted, which breaks easily, and it should be across the track at a safe height so that there is no risk of it reaching the necks of any of the athletes.

(4) Starting pistols should not be misused or tampered with when they are not being used.

Racket games

Squash and badminton are becoming increasingly popular sports and together with tennis, are available in many schools.

(1) Outdoor courts should always be checked to see that they are safe. Shale or similar nongrass courts should be watered and rolled regularly, to keep the surface firm and level. Lines on courts should be flat, level and securely fixed. A particularly keen inspection is necessary where courts may have been made slippery by rain.

(2) Teachers should carefully organize practice sessions, particularly where there are large groups, with some pupils involved in the activity and others waiting their turn. There should be no danger of a pupil being hit by a racket as a stroke is being made or, alternatively, being hit by the ball.

(3) Correct footwear is important and should be checked to see that there is no danger of a pupil tripping or slipping.

Weight training

Weight training is becoming increasingly popular, both as an aid to fitness in competitive sport, and also as an exercise in itself. To attempt weight training without understanding the various techniques and the anatomical and physiological factors involved can be dangerous.

(1) Equipment should always be checked. There should be no sharp metal parts or sharp ends, and any metal with a rough finish could be dangerous. Under no circumstances should faulty equipment be used.

(2) Equipment must always be stored safely. Weak or unstable storage racks are a great hazard. Any equipment that is not stored should be put out of harm's way.

(3) Strict discipline is essential and a pupil should never be allowed to play around with the weights.

(4) Equipment should be spaced out so that there is no risk of pupils being a danger to each other during a weight training session.

Cycling

Cycling is an increasingly popular activity and basic safety checks and sound organization and discipline are essential.

(1) All bikes should be checked for safety. It is essential to check brakes and tyres, and lights if they are needed. The cause of any strange noises should be investigated. Routine maintenance checks will discover whether brake blocks are worn, whether tyres are smooth and worn and whether they are pumped up hard enough. Spokes should be inspected to see if any are bent, broken or missing. The chain will be too loose if it can be lifted more than 2 cm, using a pencil. On the saddle, the nuts should be checked to see if they are tight and the saddle should not for any other reason be wobbly. Saddle heights should be checked to see that the rider can sit comfortably on the saddle with one foot on the ground.

(2) The leader must be sure that the children are proficient cyclists and that they understand the Highway Code before allowing them on the roads.

(3) It will usually be safe to cycle two abreast, unless there is heavy traffic on the road, in which case cyclists will need to be in single file. In any event, riders should not be too close to the person in front or too close to the rider alongside when riding in pairs. A safe distance between bicycles is at least one bicycle length. The leader should make sure that the group knows how to move safely into single file when necessary.

(4) Group riding should, if necessary, be practised on the school playground, or some other safe place off the road.

(5) Seven is the recommended maximum number of cyclists for one adult leader and, in that case, the leader should ride at the back of the group on the outside, so that whole group can be seen and instructions given as necessary. The leading pair should be two reliable riders. If there are two leaders, the best system of supervision is for one to be at the front of the party and the other at the rear.

6
SCHOOL TRIPS

There is no doubt at all that school visits and journeys are an essential element of the school curriculum, as they are a valuable part of the education provided for the children. Pupils taken outside school premises have the chance to gain new personal and social skills, and to return to school with greater confidence and enthusiasm. Many children are taken out of school for a short time to go to the local museum or library. Others are taken to the local farm, while others spend a week or more away at an activity centre or skiing in Europe. As a result of recent tragedies, most LEAs and independent schools now have comprehensive notes of guidance for teachers on school trips, and these deal with a number of issues in detail. Guidelines should make it clear that safety is never an 'extra' consideration, but is an integral part of every out-of-school activity.

In 1989, the DES published *Safety in Outdoor Education*, which replaced *Safety in Outdoor Pursuits*, produced in 1977. It includes advice about general safety principles, leadership and the safety features that should be part of preparation, as well as safety considerations once the trip is underway. The section in the book devoted to safety on land gives advice about mountain walking, rock climbing, skiing, caving, campcraft, horse riding, orienteering, rope courses and zip wires, and cycling. There is also a section dealing with safety afloat, which includes advice about swimming, canoeing, sailing, windsurfing, surfing, rafting, subaqua activities, rowing, angling and fishing. The third section on specialist activities deals with safety in the air, which sets out general safety principles applying to airborne activities, including gliding, flying and parachuting.

In 1987, the School Curriculum Development Committee produced a teachers' guide to safe practice out of school entitled *Out and About*. This book was written with the assistance of an Advisory Group consisting of union and LEA representatives, and other bodies with expertise in outdoor education. Throughout the book the emphasis is on safety being a matter of positive attitudes, rather than just rules and regulations, and there are chapters dealing with leadership, planning, residential and nonresidential trips, adventure activities, trips abroad and school and community activities.

Responsibilities for school trips

Headteacher

The head is in charge of the internal organization, management and control of the school, and is responsible for seeing that all school trips comply with the LEA's regulations. In addition and in order to discharge the duty of care towards the children, the head must be reasonably satisfied about the preparations and arrangements for the trip. This responsibility is one of general oversight and responsibility for specific details can be delegated to another member of staff, usually the teacher in charge of the trip. The delegation must be a reasonable one in all the circumstances. There has to be a first time for every teacher to take charge of a trip, but a head could put himself or herself at risk both professionally and legally by allowing a teacher to take charge of a trip without any previous experience, either as a leader or as a deputy under a capable leader. In any event, where a teacher takes charge for the first time, either the head or a senior member of staff may well have to play an active part in preparation and in the preliminary arrangements.

If the head is not involved in the trip, then he or she will be an important contact point for teachers, parents and the LEA in the event of any emergency or mishap. The head will need to have written details of the trip, which should include travel times to and from the destination, the address and telephone number of the destination, names of all those on the trip and contact addresses and telephone numbers for parents.

LEAs

The LEA's duty of care for children on a school trip is exercised through the teachers who are the LEA's employees and, consequently, the LEA is responsible for the negligence of any teacher on a school trip, when a teacher is acting in the course of his or her employment, just as if he or she were in school. The position of a teacher on a trip arranged by a third party is discussed later.

Governors

School governors now have statutory responsibilities for the school curriculum, including extra curricular activities such as school journeys and trips. In respect of those trips that specifically require the governors' consent, the governors will need to satisfy themselves that the trip has a clear educational value, that arrangements comply with LEA guidelines, and that there are no unacceptable burdens either in educational or safety terms upon the school in the absence of staff on the trip. Decisions about school trips do not necessarily have to be made by a full governing body, and responsibility can be delegated to a subcommittee if the governors feel this is appropriate.

Employing governors, that is governors at an independent school, a grant maintained school or a voluntary-aided school have the same responsibilities as LEAs.

Leadership

The quality of leadership is essential to the safety and success of a school trip, and no set of rules and regulations, however detailed, can guarantee the children's safety. On every trip there must be a teacher in charge of the group and, in most cases, there will also need to be a deputy leader standing ready to take over if necessary. GCSE is vital. This stands for Good Common Sense and Experience and, where necessary, the leader should have a nationally recognized qualification, especially where children are taken to potentially dangerous environments or asked to undertake potentially dangerous outdoor pursuits.

Experience is the great teacher and for the competent and experienced leader, safe practice will have become a state of mind. One particular skill acquired through experience is a general awareness and understanding of danger and the ability to identify a potential risk. Identifying a risk is, of course, half way towards eliminating it, and leaders must be aware of the possible risks involved in working in particular environments, undertaking certain activities or using particular equipment or facilities. An experienced leader will also be clear and confident with colleagues and be able to set high personal standards. The leader must be familiar with the children in the group, knowing their strengths and weaknesses and their general abilities; aware of their previous experience away from school or from home, as the case may be; as well as aware of their previous experience of the type of trip being undertaken.

The leader must be able to exercise full responsibility during the trip and this must be accepted by everybody else taking part, including senior colleagues. In some cases, the head may be the leader, but it should not follow that if the head does go on a school trip, he or she should automatically be the leader.

Adults on a school trip may have little or no experience of taking out a group of children. The leader will wish to offer advice such as:

(1) Get to know the children in your group as quickly as possible, learn their names and be able to match a name to a face.
(2) Find out if any of the children in your group need particular care or attention.
(3) Make yourself familiar with the site that the group is visiting and with the itinerary.
(4) Listen carefully to instructions from the teacher in charge and keep safe any written details or instructions that you are given.
(5) Listen carefully to any instructions given to you or to the group as a whole by an instructor, a guide or an official.
(6) Try and anticipate in advance any potential hazards and be alert for any dangers that you are warned about or that you notice while you are with the children.
(7) Always try to keep every pupil in your charge in full view.
(8) Never let a child linger behind the others, or go off alone.
(9) Count the pupils in your group regularly.
(10) Ensure that the children behave in an orderly and responsible way. If a pupil or a group of pupils misbehaves and does not respond to your instructions, you will need support from one of the teachers.
(11) Find out which teacher is carrying a first-aid kit or, if you are on site, where the first-aid kit is. If there is an accident, call any teacher to help, unless one of the teachers is responsible for first aid in which case, try and contact him or her first of all.

Preparation

The importance of proper preparation to secure the success and safety of a school trip cannot be overstated, however long or short the trip, and however large or small the group. Successful safety planning depends to a large extent on the leader being able to anticipate all the potential risks and dangers and the difficulties which could arise, and then making plans to avoid and eliminate them. Many school trips, particularly those involving outdoor pursuits, are by their very nature, underpinned by challenge and adventure and so can never be free of risk. Indeed, part of the educational value of these adventure activities is to make children aware of the need for safety considerations to complement initiative, excitement and the spirit of adventure. But while children should be encouraged to confront a challenge and to face adventure, they must never be exposed to unacceptably dangerous conditions and risks.

Preparation will inevitably involve the children themselves, and this is an ideal opportunity to draw to their attention the need for positive attitudes to safety. In particular, the children must be aware of the importance of good order and discipline during the trip, and it must be clearly understood that all party members should behave responsibly and be a creditable representative of the school. Before the trip, a list of rules should be drawn up and circulated to all the group. These rules are, of course, just as enforceable on a school trip as they are at school.

Parents and governors should also be involved in the planning stage and kept fully informed of what arrangements are being made. The reports into the tragedies at Land's End (in 1984) and the Austrian Alps (in 1988) both highlighted the need to keep parents fully informed at an early stage in the planning, so that they can make any decisions about the trip on a properly informed basis. This is discussed in more detail later.

So as to be able to identify potential dangers, the teacher in charge needs to know the area that is to be visited, as well as knowing the children being taken there. There is really no substitute for first-hand knowledge of the area, and at least one teacher on the trip, ideally the leader, should have this experience of the location and its immediate environment. On the trip itself, teachers should carry out reconnaissance of any new areas before the children are allowed there.

Part of the planning should deal with what happens when things go wrong, and in adventure activities in particular, there must be an emergency procedure. But emergency procedures are just as important in activities which are not so readily identified as hazardous. For example, it is plain foolish to take a group of children anywhere out of school without having thought what to do if a child falls ill, or becomes lost, or if anything else happens that seriously disrupts the normal routine. The reports into the Lands End and Austrian Alps tragedies both recommended more efficient procedures for dealing with the aftermaths of serious incidents. The priorities in these situations are to attend to the victim, safeguard the rest of the group, and inform quickly and in an appropriate and sensitive way, everybody who needs to know about the accident.

Emergency procedures on site, such as fire drills, must be fully understood and practised. When a school party arrives at a hotel or at other accommodation, the fire drill must be a priority so that the party is immediately prepared for an outbreak of fire.

Supervision

Most LEAs lay down supervision ratios in their school trip regulations and some of these are extremely complex. No trip should be allowed to start off, unless the supervision arrangements conform with the LEA regulations. But any regulations about supervision must be taken as guidelines and as laying down minimum supervision levels, which may have to be enhanced in particular circumstances, depending upon the nature of the trip, the location and the age and experience of the children in the group. In every case, it is the leader's duty to see that the group is adequately supervised at all times. The leader will have to take into account the experience of the adults on the trip, whether or not they are teachers and, if so, whether they teach at the school concerned. Parents should not be allowed to come on a trip simply as a holiday and they must be clear on their roles and responsibilities, so that there is no confusion about who should be doing what. The leader needs to find out how well any nonteacher supervisors know the children, how familiar they are with safety and emergency procedures, and whether they have any specific qualifications, such as first-aid training.

The children themselves have to be considered when decisions are made about supervision arrangements. The leader will need to consider:

(1) Their age, sex and numbers. Parties of mixed pupils should normally be accompanied by teachers of both sex.
(2) Their previous experience away from school or home.
(3) Their previous experience of the particular activities that are included in the trip's schedule.
(4) Their general capabilities, sense of responsibility and discipline, both individually and collectively.
(5) Whether any of the children have special needs. An extremely high level of care is necessary when teachers are dealing with pupils with special needs. Wider safety margins and more generous pupil-teacher ratios than normal may well be necessary.

When deciding about the role of supervisory staff, the leader has to take into account the possibility of an accident occurring that takes the leader away from the group. For example, the leader may have to take a child to hospital or back to school. In these circumstances, somebody else would have to be left in charge. Alternatively, the leader may need to stay with the group and will then have to select a suitable person to accompany the child. To guard against this contingency, it is very advisable that there are at least two teachers accompanying any group engaged in anything more than a brief visit close to school.

Supervision ratios do not in themselves guarantee safety. For supervision to be effective, there needs to be proper group discipline and effective group control and communication. If there is inadequate discipline, then any supervision arrangements will fall apart and the children's safety will be at risk. Rules and codes of conduct relating to matters such as drinking and smoking must be clearly understood and enforced. Communication within the group was one of the issues that was considered in Berkshire's Report into the Austrian Alps tragedy.

On the Altwood School Easter tour to Austria in 1988, there were forty-five boys and girls and four teachers. On 4 April, the group went up the Untesberg, which is around 6,000 feet high. It was a fine, sunny Easter Monday.

The Untesberg is one of the most popular tourist spots in Austria and all four teachers had been on school skiing trips before, the leader having led skiing trips in the Alps for the past fifteen years.

The party set off to the summit, first in a cable car and then on foot in a crocodile formation with teachers at the front, middle and rear. During the morning, the party split up with most of the party stopping in a safe area in a small hollow, but six boys went unobserved to another sliding area which was unsafe. The party reassembled for lunch in dribs and drabs and the six boys returned late, although this was not noticed. In the afternoon, the group had the choice of going back down in the cable car or staying at the top. The children had been warned in the morning not to wander off from the track or from the safe sliding slope, and this warning was repeated after lunch. But a group of six boys, not entirely the same boys as in the morning, went back to the unofficial slide. On the way, they found another slope and as they slid down it, the slope became so steep that four of the boys could not stop themselves and slid over the precipice.

The Report recommended that staff should consider carrying check lists for when parties split up, or if there is an accident. This should be reinforced by regular head counts. The Report also commented that small groups in charge of one person usually ensure better supervision than when the whole group is being generally supervised by several teachers.

Particular care needs to be taken over the children's free time, and it will be the leader's judgement about whether or not children can be trusted to act sensibly unaccompanied and, if so, the correct size of any groups of children that are allowed to go off by themselves. Despite the warning that had been given, the Altwood Report said that children should not have been given 50 minutes free time on a mountain, nor should it have been assumed that they had obeyed the instructions given to them. Children must be told clearly under what conditions they can explore unaccompanied, and the coroner at the Land's End inquest specifically recommended that wherever there is a potentially hazardous area close by, a teacher should be sent ahead for a safety check.

The Report also recommended that adjustments should be made to the staffing ratios if staff take their own children and there is a possibility of there being a conflict between the parental and teacher roles.

The Report said: 'In off-site activities, staff must have an expectation of an obedience to discipline, reasonable and responsible behaviour and common sense relating to the age and ability of the pupils. Children and parents must be made aware by schools of these expectations and responsibilities.' The Report added that teachers should exclude children from off-site adventures where they did not have a reasonable expectation that these qualities would be displayed, unless appropriate arrangements could be made to cope with such difficulties.

The report suggested that LEAs, schools and governors should provide teachers with the opportunity to acquire the skills required in the very demanding role of caring for children out of doors.

Insurance

Adequate insurance is essential for any school trip as all LEA guidelines will confirm. Most teachers are not experienced in the field of insurance and, as first recommended by the Land's End Inquiry, LEAs are increasingly making available to teachers their own experience of insurance matters.

Insurance policies are legal documents and contain a number of conditions, limitations and exclusions and these need to be checked very carefully.

LEAs will provide public liability insurance, which is cover against the risk of a legal claim by a third party. As well as this, there should be cover for the following risks:

(1) Personal accident. Personal accident insurance is extremely important. The standard insurance policies include cover for death and major

injuries, including loss of one or more limbs or eyes, as well as permanent or partial disability. It is 'no fault' insurance, so there is no need to prove liability.

(2) Medical and related expenses. Insurance cover is available to cover expenses following sickness or injury to a group member. These expenses normally include additional board or lodging for any group member or a relative or friend who remains with the injured person. Also covered are costs of a relative or friend travelling home with the injured person and other costs of transporting the sick or injured person home.

Medical cover will normally include reasonable medical costs, hospital or nursing fees and emergency dental fees. If there is a fatality, then cremation at the place of death or, alternatively, the cost of bringing the body home for burial, will usually be covered.

(3) Personal effects. Insurance companies provide cover for loss or damage to luggage, clothing and other personal effects, and for loss of money.

(4) Hired equipment. It may well be a term of the hire agreement that the hirers arrange insurance for the period of hire.

(5) Special activities. High-risk activities are often excluded from standard policies and, if so, separate insurance will be an absolute necessity.

(6) Cancellations. Cover is available for loss caused by a member falling out, so that the party loses the benefit of a special concession rate. There can also be cover to meet additional expenses if there is an unavoidable change of a centre base as a result of an outbreak of infectious illness, or any other event which makes it unsuitable. There may be a loss of deposits and out-of-pocket travelling expenses if the trip is cancelled and these losses, in certain circumstances, can be covered.

(7) Extra expenses. Insurance can be arranged to cover additional expenses reasonably incurred because of an enforced extension or abbreviation of the trip through the use of alternative transport because of strike, riot or civil commotion.

(8) Foreign activities. Special insurance arrangements will be necessary for activities abroad.

(9) Transport. There must be proper vehicle and passenger liability cover, and this needs to be looked into particularly carefully when travelling abroad. So far as travel in the EC is concerned, the insurance 'green card' is not necessary, provided that the vehicle is registered in a member state; but without a green card, only the minimum insurance cover required by the law of the country concerned will apply.

Information to parents

As already mentioned, parents should be kept informed of proposed arrangements for a school trip at an early stage in the planning. Many local trips are part of the normal school routine, and while it is not strictly necessary to have parental consent for each separate trip of this kind, it is both professionally prudent and legally wise for parents to be told in advance that their children will not be in school at a particular time.

For trips further afield, the school requires the written consent of parents, so it is only fair that parents have the right to expect all the necessary information before their consent is given. As the Land's End inquiry pointed out, it is important to have meetings with parents after they have received written information about the trip, so that they can raise any questions and clear up any uncertainties at that meeting. It is also an opportunity for the parents to meet the accompanying staff and the other adults on the trip.

One of the parents on the Austrian Alps trip is reported as saying 'Despite asking all the right questions and seeing a video of previous trips, we were never informed that the children were to be left unsupervised in such a dangerous place.' The report recommended that information should be given in a 'realistic and fair presentation'.

Parents have every right to expect information about the purpose and educational value of the trip, which includes:

(1) The name, address and any telephone number of the destination and any other bases.
(2) The composition of the party (age ranges and sex) and the name and relevant experience of the teacher in charge and the deputy leader.
(3) Where appropriate, parents should have the details of other adults accompanying the party and staff contacts at home.
(4) The date, time and place of departure and return, and arrangements for collecting and dispersing the children.
(5) Methods of travel and the name of any travel company being used.
(6) Details of the activities during the trip (specifying any hazardous activities), and arrangements for supervision both generally and during specific activities. The parents will also need to have details of any times when the children will not be directly supervised.
(7) The cost and what it covers, together with details of the deposit.
(8) The date after which the deposit cannot be returned if cancelling.
(9) Details of pocket money.
(10) Staff responsible for money.

(11) What insurance is provided and what insurance is not provided (see p. 73). The Land's End inquiry stressed the need to give parents full and specific details of what the insurance cover is. This is extremely important.

(12) Details of the rules and the code of conduct applying on the trip.

(13) Details of communication arrangements between the leader and the school in the event of an emergency.

(14) Details of any inoculations that are necessary.

(15) Whether there are children in the group who have health problems.

(16) A check list of clothing and other items to take.

Special care is needed when providing written information to ethnic minority parents, to ensure that all the information is clear enough to be fully understood.

Many LEAs provide specimen parental consent forms for parents to use and many schools also produce their own information booklets to parents.

Adventure activities

In recent years, there has been a tremendous increase in the number of outdoor activities available to young people. Pupils can be involved in walking (sometimes in mountainous or remote country), orienteering, camping and climbing activities. There are specialist activities on water such as sailing, canoeing and rowing, and pupils may also have the opportunity of flying or gliding. The DES in its advisory booklet *Safety in Outdoor Education*, points out that challenge and adventure are never free of risk, and that learning to have regard for your own safety and the safety of others is an important part of personal development. However, 'there must always be an acceptable framework of safety. It is indefensible to expose young people to dangerous conditions and unnecessary risks.'

It is particularly important in outdoor activities that potential dangers are identified in advance and either reduced or eliminated during preparation. Sound and experienced leadership is extremely valuable when young people are taken outdoors, so is proper equipment and suitable clothing. The DES also points to the need for at least one person involved with the trip, ideally the leader, to have first-hand knowledge of the area being visited so that he or she is familiar with local conditions and knows what factors have to be taken into account in the choice of equipment and clothing. So far as planning is concerned, the DES advice in the booklet is clear and simple. Having set out how planning can contribute to the success of a trip in terms of achieving objectives, the DES adds,

'Planning is also essential for safety. Participants should be involved in the task of preparation; this is the best way of engendering positive attitudes towards safety.'

Many LEAs give detailed advice about each of the main outdoor activities in their written guidelines and also have specialist advisers available. Details of relevant national organizations and their publications are given in the appendices and bibliography.

Residential trips

Many educational visits are based at residential centres and will include outdoor activities. In staffed residential centres, the centre's staff have overall responsibility for courses that are run for pupils, although teaching staff will also be involved in the various activities and will be responsible for the pupils' behaviour and general discipline. Before the trips starts, the respective roles of the centre's staff and the teaching staff should be identified and the centre should be able to satisfy the school that its staff are suitably qualified to provide whatever specialist instruction is necessary and are properly briefed about arrangements. The school will also need to make reasonable checks to see that the accommodation and other facilities are suitable. The centre will have safety rules for each of the activities involved and these should be strictly followed.

Travel abroad

The Department of Health has produced two information leaflets, SA40, *Before you go* and SA41 *While you are away*, both of which give health guidance to people travelling overseas.

SA41 says 'losing your luggage is not the worst thing that could happen to you when you are abroad. If you become ill or have an accident while on a business trip or holiday, it may not only be unpleasant and expensive, it could be fatal.' The leaflet includes a holiday health check list, which gives advice about a number of general safety matters to the traveller. For example, the traveller should check drinking water and also water for cleaning teeth and washing the mouth. Travellers are also advised to be careful with certain foods, namely raw vegetables, salads and unpeeled fruit, raw shellfish, cream, ice cream and ice cubes, undercooked meat or fish, and uncooked, cold or re-heated food, all of which could be contaminated.

There is also information about health care available for visitors in each of the EC countries, and advice on how to get emergency treatment with form E111. Some emergency medical treatment is available through reciprocal health care arrangements, and form E111 is the certificate of entitlement to this treatment.

Emergencies

Accidents and mishaps do happen, despite the most vigorous precautions. Carefully thought out emergency procedures can minimize the dangers and traumas that inevitably follow. Most LEAs now give their own advice about how teachers should handle emergency situations, and staff should be familiar with this in order to deal effectively and sympathetically with accidents and their aftermath.

Emergency procedures cannot legislate for every eventuality, and particularly difficult situations can arise when a single teacher is in charge of children out of school. For example, there may be a football match or game of netball at another school and a child is injured. The teacher will have to exercise reasonable judgement about whether the priority is to attend to the needs of the injured child, perhaps to the extent of accompanying him or her to hospital and remaining there, or whether the demands of the other children returning home must have priority. This will depend on the age of the children, the extent of the injuries to the one child, the distance that the other children have to travel in order to return home, and the nature of their route. Of particular importance is what parents have been told about the children's return from the game. The requirement to have emergency telephone contact numbers for parents will be a tremendous help in an emergency situation, and a teacher will need to have this information readily available.

Travel and transport

As the sinking of the cruise ship *Jupiter* illustrated, safety precautions have to be taken into account all the time, and teachers in charge must be constantly vigilant. The *Jupiter* sank in October 1988 as it left Piraeus harbour in Athens and collided with an Italian cargo ship. There were 470 children on board.

There are, of course, many different ways of moving a group of children locally, nationally and internationally. Each method of travel requires care and attention.

Walking in town

Many school activities and expeditions are in towns and cities, and there is no need for transport to be arranged, as the group can go on foot.

However, the urban environment can present just as many dangers as remote, outdoor country, and leading a group of children along a crowded street or a busy road carries enormous responsibilities – no less than leading a group on an outdoor adventure. There are many different kinds of potential hazards, which have to be identified and pointed out to the children beforehand.

Children should be taught to observe road safety rules, the Highway Code and the Green Cross Code. In a busy town or city, children must be kept under close supervision and, in most cases, at least two adults will be required, one supervising at the front and the other at the rear. There may be circumstances in which the teacher is able to decide that the group is small and capable enough for one teacher to be sufficient to ensure safe supervision. If this arrangement complies with LEA guidelines, the group can proceed on this basis with senior children positioned at the front and back of the group to act as markers, while the teacher moves up and down the line, seeing that all is in order. Supervision should be maintained at all times, and the teacher should not be distracted, for example, by a child wanting to stop to look at something or to talk about something.

Urban field work requires particular care during preparation, and should not in any event be sanctioned unless the children concerned are old enough and capable enough to be left unsupervised on the streets. They must have clear instructions on where to go, when to return, and where to return to and what to do if there is an emergency. It should be made absolutely clear that children should not accept any form of invitation or any kind of gift from strangers. They should be directed to ask for help from a policeman if they get in difficulties or become lost.

Coaches

Coach travel is cheap travel, and because children are in a small, confined space, supervision is generally easier. While teachers are not required to make meticulous inquiries about the suitability of the coach firm, or of the particular coach, the leader should be satisfied that the firm is a reputable one and can accommodate all the group's requirements. A number of recent accidents in this country and abroad have caused concern about coach safety standards.

There are a number of basic safety rules when travelling by coach which children should know and follow. They should never attempt to get on or off a moving coach or a coach held up in traffic or at traffic lights. While the coach is moving, nobody should run about inside or do anything to impede the driver's vision or distract his attention.

It is the leader's responsibility to know the position of the emergency door and where the first-aid equipment is kept.

Trains

Rail travel is quick and can be relatively cheap. Children are not confined to their seats as much as they are in a coach or aeroplane, and there is ready access to toilet facilities and refreshments.

A number of basic safety rules have to be observed. At the station itself, children should be kept well away from the platform edges, and when getting on and off trains, they need to be warned to watch the gap between the coach and the platform. Under no circumstances should a child attempt to get on or off a moving train, or to touch door catches, or lean out of windows while the train is moving.

Air and sea travel

More and more children and young people are travelling by air, but taking a school group on to an aircraft nevertheless requires careful planning and preparation. Most of the airlines provide their own information and practical advice for travellers and groups of travellers.

Educational cruises and sea crossings are commonplace, and the normal safety precautions should be taken. Teachers must not regard days at sea as holidays, and proper discipline is essential.

In late 1990, a report was prepared by a group of teachers for Sea Link, the ferry operator. The report was in response to complaints by Sea Link about the misbehaviour of pupils on the ferries, including allegations that there were unruly pupils running around while the teachers settled down in ferry bars. The pupils often presented a safety risk to themselves and also others, distracting the crew from their duties, causing damage and sometimes committing theft.

The report contained a number of suggestions about tackling the problem. These included setting up a club for schools using the ferries, with members undertaking to abide by a code of conduct, which included a requirement that teachers should wear identifying badges and that pupils should either wear a badge or a distinctive uniform. The code lays down a maximum pupil-teacher ratio of 12 to 1, and is heavily critical of teachers spending their time in bars.

Membership of the club should be revoked for a year for any breach of the code, and the report also recommends that any serious misconduct should be reported to the school's head, the LEA and, perhaps, given press publicity.

Minibuses

There are a number of safety aspects to consider in relation to minibus driving, and these are dealt with in Chapter 10.

Third party trips

Sections 106 to 111 and Sections 117 and 118 of the Education Reform Act 1988 and the DES Circular 2/89 'Education Reform Act 1988 – Charges for School Activities', set out the changes in the financial arrangements for school trips which took effect from 1 April 1989.

The Act does not allow parents to be charged for education during school hours, except in the case of individual instrumental music tuition not being part of the National Curriculum or a prescribed public examination, materials and ingredients for practical subjects where parents have indicated in advance that they want the finished produce, and transport not provided by the LEA or the school. All activities outside school hours are 'optional extras', except for those required by the National Curriculum, or a prescribed public examination, or those relating to religious education. Charges can be made for 'optional extras' and voluntary contributions, provided that they are genuinely voluntary, can be invited from the parents at any time.

Although parents cannot be charged by the LEA or school for education in school hours, there is no restriction on charging for activities during school hours which are arranged by a third party, in which case the third party charges the parents direct. Staff and pupils who go on the trip are given leave of absence from school. Circular 2/89 sums up this arrangement as follows,

> the LEA and the school governing body would not take part in the transaction and it would be for the parents and any staff members similarly released for the activity to satisfy themselves about the adequacy of the arrangements made by the third party to secure the safety and welfare of the children.

LEAs that have produced written procedures for staff involved in school trips arranged by third parties set out the role of the governors and of the LEA, and they also deal with the organization of the trip, as well as the important issue of insurance. The DES has indicated that it does not regard these trips as school activities but, nevertheless, the governors will have a role to play, because they will be required to give approval for any staff or pupils at the school to be released in order to go on the trip. In order to reach this decision, the governors will need to have detailed information about the proposed activity, and that will give them an opportunity to express any reservations it may have on safety issues. Similarly, written details should be sent to the LEA, so that it has an opportunity of making any such reservations known to the governors.

Staff involved in activities should see that parents are supplied with clear written details of the nature of the activities involved and the levels of supervision that will be provided. If the company concerned has a set of procedures or code of practice, then copies should be provided for the parents. Meetings with parents are required, just as they are in normal school activities, and meetings may well involve the organizers.

Insurance cover for a trip organized by a third party must be studied closely to see that all the heads of cover mentioned earlier in this section (see p. 73) are included as required. Parents should be told in writing what the insurance cover is so that they have an opportunity of taking out additional insurance cover if they wish.

It is likely that most LEAs will have arranged for their existing public liability cover to operate should a claim be made against a teacher acting as a party leader or supervisor on a trip organized by a third party. This must be checked in every case, and teachers also need to find out whether the insurance package taken out by the organizer for pupils includes supervisors as well.

It is too early to assess the impact of this new legislation on school trips, but the immediate response of many teachers to third party trips has been an extremely cautious one.

Industrial visits

School children visit factories and workshops as part of the curriculum, as well as going to firms for work experience (see p. 83). However brief the visit, children are inevitably exposed to hazards because the industrial environment is a dangerous one. There are heavy items of machinery and dangerous materials and equipment on site, and there may also be extremes of either heat or cold. It should not have to be emphasized that safety planning is critical before pupils are taken on to work premises. In particular, there must be:

(1) Liaison with the organization concerned. It may well be necessary for the teacher in charge to arrange a site visit and a meeting to confirm details. The teacher needs to be assured that the premises comply with safety regulations made under the Health and Safety at Work etc Act 1974 and related legislation, and also that the children will be properly attended to. LEA safety officers and local health and safety offices will be able to advise on safety matters.

(2) A clear agreement on the allocation of supervision duties between teachers and any party guides or supervisors. A teacher can only safely delegate supervisory responsibilities to a guide if he or she is reasonably satisfied that the guide is fully competent and understands his or her role and responsibilities.

(3) Confirmation that all necessary protective clothing and equipment will be available.

(4) A full briefing for children about the objectives of the visit, the potential dangers and the firm's safety regulations, including accident and first aid procedures.

(5) Full details of arrangements supplied to parents and their consent to those arrangements.

(6) Adequate insurance arrangements. The DES, in Administrative Memorandum No. 22/67 'Liability for Pupils and Students Visiting Industry', advises LEAs to make sure that their own insurance arrangements are adequate to cover visits.

Work experience

Under the Education (Work Experience) Act 1973, pupils in their last year of compulsory schooling are allowed to participate in work experience schemes, which may be organized by individual schools or those arranged centrally through the authority's careers service. Pupils may be involved one day a week over a period of time or for a more concentrated, but shorter, period. Any LEA regulations must be strictly followed, and LEA guidelines will normally include advice on what should be included in a letter to the employer authorizing the arrangements.

A number of matters should be covered in this letter. For example:

(1) Pupils will be given meaningful work and be placed under the guidance of a responsible person who will give proper instruction and supervision if machinery or equipment is used as part of the work.

(2) No pupil will be required to operate dangerous machinery or work in a hazardous environment. Any special or protective clothing required by pupils must be provided for them.

(3) No pupil will be exposed to conditions of work for which he or she is not medically suited. The employer may need medical or other information about a pupil if this is relevant to his or her health and safety.

(4) The employer will confirm insurance cover against death or injury to a pupil caused by the employer's negligence or the negligence of an employee. LEAs will normally provide personal accident insurance cover for pupils.

This letter will not necessarily be a substitute for a visit to inspect the premises and to discuss safety issues, so that the school is clear about what working conditions will be and the employer understands what the school expects. Both pupils and parents should be fully briefed about the arrangement and parental consent should be given on an informed basis.

The legal requirements contained in the Education (Work Experience) Act 1973 are explained in DES Circular 7/74, 'Guidelines for the Work Experience Act 1973'.

7
ACCIDENTS AT WORK

Compensation and liability

Around 500 people are killed at work each year, and 400,000 seriously injured. These figures are probably a great surprise to many members of the public, and the number of accidents that befall teachers at work would also astonish many people. There are tripping accidents, falling accidents, slipping accidents and cases where teachers are let down by a piece of school furniture or a piece of equipment. In some cases, the teacher is shaken, perhaps bruised or even bloodied but, nevertheless, fully recovers sometime later. But there are other accidents from which teachers do not fully recover and are left with some form of permanent injury. In some cases, teachers have had to take early retirement and leave the profession on grounds of ill health because of the lasting effects of an accident. A fracture is painful and very inconvenient, and there is also a lingering doubt about possible problems in the future, particularly the problem of osteoarthritis in later years. In some cases, a relatively minor injury can have serious effects. A finger injury to a music teacher or a knee injury to a PE specialist can put that teacher's career in jeopardy.

The back is particularly vulnerable to serious injury, and back injuries at the base of the spine can be particularly disabling. A serious back injury can completely change a person's life. The National Back Pain Association is a national medical charity set up in 1968. It has a number of local branches through which back pain sufferers, and those who care for them, can receive information, advice and mutual support. It also provides information and advice to educate people to avoid back injuries and back problems, both at home and at work.

The priority must always to be to prevent accidents to staff, but if there is an accident and a teacher is injured, then a number of issues must be addressed.

It may be that the teacher needs time off work. Except in the case of the most serious injuries, this will not normally present a problem, because teachers in maintained schools are entitled to generous sick pay arrangements, which give maximum benefits of 100 working days on full pay and the same number of days on half pay.

An accident at work is an industrial injury, and there is a state benefit called disablement benefit paid by the DSS to someone who is disabled as a result of an industrial injury. If a medical examination reveals a disability of at least 14 per cent for longer than fifteen weeks, then a weekly pension is payable. The weekly benefit ranges from around £15.00 to over £75.00, depending on the extent of the disability. This is purely a medical issue and the DSS do not consider how the accident happened and who was to blame.

The DSS regulations relating to disablement benefit use the expression 'loss of faculty', which means that the injured person has suffered an impairment of the proper functioning of part of his or her body or mind. The regulations also give some guidance on how to assess the degree of disability arising from a loss of faculty. Disablement is assessed as a percentage, and loss of both hands or loss of sight would produce 100 per cent disablement, the loss of one hand would mean 60 per cent disablement, and loss of an index finger, 14 per cent. Where a loss of faculty cannot be categorized in this way, then all the medical evidence is assessed to see what, in practice, is the effect of the injury on the person's ability to enjoy a normal life.

If a claimant is dissatisfied with the DSS decision either to reject an application or as regards the assessment of the extent of the disability, then he or she can appeal to the local Medical Appeal Tribunal. There are regional Tribunals throughout the country and each Tribunal has a legally qualified chairman, but it is not a court of law and there are no court fees. Most teachers who appeal in this way attend the Tribunal with a friend or union representative.

As well as claiming financial compensation from the State for an accident at work, the teacher can also seek compensation from the employer, but to do this, the teacher has to show a breach of the employer's common law duty of care or, alternatively, a breach of statutory obligations under the Health and Safety at Work etc Act 1974, or under the Occupier's

Liability Act 1957. A teacher who wishes to take advice on the prospects of succeeding with a claim and contacts his or her union will need to have the following information:

(1) A full statement, including the time and place of the accident and what happened. In most cases it will be relevant to know what the teacher was wearing, particularly in the case of a falling or slipping accident, where footwear is significant.

(2) It is very important to gather together any evidence before it disappears. In some cases a photograph may be sufficient to record the condition of an area of floor, or a section of playground or playing field, where an accident took place. In some cases, independent expert opinion will be needed to prove that a particular piece of equipment or machinery was dangerous. An actual inspection may be needed to do this. In the case of a slipping accident, as much information as possible is needed about the composition of the floor, how it is cleaned and polished and with what. The central question is whether or not nonslip polish was used.

(3) It may be that the injured teacher did not remember what happened or, alternatively, his or her account is disputed by the LEA. It is very important to have witness statements from any adult who saw what happened.

(4) If the accident was not the first mishap of its kind in the school, then that will help to show that the accident was foreseeable. An LEA cannot claim that it was unreasonable to expect it to have anticipated the accident if, in fact, there had been a similar accident or near accident before which had been reported. So evidence from a colleague involved in a previous incident of a similar nature is very helpful. The school's health and safety representative may also have useful evidence.

(5) Other evidence may be available from colleagues to support the facts being relied upon to claim negligence. For example, a colleague may be able to confirm lack of training given to staff on a particular safety issue, or to confirm the details of polishing, cleaning or maintenance arrangements. It can be difficult for a colleague to give evidence against an LEA that employs him or her, and the wishes of a potential witness in these circumstances should always be respected. In many cases, evidence may be available in other ways. For example, the accident book and accident reports will confirm details of any previous accident that can help a claim.

Most compensation claims are settled between the teacher's representatives and the LEA's insurers, without having to go to court. If a case does go to court, then it could be many years before judgement is given.

For a number of years, critics of the present system, which is based on what is known as tort liability, have claimed that it is unfair in that the law appears to be only concerned with apportioning blame and awarding compensation, rather than initiating changes to eliminate accidents. Two employees could be injured in the same way and have the same needs as a result of the accidents. If one can successfully claim that the employer was negligent, then he or she will be compensated, but if the other is unable to do so, he or she will get nothing.

In 1973, the Royal Commission on Civil Liability and Compensation for Personal Injuries (the Pearson Commission) was set up to consider the existing system and any possible alternatives. The Commission decided that the present system was fundamentally sound and no substantial changes were necessary. It concluded that the benefits provided by the State, in the form of benefits for industrial injuries, could be extended and improved, but that the common law system of tort liability needed minor changes only.

Damages

Where compensation is paid for personal injuries, then the pain and suffering caused by the injury is taken into account as well the continuing pain, inconvenience and, in some cases, future disability. Also, if the claim is successful, the injured person can recover any losses or expenses directly incurred as a result of the accident, such as medical expenses including prescription costs and, in some cases, loss of earnings or loss of future earnings. Compensation has to be assessed in each particular case, and there are no set figures as there are with DSS compensation. Although no two injuries, however similar, have exactly the same effect on different people, there is a considerable amount of case law which acts as a useful guide in fixing the figure in any particular case, and the following examples give some idea of the range of compensation that can be awarded.

A thirty-nine-year-old man who suffered a tear of the right knee, which left him with some residual pain and occasional swelling, was awarded damages of £2,250 in 1984. In the case of a fifty-seven-year-old woman who injured her big toe when a heavy lid from a shredding machine fell on her foot, the court made an award of £2,750 in 1986. The toe was badly swollen and bruised, and the injury increased the chances of osteo-arthritis in later life. A thirteen-year-old-school-boy who fell against a metal pole and needed twelve stitches to a cut in his shin, was awarded £500 in 1989. He made a full recovery, but was left with a small scar.

In 1985, compensation of £2,500 was awarded for a broken arm which completely healed after several months. A man who injured his right leg when he slipped on a polished floor was awarded £4,000 in 1984. He tore a ligament in his leg and this left a problem with bending his right knee. A woman who damaged her knee leaving her with stiffness problems and osteoarthritis, was awarded £4,250 in 1986. In 1987, the court awarded £1,500 to a teacher who was hit on the shoulder and neck by a blackboard that fell on her. There was minor soft tissue damage and some residual discomfort, which was expected to disappear with time.

A thirty-five-year-old woman was awarded £4,250 compensation in 1986 after an accident which resulted in the tip of her left index finger being amputated. The finger was 2 cm short and this made simple tasks such as opening jars or holding dishes difficult.

More serious injuries will attract larger amounts of compensation. A forty-two-year-old teacher injured her right leg when she fell on a polished floor. At the trial in 1988, she was awarded £10,000 for her injuries, as it was noted that the injury had cause some degeneration of the lumbar spine, forcing her to take an infirmity pension.

Similarly, serious disabilities will warrant large amounts of compensation. In a 1984 case, the court awarded £12,000 to a 64-year-old man who slipped and fractured his left femur. The head of the femur had to be replaced by a steel ball and at the date of the court hearing, a hip replacement was seen as the only realistic solution to the problem. The hip was painful and he walked with a stick and a slight limp.

Accident reports

It is very important that accidents are properly reported, both to ensure appropriate action in particular cases, and also to enable the employer and others, such as the Health and Safety Executive, to identify recurring types of accidents and take appropriate action to stop further accidents.

The requirements for the reporting of accidents are set out in the Reporting of Injuries, Diseases and Dangerous Occurrence Regulations 1985, which came into force in April 1986 and failure to comply with these Regulations is a criminal offence. The Health and Safety Executive has produced a small leaflet entitled 'Report that Accident', which summarizes the main requirements of the Regulations.

If anybody is killed or seriously injured (including being kept in hospital for more than twenty-four hours) in an accident at work, the employer must notify the appropriate authority as soon as possible. In the case of an office, shop or residential accommodation, the appropriate authority is the local Environmental Health Department. In other cases, it is the local Health and Safety Executive.

These occurrences must be formally reported and so must any accident at work which causes an employee to be off work for three or more days. A report form must be completed and sent in to the appropriate authority within seven days.

The employer must keep a record of any accidents or occurrence which have to be reported. The record must include the date and time of the accident, place, how the accident happened and details of the person's injury.

The form that has to be used for reporting accidents and dangerous occurrences is form F2508.

In 1986, the Health and Safety Commission's Education Service Advisory Committee produced a booklet, *Guidance on a voluntary scheme for the collection, collation and analysis of injury, disease and dangerous occurrence data in the education sector*. It points out that the substantial number of incidents involving pupils, students and visitors are not reportable under the Reporting Regulations and it recommends that LEAs should collect data covering the following:

(1) Dangerous occurrences as defined in the Regulations.
(2) Fatalities as defined in the Regulations.
(3) Injuries and conditions as defined in the Regulations.
(4) Injuries causing incapacity for work for more than three days as defined by the Regulations.
(5) Diseases, as defined by the Regulations.
      And also:
(6) injuries to pupils as (4) and (5) above.
(7) Near miss incidents. A near miss is where a culmination of events could have led to an injury or where there was an incident, but the injury caused was not reportable under the Regulations, but could be much more severe if the incident were to happen again.

The Social Security Act 1975 lays down requirements for accident books in workplaces where at least ten people are normally employed, but in schools, regardless of teacher numbers, all accidents should be logged in the accident book. Like the reporting procedures, recording an accident is of no benefit in itself to the injured person, but it does serve as a record of what happened and is, therefore, available as evidence if needed. Where a claim for negligence is based upon the LEA's failure to act following a similar accident, the accident book will be good evidence of that similar incident.

8
SCHOOL BUILDINGS

Legislation

In 1972, the Robens Committee, which looked into health and safety at work, included in its Report an observation about school buildings and also hospital buildings. It noted that despite much rebuilding in recent years the nation's stock of hospitals and schools still included old and unsuitable premises which could be improved or replaced only gradually and at very considerable cost. The Report added that in expending the resources available at any given time for the improvement of standards in such premises, the needs of employees, patients, pupils and students must all be taken into account.

There is some very detailed legislation on the statute books about the layout of offices and shops and factories. In the case of educational establishments, there is only the Education (School Premises) Regulations 1981, which replaced the School Premises Regulations 1972 and implemented a number of recommendations in the 1977 Report by the DES 'A study of School Buildings'. These Regulations were made under the authority of section 10 of the 1944 Education Act, which requires the Secretary of State to make Regulations about standards to which school premises must conform. The section also requires LEAs to observe these standards. But as will be noted in the context of fire safety (see pp. 120–1), the Secretary of State is able to waive any of the Regulations for a particular school where 'having regard to the nature of the existing site or to any existing buildings thereon, or to any other special circumstances affecting the school premises, it would be unreasonable to require conformity with a requirement of the Regulations'. There is a transition period for schools in respect of certain requirements which did not appear in the 1972 Regulations, and any school which needs to carry out work to bring it in line with the 1981 Regulations has until 1 September 1996 to do this. Meanwhile, the DES is carrying out a review of the Regulations in the light of educational changes since 1981.

The Regulations themselves cover nursery schools, primary, secondary and special schools, and they have recently been extended to cover grant maintained schools. They make provision for the structural requirements of schools, including weather and safety protection, lighting and acoustics, heating, water supplies and drainage.

The Regulations also deal with recreation areas, playing fields, the overall size of school land, as well as with school buildings. So far as school buildings are concerned, the Regulations say that they should be large enough to accommodate the following:

(1) The convenient passage of persons and movement of goods within the buildings.
(2) The storage of teaching apparatus and equipment, etc.
(3) The storage of general nonteaching items.
(4) Separate storage of any fuel required for the school.
(5) The storage and drying of pupils' outdoor clothing and storage of their other belongings.
(6) The preparation of food and drinks and the washing of crockery, etc.

The Regulations also cover washrooms for both staff and pupils and, so far as medical accommodation is concerned, the stipulation is that 'every school should have accommodation for the medical or dental examination, treatment and care of pupils and the accommodation should include a wash-basin and be reasonably near a water closet'.

There are provisions relating to structural requirements which are as follows:

(1) Load-bearing structure. Any load-bearing structure in the school building should be capable of safely sustaining the load and the imposed loads and the horizontal landing forces to which it is likely to be subjected.
(2) Weather protection. School buildings should be of such design and construction so as to provide reasonable resistance to rain, snow and wind as well to moisture rising from the ground.
(3) Safety Protection. Every part of the school building should be designed and built so as to reasonably assure:

(a) The safe escape of the occupants in case of fire.

(b) The health and safety of other aspects.

In Scotland, the School Premises (General Requirement and Standards) (Scotland) Regulations (1967), amended in 1973 and 1979, lay down general standards for school buildings, and there are also the Building Standards (Scotland) Regulations 1981. But as in England and Wales, these Regulations are not backed by vigorous enforcement policies.

The Occupier's Liability Act 1957, imposes a duty on occupiers of premises to take reasonable care for the safety of visitors to the premises, and Section 3(a) of the Act says that an occupier must be prepared for children to be less careful than adults.

The Occupier's Liability Act 1984 extends this occupier's duty of care to trespassers. Many school fields are used out of school hours by dog owners and young children from the area, and it is not possible for the school's boundaries to be completely secured to stop this happening. Schools that are aware of this practice are required to keep the school field in a safe condition and clear of any dangerous obstructions or equipment that could injure anyone walking across or playing on the field. Some LEAs have signs outside their schools warning trespassers not to come on the premises.

It was a surprise to nobody when the 1988/89 annual report by the Senior Chief Inspector of Schools published in January 1990 found that poor accommodation and out-of-date and badly-maintained equipment was common in schools. In two-thirds of the secondary schools inspected, the accommodation was unsatisfactory, and in just under half of those schools the problems were serious. They included temporary and dispersed buildings, overcrowded classrooms and poor maintenance. There were many examples of a shortage of accommodation or unsuitable accommodation for science, home economics and craft design and technology.

The majority of primary schools visited by the Inspector had suitable and adequately maintained accommodation, but the report drew attention to the need for primary schools to have suitable accommodation for science and technology work in the National Curriculum. At present, said the report, many schools do not have enough space or sufficient equipment in physical science and information technology.

Shortly after the Inspector's report was published, Alex Carlisle MP put down a Preliminary Question in which he asked the Secretary of State for Education and Science what proposals he had for renovating secondary schools. The reply indicated that it was for LEAs to decide what building projects were necessary. In 1990−1, £485 million is available by way of capital allowance for schools and colleges in England and Wales, and there is also £118 million available in grants for voluntary-aided, special-agreement and grant-maintained schools.

The severe weather early in 1990 forced many pupils to miss schooling because of damage to school buildings, and the DES estimated that over 100,000 pupils had to stay at home. Many LEAs still struggling to repair the damage of the 1987 hurricanes are now facing further large repair costs.

Temporary school classrooms appear to have been particularly affected by the high winds, and this has raised the question of whether or not they can continue to be used on anything other than a short-term basis. In some LEAs, temporary classrooms are widely used. In Surrey, for example, around 12 per cent of classroom space is temporary.

On 27 March 1990, there were a number of Parliamentary Questions about the condition of school buildings. The Secretary of State was asked to make an estimate of the current outstanding repairs in schools in England and Wales. The answer was as follows:

'The DES school building survey in 1987 estimated the cost of implementing the main structural requirements related to the Education (School Premises) Regulations 1981 and other physical requirements in primary and secondary schools in England was about £1.1 billion. Substantial sums have since been devoted to improving school premises. The repair of schools in Wales is a matter for my Rt Hon. Friend the Secretary of State for Wales.'

Also on 27 March, the following question and answer emerged:

Mr Mullin: 'To ask the Secretary of State for Education and Science what action he is taking to ensure that schools are in good repair, prior to the enactment of local management of schools.'

The Parliamentary Under-Secretary of State for Education and Science (Mr Alan Howarth): 'It is the responsibility of local education authorities to carry out necessary repairs to county and voluntary controlled schools. Governors of voluntary-aided schools receive grant aid from the Department for necessary external repairs.'

The Secretary of State was asked further questions about the Government's funding for school buildings dealing with two contemporary issues, City Technology Colleges and local management of schools. These questions are recorded as follows:

Mr Mullin: 'Is the Under-Secretary of State aware that next financial year the capital allocation from the Department for Gateshead city technology college is three times that for all 145 schools in Sunderland put together? How can that be justified when many of the schools in my constituency and elsewhere are falling to pieces?'

Mr Howarth: 'The Hon. Gentleman may be aware that officials from my Department recently had a meeting with officers of Sunderland local education authority. We are anxious to look as helpfully as we can at the capital needs of Gateshead. The capital guidelines issued to authorities are based on objective criteria and standards that are well understood by the authorities. If the bid from Sunderland failed to match our national priorities it is the responsibility of the authority. We are anxious, however, to look with the authority at its needs.

'I am sorry that the Hon. Gentleman is not prepared to welcome the establishment of a city technology college to his area which will provide a magnificent educational opportunity for children in Sunderland. It is sad that such a negative, grudging attitude should be shown to the generosity of the sponsors and the willingness of the Government to establish the highest standards of educational provision for all children in his area.'

Mr Sayeed: 'Is my Hon. Friend aware that I recently visited St George's school in my constituency, which is operating the full local management of schools system and which is extremely happy with it? Is my Hon. Friend aware that that school now gets its repairs done speedily by outside contractors which cuts down the costs to the school and that, next year, it will be able to carry over £70,000 of its budget? Will the Minister tell my right Hon. Friend how pleased that school and other schools are with the 100 per cent carry-over rules now permitted by the Department?'

Mr Howarth: 'My Hon. Friend is absolutely right. The flexibility that LMS will allow head teachers and the chairman of governors to enable them to get work done is enormously welcome. Those people have welcomed LMS because it offers them an enhanced opportunity for responsibility and to get things done at a practical level. Many headteachers have told me how difficult it has been to have every decision that they needed to take about repairs and maintenance of their school second-guessed by their authorities. They are pleased to have the opportunity for flexible, rapid response.'

Whatever party political line one takes, it remains the sad truth that the present standard of school buildings is intolerably low. This creates an inevitable risk to staff and pupils in schools, and the remedy requires a concerted and expensive programme of repair and restoration. This view was endorsed by the Commons Select Committee in Education in its May 1990 report 'The Supply of Teachers for the 1990s'. The Committee recommended that resources should be made available urgently to bring all schools up to a standard of good repair and to maintain good levels of equipment. Until such an investment is made in school buildings, there will be the continued risk of fatalities in severe weather as happened at the start of 1990, and also of incidents like the death of a five-year-old pupil at a Clapham school in November 1989, when a gate pillar gave way, bringing down a fence and a wall.

Every part of the school building must be properly maintained and looked after so that those who use each part or pass through it will be safe. A number of different points have to be considered and different points have to be considered in different areas (see pp. 31−2 in relation to classrooms), and safety precautions should be observed, even in places that appear to be safe and free of risk.

Offices

School offices are subject to safety legislation. In the Office, Shops and Railway Premises Act 1963, an office is defined as a building or part of a building, sole or principle use of which is as an office for office purposes. The expression 'office purposes' is in turn defined to include administration and clerical work which in turn includes typing, duplicating, book-keeping and sorting papers. The 1963 Act deals with matters such as temperatures, ventilation, lighting and over crowding.

It is beyond comprehension why school buildings occupied by pupils are left outside safety legislation, while offices in the school occupied by a small number of adults are protected by legislation.

Although, on the face of it, offices do not appear to be particularly dangerous places, a number of hazards do exist and among the safety precautions that should be taken are the following:

(1) Good housekeeping and tidiness are as important in school offices as elsewhere in the school. Floor areas should be kept clear of obstructions, such as files, piles of documents, briefcases and handbags.

(2) There may be dangerous substances, such as substances for photocopying or duplicating machines, and these should be safely stored away when they are not being used. These substances will be included in assessments under the Control of Substances Hazardous to Health Regulations 1988 (see pp. 24−6).

(3) If smoking is allowed, then there should be ashtrays available, and waste bins provided for cigarette ends should not be used for waste paper.

(4) There may be a variety of machinery and equipment in an office, and care should be taken that there are no trailing leads or wires which could cause a falling accident.

(5) Office furniture should be safe, and it should be checked to see that there are no sharp edges or open draws that people could walk into. Keys should not be left in furniture locks for the same reason.

(6) Heater outlets should be kept clear, and they should not be used for drying clothes or tea towels. If any supplementary heating is brought into the office, it should be checked for safety.

Staff room

Again, staff rooms are not areas that one would imagine to be particularly dangerous places. Nevertheless, attention should be paid to tidiness, the proper placement of books, files and other personal belongings, so that they are not an obstruction or otherwise dangerous. Care should be taken with any electrical equipment being used.

Kitchens

The Education (School Premises) Regulations 1981, unlike their predecessor the Standards for Schools Regulations 1972, do not contain detailed specifications about kitchens. The reason for this which is set out in the DES Administrative Memorandum 2/81 'The Education (School Premises) Regulations 1981' is that the Education Act 1980 released LEAs from the legal obligation to provide school meals of a prescribed standard for all pupils who wanted them. LEAs do still have a duty to discharge to any pupil from a family in receipt of a supplementary benefit or family income support and LEAs are also required to provide such facilities as they consider appropriate for the consumption of meals or other refreshments brought to school by pupils.

A person must keep all parts of his or her person that come into contact with food as clean as is reasonably practicable, and the same applies to all parts of his or her clothing or over-clothing. Any open cut or abrasion on any exposed part of the person should be covered with suitable waterproof dressing, and persons in contact with food should refrain from spitting and from smoking tobacco or any other smoking mixture when handling open food, or while in the food room where there is open food.

Kitchen walls, floors, doors, windows, ceiling and woodwork must be kept clean and in good order.

Various forms of food poisoning have been brought to the public's attention in the last few years, and this underlines the need for meticulous standards of hygiene. There are several groups of bacteria known to cause food poisoning, one of which is *Salmonella*, which has been the subject of recent public and media interest. *Salmonella* is one of the most common bacteria groups and the Institution of Environmental Health Officers advises that all new red meat and poultry should be treated as if it were infected with *Salmonella*.

Foods with just a small number of *Salmonella* bacteria are not harmful, but the bacteria can develop very rapidly, with a single cell capable of producing 7,000 million cells in 12 hours. Lightly-contaminated food left in a warm room is a good breeding ground for *Salmonella* as is frozen poultry left to thaw for too long at room temperature.

A number of simple rules and precautions should be observed to ensure hygiene and safety. For example:

(1) Is there enough space for the catering staff, especially in areas around kitchen machinery, such as cutting, mincing, chopping and slicing machinery? The kitchen must be organized so that there is no risk of people colliding with each other, bumping into things, or tripping over things on the floor. All parts of the kitchen must be clean and in good repair, particularly those surfaces used for preparing food.

(2) All gangways and exits should be clear of equipment and any other obstacles such as, materials, rubbish or trailing cables. Floors need to be kept in good condition and be nonslip.

(3) There should be adequate storage space and a procedure for seeing that when goods are delivered they are not piled up around the work area. There should also be a procedure for quickly disposing of empty cans, food containers, etc. from working areas. All refuse must be removed to dustbins at the end of the day.

(4) Proper drainage is necessary around washing machines, sinks and other areas where water could accumulate and become a slipping hazard. If mats are put down on the floor, they must be positioned safely and maintained in good condition.

(5) Staff need to wear suitable footwear at all times and should not wear jewellery when handling food. All clothing should be correctly fitting and protective clothing must be worn when necessary.

(6) Particular attention needs to be given to knives and other sharp-edged tools. They need to be in good condition with the handles firmly fixed, clean and free from grease. There must be enough space for the person using the knife to work safely and comfortably, and that person must be using the correct knife for the particular work being done. Knives should be washed carefully and stored safely when not being used.

(7) Microwave ovens should comply with British Standard BS 5175: 'Specifications for safety of conventional or electrical appliances using microwave energy for heating foodstuffs', which sets out the requirements for testing ovens with or without additional forms of heating. As well as this, BS 3999 sets out methods of measuring the performance of household electrical appliances and, in addition to information about microwaves, there is information about electric

kettles, food preparation machines, electric cookers, dish washing machines and freezers.

(8) Individuals should not be required to lift excessively heavy loads. There should be proper training in correct lifting procedures and wherever possible, trolleys should be provided.

(9) Food hygiene is particularly important in the cooking, preparation and storage of food. Foodstuff should not be kept either too hot (above 63°C) or too cold (below 10°C), because that can breed bacteria.

(10) All cookers should be switched off when not in use, and when the kitchen is not being used, all doors and hatches should be securely closed.

(11) All electrical appliances should be disconnected when not in use, and electrical points should not be overloaded. All plugs should be switched off and removed from sockets when they are not being used.

Safety in school kitchens must be taken seriously as a significant proportion of accidents to staff in the education sector involve catering staff, with common accidents being burns, scalds, falling accidents, cut fingers and back injuries. The Education Advisory Committee of the Health and Safety Commission has produced an information sheet 'Health and Safety of Catering Staff in Educational Establishments', which gives details of sources of advice and guidance on kitchen safety.

Boiler room

The Health and Safety Commission Education Service Advisory Committee has produced a booklet *Fumes in Solid Fuel Boiler Rooms at Educational Establishments* in response to a number of surveys which have shown that school caretakers can be exposed to a high concentration of fumes from boilers. Caretakers may have to remove debris and ash from boilers several times a day, and the risk of exposure is increased from poorly designed or poorly maintained installations.

Surveys that have identified this problem have shown concentrations of sulphur dioxide, carbon monoxide and oxides of nitrogen, which can cause respiratory tract irritation, malaise and headache if exposure is at a low level, but repeated exposure can cause chronic lung disease, such as bronchitis, and high concentrations can cause death.

The ESAC gives practical advice about the planning of new boiler rooms, the selection of fuel, and suggests ways of alleviating the problem of exposure if the existing boilers are causing concern. It recommends good working practices for caretakers, and advises that information should also be obtained from the suppliers so as to operate good working practices.

As well as seeing that the boiler is safe and properly maintained, there should be a regular check to see that there is no rubbish, waste paper or other combustible material stored in the boiler room, and that any hazardous substances such as cleaning materials are properly stored.

Floors and corridors

Floors that are excessively polished look clean and sparkling, but at the same time they can be dangerously slippery, particularly if layers of polish have been allowed to build up. Different types of polish and different polishing procedures are necessary for different types of flooring. Manufacturers' recommendations and instructions on polish should be followed.

Ideally, floors should be cleaned outside school hours, but if that is not possible, then barriers and warning signs should be used so that nobody will walk over the floors while they are being cleaned and after they have been cleaned but before they have dried properly. There will be some corridors that simply cannot be closed off during school hours, and here the best procedure is to polish one half of the width of the corridor at a time. If a chemical cleaner is used, it must be thoroughly washed away with clean water. If the floors are hand washed or mopped, then they should be left as dry as possible.

The Health and Safety Executive has produced a booklet *Watch your step — prevention of slipping, tripping and falling accidents at work*, which gives extensive advice about how to reduce the risk of these types of accidents. There is detailed advice about the care and maintenance of floor surfaces and stairs, indoor corridors and outside pathways. The booklet concludes by saying that if slipping, tripping and falling accidents are to be avoided, both employers and employees must be committed to an effective strategy of prevention. The employer's responsibility is to analyse potential risk areas and, with the employees' support, work towards eliminating actual and potential risks.

Floors close to entrances need particular attention, especially if they are smooth and can be slippery when they are wet. Door mats should either be recessed so that they are flush with the floor surface, or have a nonslip rubber backing. Unsecured mats can be tripping or slipping hazards, particularly if they are on smooth polished floors. A change in floor levels, either on account of single steps or a slope, can also be a hazard and they should both be made clearly visible.

Where a floor is tiled, the tiles should be even and in good condition and firmly stuck down, so as not to be a tripping hazard.

It is important that falling accidents are properly recorded and investigated, so that contributory factors can be identified and then attended to. It could happen that a number of factors contributed to a particular falling accident where, for example, a teacher wearing inappropriate footwear trips over a loose floor tile in a poorly-lit area (see p. 89). It will be the most common contributory factors which will need the most urgent attention.

Ladders are popular because they are relatively cheap, light and easy to carry and easy to store. Surveys have shown that there are four main causes of ladder accidents. First, there are accidents where the ladder itself is defective. Second, there are accidents caused by the ladder slipping at the top or, third, slipping at the bottom. Finally, there are accidents where the person using the ladder falls off, usually when doing something with both hands and then losing a foothold. When ladders are used in schools, they should be of a good standard and properly maintained, and should always be securely fixed before anybody starts to climb. The ladder must, of course, be fixed to something that is itself secure. Where extension ladders are used, they should overlap the main ladder sufficiently far to be secure.

It is sometimes easy to forget that ladders may be used near dangerous equipment or other hazards overhead. Metal ladders, in particular, need to be manoeuvred very carefully if they are in the vicinity of live, uncovered electrical conductors.

Outdoor areas

Paths and other means of access to school must be kept in a safe condition because every day, a large number of people, both adults and pupils, will pass along them. The following checks should be made:

(1) Paving slabs should be checked to see that they are not cracked, broken or uneven.
(2) Outside steps must be in good order and secure. Where there are hand rails, these should be firmly fixed and have no sharp or broken edges.
(3) Any outside lights must be in working order. Outside lighting for footpaths and walkways, especially if they are across uneven ground, can help reduce the risk of someone falling over on their way to, or out of, the school.
(4) Any dangerous equipment should not be left lying around pathways or on the grass.
(5) Walkways should drain properly so as not to collect surface water,

which can be a slipping hazard, especially if frozen over. There should be an effective procedure for putting down sand or salt on areas likely to get icy or snowed up. If dead leaves are allowed to accumulate on pathways, they can be a hazard when the pathway becomes wet.

Playgrounds

All children at some time fall over and suffer minor bumps and bruises in a playground, and that is part of the learning process. But there is a growing concern that the condition of many school playgrounds creates unnecessary risks.

The British Standards Institution has produced a new standard (BS 7188), which sets out five methods of testing playground surfacing. One aspect that is tested is the shock absorption qualities of the surface, and the BSI is available to conduct tests for schools. If any contract for playground surfacing work is put out to tender, then manufacturers should be asked to give information about the BSI test report, or a similar report from any other recognized tester.

BS 5696, which deals with playground equipment, includes a code of practice on how to install safety surfacing.

The BSI strongly recommends that those responsible for purchasing playground equipment should ensure that impact absorbent surfaces are provided, so as to reduce the risk of serious head injuries caused by children striking hard ground.

According to the Centre for Sports Technology, a vertical drop of more than one foot on to a hard, unyielding surface can result in death.

The BSI's safety specifications for playgrounds include the following:

(1) The overall height of fixed equipment should be no more than 2.5 m.
(2) If access to a slide platform is over 2.5 m, there should be intermediate platforms, except on spiral staircases.
(3) Slides should contain no joints.
(4) The spaces between guard rails and equipment should be filled in, so as not to provide any more head traps.
(5) All equipment should be visually inspected once a day, recorded inspection taking place at one to three month intervals, and a certified inspection should occur at intervals not greater than twelve months.
(6) Impact absorbing surfaces should be provided in at least the operating area around equipment, particularly those items from which falls are possible.

The National Playing Fields Association has produced a booklet entitled *Playground Planning for Local Communities*, which includes a section on surfacing that discusses each of the different types of surfacing in turn. Loose-fill tree bark or gravel is effective in absorbing impact and is relatively cheap. However, the depths needed to ensure safety are variable and expert advice is needed. The National Playing Fields Association recommends a depth of at least 300 mm. This type of covering does also need maintenance and it can hide dangerous objects like glass or other sharp objects. Other loose-fill materials include sand, lightweight ceramics and wood chips. However, according to experts, including the National Playing Fields Association, these should not be considered seriously.

Synthetic surfaces such as carpet or wet-paur surfaces are becoming increasingly common, and they are considered to be generally effective, more permanent than loose-fill materials and requiring less maintenance. They are, however, more expensive and can be difficult to lay.

The South Warwickshire Health Authority, which has for some years been campaigning for better playground standards, carried out an investigation into the incidence of playground accidents in the Warwick district during the period 1980 to 1982, and again from July 1988 to June 1989. In the second survey, it was discovered that some 56 per cent of the accidents were the result of a simple fall on to a hard surface. Consequently, one of the inclusions of the report was that more attention should be applied to the development of a cheap, hard-wearing and relatively safe playground surface.

In 1990, the National Playing Fields Association and the Municipal Mutual Insurance Company jointly launched a scheme to enhance safety standards in playgrounds. A service is offered to local authorities which includes a full audit of existing playgrounds, a full inspection of a new site and half yearly or annual inspections which can cover sites, equipment and surfacing. Advice on current safety standards and legal requirements is also offered.

The NPFA's involvement provides the highest standards of playground inspection, and Municipal Mutual is the principal local authority insurer.

Reversing vehicles

Reversing vehicles have long been recognized as a hazard and the big threat is not so much on the road, but in off-road situations, including school precincts where the danger to young children is most real.

A large number of vehicles regularly visit schools to deliver necessary foodstuffs and equipment, e.g. milk and bread vans, local authority vehicles, school buses and waste collection vehicles. Frequently, if not nearly always, they are obliged to reverse at least once during their visit. Drivers reversing their vehicles will only have a limited visibility behind them, and that is one of the reasons why this manoeuvre has a high record of accidents.

Whenever there is an alternative to the reversing manoeuvre, it should be used. If reversing cannot be avoided, then the school may nevertheless be able to minimize the risk of accidents, and the way of doing this is to separate vehicles from pedestrians as much as possible. If the driver's mate is able to direct the vehicle as it reverses – provided both the driver and the mate are clear about where the latter stands, what signals he gives the driver and what they mean – then this will help to increase safety.

The National Reverse in Safety Campaign was formed in 1988 to promote measures to reduce reversing accident and one of its earliest initiatives in terms of research into the problem was to circulate a questionnaire to every school in the country to establish the level of the reversing problem in educational establishments.

Several thousand completed questionnaires were returned, identifying a major problem in schools. Reports of several deaths, numerous accidents and a considerable number of 'near misses' confirmed to the Campaign that our school children are extremely vulnerable to reversing accidents.

The National Reverse in Safety Campaign has recently launched a major campaign to raise awareness in schools of the reversing hazard. Campaign President, Stirling Moss, the well-known motor racing personality, is spearheading the Campaign with a programme of television, radio and newspaper publicity.

School Principals and teachers who are keen to learn more about the Campaign and its plans are invited to write to National Reverse in Safety Campaign, c/o Central Public Relations, Kings Chambers, Queens Road, Coventry CV1 3EH.

Temperatures

In the Factories Act 1961, the obligation in relation to the temperature at the workplace is specific: 'In every workroom in which a substantial proportion of the work is done sitting ... a temperature of less than 60 degrees (Fahrenheit) shall not be deemed after the first hour to be a reasonable temperature'. There is no equivalent legislation covering schools.

DES Design Note 17 'Guidelines for Environmental Design and Fuel Conservation in Educational Building', recommends that school heating systems should be capable of a minimum of 10 m^3 of fresh air per person per hour, and lays down minimum temperatures that the system should be able to maintain. These temperature are:

(1) 19°C in areas where occupants are lightly dressed and inactive (for example, medical inspection rooms).
(2) 18°C in areas where there is an average level of clothing and activity (for example, classrooms).
(3) 15°C in dormitories.
(4) 14°C in areas such as gymnasia, where occupants are lightly dressed, but activity is vigorous.

The Design Note also recommends that the temperature in circulation spaces should not be more than 3°C below the temperature of the spaces they serve.

In the summer, when the heating system is not operating, the recommended temperature for all spaces is 23°C with a swing of not more than 4°C from that optimum. The Design Note points out the possibility of undue temperature rises in warm weather, and refers to the need for good ventilation to help combat this.

A number of schools have to use portable gas heaters to supplement the school heating. It is important that these heaters are safe and that the pupils are told to be careful around them. The Health and Safety Commission Education Service National Industry Group has produced a document, 'Temporary use of liquefied petroleum gas heaters in school', which gives guidance on how to use heaters safely, where to place them, how to maintain them and how to store cylinders. It also gives advice about ventilation around heaters and what to do if there is a leakage.

The Committee advises that as it is normally foreseeable that the need for emergency heating will arise from time to time, written procedures should be drawn up. Heaters should only be brought into a room when required for immediate use and should be removed when they are no longer needed. The number of heaters in a room should be kept to a minimum. Each heater should be located so as not to obstruct a means of escape, and should not be exposed to draughts. There should be at least one metre of clear space around it, but a heater can be placed against a wall, provided the hot surface faces away from the wall with no curtains or other combustible materials within the metre space. Special care needs to be taken when replacing heaters in laboratories, art rooms and work rooms where there will be highly flammable materials. When a suitable location has been found, then everybody should understand that the heater should not be moved without proper authorization.

Lighting

Inadequate lighting as a result of poor lighting, excessively bright light or incorrectly placed lights, is often a contributory cause of accidents, particularly tripping or falling accidents. DES Design Note 17, 'Guidelines for Environmental Design and Fuel Conservation in Educational Buildings', recommends that in day time the main source of light should be daylight, so each teaching area should have a window area of at least 20 per cent of the total area of the external wall. Illumination, supplemented by electric light as necessary, should be maintained at least at 150 lux. When fluorescent lighting is used then illumination should be maintained at not less than 300 lux. The Design Note recommends that in primary schools, normal filament lighting is sufficient, but that fluorescent lighting of not less than 300 lux should be provided.

There are certain areas where correct lighting is essential. For example, lighting on stairs must be adequate, and it is unsatisfactory to have a switch at the bottom of the stairs so that a person has to walk down the stairs in darkness before the light can be switched on.

There needs to be suitable lighting in all store rooms and stock cupboards, and all light fittings need to be regularly cleaned and maintained. Dirt that is left to accumulate in fittings can cut out a significant amount of the light.

Electricity

Detailed advice is available from the Health and Safety Executive in its guidance note GS23 'Electrical Safety in Schools', which was originally produced in 1983 and updated in April 1990.

The Executive offers general advice about electrical apparatus in schools. Among the advice it gives is the following:

(1) All electrical equipment including socket outlets and other fittings, for example, light fittings, should be chosen to take into account what they are to be used for and also the possibility of being meddled with. Electrical equipment which is close to where pupils are sitting is at risk of being meddled with, and so wherever possible it should be positioned away from pupils.

(2) Fixed electrical installations should be properly inspected and tested

at least every five years, or more frequently if subject to damage and abuse.

(3) Socket outlets should be positioned so as to minimize penetration by water and, if necessary, special socket outlets may be needed. Where water outlets are close to electrical socket outlets, a high standard of electrical protection will be necessary.

(4) Plugs and sockets should be chosen to prevent an accidental connection to the wrong supply. For example, it should not be possible to plug a 110 volt apparatus into a 240 volt socket outlet.

(5) Where pupils are required to set up a project or an experiment, special precautions must be taken if there could be contact with live parts of more than 25 volts. Before any electricity supply is connected, a teacher should have checked that the equipment has been set up so that there will be no danger when the supply is connected. If any fault occurs during an exercise involving electricity, all supplies should be cut off before the fault is investigated.

(6) Schools should keep an inventory of electrical apparatus and the apparatus should be examined to see if it is obsolete, redundant or defective.

(7) All portable electrical apparatus should be regularly inspected and checked. A record should be kept of portable apparatus, together with details of checks and inspections. There should be a visual inspection before the start of every term, which could reveal common faults such as broken plugs, frayed leads or loose or damaged casings. As well as this, all such equipment must be serviced at least once a year by a suitably qualified person.

The new Electricity at Work Regulations 1989 replace the existing regulations dating back to 1908, and impose obligations on employers and employees to eliminate danger from electric shocks, electric burns, electrical explosion or arising from fires and explosions caused by electrical energy. The Health and Safety Executive has produced a small leaflet 'Electricity at Work' and also a 'Memorandum of Guidance on the Electricity at Work Regulations 1989', which give further details. There is also the Guidance Note 'Electrical Safety in Schools' already referred to, which takes the new Regulations into account.

The Regulations came into effect on 1 April 1990 and noncompliance with these Regulations is a criminal offence. Responsibility for complying with the Regulations rests on all those who are able to exercise control over matters covered in the Regulations, and as the Regulations cover all electrical equipment and systems, this means that many staff in schools, including nonteaching staff, will be affected to some extent. The Regulations state that no employee can carry out any work where technical knowledge or experience is necessary to prevent danger, unless they have that knowledge or experience. LEAs will need to establish what this means in relation to maintenance and upkeep of electrical equipment in schools and, in particular, who is competent to deal with each type of electrical maintenance or repair.

Children should be advised to be careful with and respect electricity. In home economics, for example, there must be safety rules which should include.

(1) Never handle plugs, switches or any electric appliances with wet hands.
(2) All appliances should be switched off and unplugged before being cleaned.
(3) Never let a flex touch hot parts of a cooker or a toaster.
(4) If bread is stuck inside the toaster, the toaster should be switched off and unplugged, then allowed to cool before any attempts to remove the bread.
(5) Nobody should poke around a toaster with a metal implement.
(6) Kettles should be switched off and unplugged at the wall socket before being filled or before water is poured from it.

The Health and Safety Commission Education Science Advisory Committee has produced a summary of 80 electrical accidents on educational premises between September 1984 and September 1989. The summary is used as a training aid and includes the following examples:

IP [injured person] was operating photocopying machine in school office – machine stopped, IP pushed plug firmly into two socket adaptor. Machine operated then stopped again. She then held plug in while operating machine and received electric shock. Adaptor in use at double socket, apparently lose fitting in socket.

Member of teaching staff received electric shock at mains voltage while emptying coins from a coffee machine rented by the staff association. He removed the coin collection drawer and reached inside to retrieve additional coins, thereby contacting live wires at rear of on/off switch.

Auxiliary teacher received electric shock when switched on electric light switch. County Council report that coverplate of switch did not properly overlap hole cut to receive box and water had entered causing short circuit. Also switch box had become loose and earth terminal was not tight.

Electrical burns to two fingers of hand suffered by fifteen year old school pupil in chemistry lesson demonstrating electrophoresis. Leads fastened by crocodile clips to glass slide with wet tissue on top, connected to 300 v, 100 mA DC supply of Labpac transformer. About eight groups of three children conducted experiment with colour change of crystals spread across tissue.

Pupil suffered burn to hand when two-pin mains input plug split open exposing live contacts. Plug fitted into rear of electronic keyboard. IP received electric shock from mains voltage socket outlet when switching on a food mixer. Extraction fans not in operation for three months resulting in condensation on walls with evidence of moisture ingress to socket.

IP, a school meals kitchen assistant, touched metal saucepan on electric cooker and received electric shock − off work for one week. Electrician from LA found that earth wire to element had broken allowing electrical potential from ring to earth through IP at a voltage between 0−240 v.

School cleaner buffing gymnasium floor. Leads from two machines became entangled, cleaner received an electric shock and was thrown against a wall. IP received electric shock from handle of floor scrubbing machine. 240 v electric lead of machine damaged, apparently caused day or so earlier by machine itself running over lead. IP thrown away from machine and received strain injuries.

Safety signs

All safety signs must comply with the Safety Signs Regulations 1980, which in turn say that any safety signs giving health and safety information or instructions to employees must comply with British Standard 5378 'Safety Signs and Colours'. There are four categories of safety signs which are:

(1) Warning signs. These are triangular with a black border and a yellow background. These include signs giving warning of the risk of fire, risk of explosion, a toxic hazard, warning of a corrosive substance, warning of the risk of ionizing radiation, the risk of electric shock, the risk of a laser beam and the risk of danger generally.
(2) Prohibition signs. These are circular with a red border and cross bar and a white background. The symbol is in black. Examples include 'no smoking', 'no naked flames', 'do not extinguish with water', 'do not drink the water' and 'pedestrians prohibited'.
(3) Mandatory signs. These are circular with a blue background and a white symbol. These signs indicate that protective equipment and clothing should be worn, including eye protection, respiratory protection, head protection, foot protection, hearing protection and hand protection.
(4) Safe condition signs. These signs are square or oblong with white symbols on a green background. The two signs under this heading indicate first-aid posts and the direction of an emergency route.

Asbestos

There has been a considerable amount of recent concern about the possible health risks from asbestos, and it is now known that a number of serious illnesses can be caused from exposure to asbestos fibres.

A number of cases of lung cancer have been linked to asbestos, and although medical research is continuing in its investigations into this link, the number of confirmed cases is far less than, for example, cases of lung cancer linked to smoking. Similarly, cases of asbestosis, which is a form of scarring of the lungs, are relatively small in number. The third illness linked to asbestos is mesothelioma, which is a cancer of the lining of the lungs and which has been linked in particular to short periods of high exposure to blue asbestos.

The three main types of asbestos are blue asbestos (crocidolite), brown asbestos (amosite) and white asbestos, (chrysotile). Only white asbestos is used in manufactured articles and it is found mainly in asbestos cement products such as tiles and sheets. The Asbestos (Prohibitions) Regulations 1985, prohibit the importation of blue and brown asbestos and products containing them. Since 1969, blue asbestos has been banned as a building material.

Asbestos appears in three different forms. It can be sprayed, in materials like paint, it can be in the form of a hard panel or tile, or it can be in the form of soft board, such as insulation board. So in schools, asbestos may be present in asbestos boarding used for fire protection or heating insulation as well as in ceiling tiles, roof tiles, pipes and guttering.

In its advisory booklet *Asbestos and You*, the Health and Safety Executive says that there is no known safe level of asbestos dust. However, when asbestos is in a stable condition, asbestos fibres are not released into the atmosphere and undisturbed asbestos materials in good condition should present little risk. The risk of asbestos fibres being released into the atmosphere arises when the asbestos is disturbed or damaged, or for some other reason, begins to crumble.

So asbestos fibres in a roof space above a classroom should present no problem at all unless they become unstable or are disturbed by building work, in which case, careful precautions should be taken. A number of LEAs are attempting to systematically remove as much asbestos material from schools as possible, particularly in highly populated areas such as classrooms, halls or corridors. Removing asbestos has to be carefully planned and carried out, and those parts of the school affected will have to be shut off. So in some cases, it may be best to leave stable asbestos materials where they are. If removal work is undertaken, this should be done in holidays whenever that is possible, and air monitoring should take place before staff and pupils are allowed to return to the affected buildings.

The contractor carrying out the removal work must be licensed under the Asbestos Regulations, and must supply a certificate stating that air sampling has shown that conditions are safe. There are safety levels of asbestos in industrial environments, the maximum level for blue and brown asbestos being 0.2 fibres per millilitre of air and, in the case of white asbestos, the limit is 0.5 fibres. Asbestos levels in schools should not be allowed to even approach these levels, and an acceptable level would be 0.01 fibres.

The DES has produced an Administrative Memorandum (3/86), which is entitled 'The use of Asbestos in Educational Establishments', and this recommends the following procedure where asbestos is found:

(1) Identify the presence of asbestos and establish its extent, type and location.
(2) Assess the potential fibre release. This will need to take into account the location of the asbestos, its condition and how accessible it is to staff and children.
(3) Decide what remedial action is necessary and in what order of priority.

Many LEAs will have their own written guidelines which will set out each of these steps in some detail. Where asbestos is present in schools, then it should be treated carefully. It should not be drilled, sawn, sanded or have holes knocked in it. On no account should asbestos dust be swept up or brushed up, and small quantities should be picked up with a moist swab, which should then be disposed of in a sealed plastic bag. Under no circumstances should asbestos be dumped in a skip or a dustbin.

Although asbestos in equipment does not pose a hazard, asbestos products should be replaced as soon as possible. Schools should keep records of all asbestos products in school, including details of asbestos tests and asbestos work.

Formaldehyde

Formaldehyde is a widely used cavity wall insulant. It is cheap, quick to install and, if there is a fire, then it will help to prevent the rapid spread of flames. Urea formaldehyde (UF) was first developed as insulating materials in the early 1940s, and it was only relatively recently that questions have been raised both in this country and in the United States about the possible health hazards of UF.

In May 1982, the Under Secretary of State for Environment said in the House of Commons that formaldehyde vapour can sometimes cause irritation of the respiratory tract and eyes. These symptoms have subsequently been shown to be the common reaction to exposure to lower levels of formaldehyde, but these problems usually disappear when the exposure ends. However, some people are more sensitive to the substance than others, and they will experience more serious symptoms, such as stinging eyes and a sore or tight throat. The only effective solution in these circumstances is to seek a formaldehyde-free environment, but this can be difficult, because formaldehyde is present in many different materials.

Any teacher who has been exposed to relatively low levels of formaldehyde, but has experienced serious symptoms, should be advised to take medical advice straight away to see whether this means that he or she is hypersensitive to the substance. If that is the case, then reasonably practicable precautions have to be taken to eliminate or reduce that teacher's contact with formaldehyde.

Visual display units

Modern technology is advancing in leaps and bounds and sophisticated computers and word processors are now used by a wide cross-section of the public, both at work and at home. Vast amounts of information can be stored up and then retrieved in an instant by the press of a button. This new technology is available in schools, both as a teaching aid and as an administrative tool. Teachers are therefore both users and providers.

There has been a fair amount of recent research into the possible health effects of VDUs, and while it is clear that VDUs do not represent a serious health risk for the casual user, teachers do need to be vigilant for the health and well being of pupils using VDUs, and to be familiar with the relevant advice given by the experts.

The European Community's Committee of the House of Lords carried out an inquiry into the European Community Directive on VDUs and its Report, which was debated by the House of Lords in February 1989, concluded that there was no need for a mandatory directive on VDUs, but that employees should be entitled to have eye tests.

In summer 1990, the Health and Safety Commission nevertheless announced that it would be considering what proposals would need to be drawn up to give effect to the directive, and the Commission expects to publish consultancy documents during 1991, containing its proposals for implementing the directive. When the directive is implemented, the entitlement to an eye test will apply before an employee starts working at a VDU, at regular intervals thereafter, and if he or she experiences visual difficulties at any time. Employees will also be entitled to an ophthalmological examination if the eye test shows this to be necessary, and they must be provided with special spectacles if these are needed for their work and normal ones cannot be used.

The Health and Safety Executive has produced two booklets on this subject, *Visual Display Units* and *Working with VDUs*. They deal with possible health risks of VDUs and how to tackle them. There are a number of points to note:

(1) There is no medical evidence that using a VDU has a long-term effect on eyes, but some people can find that it is particularly tiring to work from a VDU screen for any length of time.

(2) There are a number of minor health problems and irritations which have been linked to some degree with VDUs. Conditions such as migraine headaches, itching skin or redness of the face and/or neck have been identified. The cause appears to be a combination of a dry atmosphere in the room and static electricity near the VDU. These are not common complaints, and they appear to be confined to those who are particularly sensitive but, nevertheless, teachers should be aware of these complaints.

(3) Neckache and backache can be caused or aggravated by badly designed workplaces. Teachers should be careful to see that pupils are sitting comfortably, and that they are not having to make awkward head movements to read from source documents or from the screen itself. In March 1990, three women who worked as data clerks for the Inland Revenue were awarded a total of £107,500 damages. All three worked at VDUs and suffered tenosynovitis, which is a repetitive strain injury, causing pain in the wrist and lower arm, attributable to repetitive typing at the keyboard.

(4) The Executive draws attention to a number of steps, most of which are nothing more than common sense, which can be taken to reduce the risk of an operator suffering any irritation or discomfort.

(a) The choice of VDU is obviously the most significant factor. Different screens have variable display contrasts, which means the contrast between the bright word characters and the darker background can be varied. In any case, the operator should have some form of control over the contrast, so as to find his or her preferred level. Flickers on screens are becoming less common, but if flickering does occur because of a fault, it should be corrected immediately.

(b) Nobody should be allowed to work at a VDU screen for excessive periods. It is felt to be unnecessary to give specific guidance on rest pauses, because everything depends on the particular circumstances, and so a teacher will be expected to exercise good judgement.

(c) There are a number of points about keyboard design which can both make the system operate more efficiently and also prevent fatigue and discomfort. Ideally, the keyboard should have a matt surround and the keys should have low reflectance surfaces with concave tops. The key legend should be legible under the room lights. The advantage of detachable keyboards is that they allow the operator to find an ideal working position.

(d) The Executive recommends that in order to provide as comfortable a working posture as possible, the underside of the work surface should be high enough to allow adequate thigh clearance of the operator and the top of the work surface should be low enough for the 'home row' of keys on the keyboard to be at elbow height for the seated operator. Chairs should be adjustable, both in height and tilt, with adjustable back rests and good support for the back, pelvis and buttocks.

(e) There should be a comfortable room temperature and there should be no drafts in the room.

Good housekeeping and tidiness is again important in VDU rooms. For example, there should be no trailing cables or leads, either across the floor or underneath an operator's feet, because these can cause accidents.

Building work on school premises

It can be an anxious time for the head, staff and governors when there are building contractors in school. The contractors will bring with them materials, equipment and machines which can attract children, and there will also be potential hazards such as holes, piles of debris and other things to fall down or trip over. There is currently a great deal of national publicity which spells out the dangers of children wandering on to building sites and the same dangers are present when contractors are in school. It is essential that it is made absolutely clear to children that all building areas are out of bounds.

The Education Service Advisory Committee of the Health and Safety Commission has produced a package of information leaflets giving advice on how to safeguard the health and safety of pupils and staff when building work is being carried out on school premises. The package is called 'Working to Keep Work Safe' with the sub title 'Building Contracts Undertaken on the Education Premises – Strategies for the Health and Safety of Staff and Pupils'.

One of the leaflets, which is entitled 'Guidance to Safe Working Practices', gives practical advice on how to minimize the risk from work in and around occupied school buildings. Whenever possible, work areas should be physically separated from parts of the building used by pupils and staff, but there will still be situations where there is no alternative but to have equipment and materials around occupied buildings. The leaflet gives advice on the demarcation of ladders, scaffolds, cradles, etc., both when they are in position for less than a working day, and for more than a working day. The need for proper communication between the school and the contractors is emphasized, so that each knows what the arrangements are. For example, scaffolding should only be erected or dismantled when the surrounding areas are clear of pupils and staff.

The danger of injury from falling objects is also pointed out and there is advice on how to avoid this. Similarly, there is a potential danger from contractors' vehicles, and the advice is that wherever possible, there should be separate access to the site for contractors, their plant and equipment. The risk of children being knocked down by vehicles is greater where there are vehicles reversing, so wherever possible, the need to reverse should be reduced or eliminated.

Another of the leaflets gives advice on strategies for smaller work in occupied premises. This includes glazing work, work on heating and ventilation and roof repairs. Other leaflets contain advice to LEAs on arrangements with contractors to ensure that all proper allowances have been made for the added risks of having so many children about while the work is being carried out.

Before contractors come into school, the head will need to have information about the work, including:

(1) The nature of the building work, the start date and the estimated duration. The head should have the name and telephone number of the LEA's supervising officer responsible for the contract.
(2) Any regulations governing the building work.
(3) Whether the contractors' vehicles will need to pass through open access areas and, if so, whether they can be segregated from staff and pupils, either by briefing the contractors on when to bring their vehicles through or, if that is not possible, by barriers.
(4) Details of the potential risks that the contractors' work will create

and, having done so, to establish what precautions the contractors intend to take. Possible risks will be:
(a) Objects falling from heights.
(b) Materials obstructing passage ways and fire escapes.
(c) Ladders, scaffolds, tools and plant being left unattended. The contractors may be using gas cylinders and these require particular care.
(d) Excavations.
(e) Electrical leads running through the school or across the playgound
(f) The storage and transport of materials and waste could create risks for staff and pupils, and the head should know what these arrangements are.
(g) Dust or fumes.

(5) Whether the contractors need to have any health and safety information from the school, such as information about where the fire alarms are, where the normal access points are, and the emergency access points and exits.

The contractors will also need other information so that they can adjust their work arrangements for the safety and convenience of pupils and staff. Among the information that the head will need to provide is:
(a) Details of accesses and exists to the school and when they are most heavily used.
(b) Details of access and exits within the buildings and when they are most heavily used.
(c) Details of the playground facilities and times of breaks.
(d) Details of arrangements for service deliveries to the school.
(e) Details of emergency services within the school and emergency exits.

(6) Whether or not the school needs to take any precautions itself. The head will need to decide what instructions and information have to be given to the children. Whether it is necessary to have daily announcements in assembly, as well as a general announcement at the start of work will depend on the type of work, the ages of the children and how the work is progressing. Similar factors will determine whether lunch time supervision needs to be increased.

As well as the information package, the Health and Safety Commission has produced a video with the assistance of a construction safety adviser working in the education sector. The video, which is entitled *Kids on Site*, lasts eleven minutes and is designed to accompany the written guidelines by illustrating the points made in the leaflets about dangers during building work, and also giving illustrations of good practice to eliminate the risk of accidents. The video costs £40 including VAT and it can be hired. In both cases, it is available from CFL Vision, PO Box 35, Wetherby, Yorkshire LS23 7EX. Telephone 0937 541010.

9
FIRE

Legislation and codes of practice

There is an enormous difference in terms of fire safety legislation between schools on the one hand, and offices, factories and other work premises on the other hand.

Two questions in Parliament in October 1989 illustrate this. John Cartwright MP asked the Secretary of State for the Home Department what steps he was taking to improve fire safety in (a) offices and (b) schools. The reply was as follows:

Offices where more than twenty persons are at work at any one time or more than ten persons are at work elsewhere than on the ground floor, are already required to have a fire certificate unless they have been exempted by the fire authority from this requirement. Fire authorities have powers to enforce the requirements of fire certificates which require offices to be provided with adequate means of escape and means for fighting fire and to provide training for employees in action to be taken in the event of fire.

The Minister then went on to explain that in offices which do not require a fire certificate, the occupier must by law provide such means of escape in case of fire and such means for fighting fire as may reasonably be required.

He referred to a recent code of practice for fire precautions in factories, offices, shops and railway premises not required to have a fire certificate. The Minister then referred to the position in schools rather briefly: 'Fire safety in schools is primarily a matter for my Rt Hon. Friend the Secretary of State for Education and Science.'

John Cartwright had previously asked the Secretary of State for Education and Science what steps he had taken or proposed to take to establish the effectiveness of fire safety arrangements in schools, and the answer was:

> To ensure the safety of occupants of schools in the event of fire, the statutory provisions, and guidance regularly issued in support of them, emphasize the importance of maintaining adequate means of escape. The day to day responsibility for properly maintaining safety rests locally, but the Department issues guidance such as Building Bulletin No. 7 'Fire and the Design of Education Buildings' and 'Safety in Education', Bulletin No. 5.

The reason for these vastly different replies so far as offices and schools are concerned, stems from the Fire Precautions Act 1971. This legislation demands that designated premises have a fire certificate. The procedure for applying for a fire certificate is set out in Regulations made under the Act, which say that while an application for a fire certificate is pending, the owner/occupier must see that there are safe and effective means of escape from the premises in the event of fire, adequate means of fighting fire, and that all employees in the premises have received instruction and training on what to do if there is a fire. Following the application for a fire certificate, the premises will be inspected by the fire authority, which will grant a fire certificate if satisfied that the means of escape from fire and related fire precautions in the premises are adequate. Once issued, the fire certificate will specify the fire escapes and the means of ensuring that they can be safely and effectively used at all material times.

The certificate will also specify the type, number and location of fire fighting equipment and the type, number and location of fire alarms. The fire authority can also incorporate in the fire certificate specific requirements, such as that fire escapes must be kept clear, that fire equipment must be properly maintained and that employees are properly trained. The certificate can also limit the number of people on the premises at any one time. If on inspection, the fire authority is not satisfied about the fire safety aspects of the premises, then a notice can be served on the occupier stating what has to be done before a fire certificate is issued and setting down a time limit.

Office premises include buildings or parts of buildings, the sole or principal use of which includes administration, clerical work, handling money, telephone and telegraph operating, writing, drawing and editorial preparation.

Shop premises are also covered by legislation and include buildings or parts of buildings, the sole or principal use of which is carrying on a retail trade or business; buildings occupied by wholesalers and buildings where members of the public can take goods for repair or treatment. It also includes certain types of covered markets.

Railway premises are also covered and include signal boxes and buildings in station and goods yards where people work. Railway platforms are also included.

The 1971 Act says that a factory, office, shop or railway premises that employs less than twenty persons at any one time and with not more than ten employees elsewhere than on the ground floor at any one time, does not require a fire certificate. Most schools have more than twenty employees and hundreds of children working in old buildings, often on split sites.

The 1971 Act gives the Secretary of State power to require any premises 'used for the purposes of teaching, training or research' to be designated but, as yet, no order has been made relating to schools. In the debate on the Education Reform Bill in the House of Lords in May 1988, when this issue arose, Lord Glenamara described this as 'nothing short of disgraceful'.

Regulation 24 of Education (School Premises) Regulations 1981 deals with safety protection. It says that every part of a school building should be of such design and construction as to reasonably ensure the safe escape of occupants in the case of fire and their health and safety in other respects. Particular matters that have to be considered are the likely rate at which flames would spread across exposed surfaces, the building structure's resistance to fire, and the fire resistance of materials used in the building. The Regulations do not become fully operative until 1996 (see p. 92) and, in any event, their enforcibility is subject to Section 10 of the Education Act 1944, which allows the Secretary of State to waive any part of the Regulations in the case of a particular school where 'having regard to the nature of the existing site, or any existing buildings thereon or to other special circumstances affecting the school premises, it would be unreasonable to require conformity with requirements with regulations'. For this reason, the Regulations have been described as a paper tiger.

DES Building Bulletin No. 7 'Fire and the Design of Educational Buildings' was revised in 1988. This Bulletin contains recommendations to do with means of escape, structural fire precautions, fire warning systems and fire fighting, but the recommendations are primarily aimed at new constructions and at adaption or renovation work to existing buildings. The Bulletin also includes very helpful practical advice and recommendations about fire prevention and everyday fire precautions but, as the Bulletin itself says, 'its main emphasis is on proper design and construction to ensure the safe escape of the occupants in the event of fire'. The

Bulletin does not directly refer to the failure to have school premises designated under the 1971 Act, but it points out one of the absurd consequences: 'Some parts of educational buildings which are used as offices or shops may also be subject as regards means of escape to the Fire Precautions Act 1971. In these cases, the local Fire Authority should be consulted.'

The DES Safety in Education Bulletin No. 5, referred to the in Parliamentary Answer on p. 119 was produced in October 1987 to coincide with a national fire safety week. The Bulletin contains recommendations about foam products, combustible materials, flammable liquids, security and fire and the public in school. It also contains advice about fire inspections and fire drills. At the end of the Bulletin, the small print says 'recommendation of a safety measure in this Bulletin or in the safety booklets does not imply Government commitment to the provision of extra funds'.

The Fire Precautions Act is enforced by the criminal courts. For example, in November 1989, the Hilton Hotel in London was served with 46 summonses under the Act dealing with complaints, such as emergency staircases and fire fighting accesses being blocked by rubbish, self-closing devices on fire doors being faulty, and other items causing material obstruction, which could have caused disaster as occupants rushed to safety. There are absolutely no criminal sanctions of this type to enforce fire safety standards in schools.

This disparity has been highlighted by the two Codes of Practice dealing with fire precautions, which were produced in 1989 by the Home Office and the Scottish Home and Health Office. One Code of Practice relates to fire precautions in work places that require a fire certificate. It gives detailed advice about the procedure for fire certification, as well as practical advice on matters such as fire resistance in buildings, how to assess the fire risk, fire-fighting equipment, fire drills and means of escape. There is specific advice to management on fire instruction and fire drills, and also particular advice on ensuring that physically disabled and sensory impaired people are safe. The other Code of Practice covers fire precautions in factories, offices, shops and railway premises that are not required to have a fire certificate. This also gives detailed practical fire safety advice. These Codes of Practice are not legally binding but, like the Highway Code, they can be referred to in court proceedings.

Also in 1989, the Home Office and the Scottish Home and Health office produced a booklet *Fire Safety at Work*. The practical advice it gives includes advice on fire escapes, fire warning systems, and fire-fighting equipment, and there is also information about staff training, including advice on special precautions for staff with impaired vision or impaired sight, and wheelchair users. There is a section dealing with good housekeeping and the prevention of fire, and a check list giving examples of good housekeeping.

Under local management of schools (see pp. 135−7), governors will have increased health and safety responsibilities as a result of their control over how the school budget is spent. Whether or not a particular structural or internal alteration, which may be necessary for fire safety, is the financial responsibility of the governors or the LEA will depend upon how responsibilities for the school building are divided between the LEA and the governors. This division of responsibility will be set out in the LEA's local management scheme, and the DES model is reproduced in Appendix IV. The division is broadly on the lines of a landlord/tenant arrangement, with the LEA responsible for the main structural items and external works, and the governors being responsible for internal matters. So the governors will be responsible for the maintenance of fire fighting equipment such as extinguishers, fire blankets and hoses.

Many LEAs have their own fire safety procedures. These procedures will say that a person who discovers a fire, no matter how small, should raise the alarm at the nearest alarm point, and warn people in the vicinity of the fire. While any available fire-fighting equipment can be used to try and put out the fire, this should not be attempted if there is any personal risk involved, and if there is any doubt then the building should be evacuated. When the fire warning signal has been sounded, nobody should disregard it or delay evacuation by collecting personal belongings. Schools will have their own evacuation procedures, and staff should know to where they must report with the children for a roll call to check that everyone is accounted for. There will have to be separate procedures for breaks and during lunch, and supervisors should know what areas they are responsible for checking if there is an evacuation. These procedures should be tested by regular fire drills, and the first drill in a school year should take place as soon as possible because there will be pupils and, perhaps, some staff new to the school.

It is very important that schools have accurate registers of pupils in schools. Pupils marked in may subsequently have left school to go to the dentist or have gone home sick, so it is important that they sign out before they leave.

Individual teachers must be familiar with the following information about fire precautions:

(1) Where all the school alarm points are situated.
(2) How to operate the alarms.

(3) What the alarm signal is, particularly if it is similar to other bells used in the school.

(4) What to do when the alarm bell sounds.

(5) Where all fire extinguishers, fire blankets and other fire fighting equipment are located.

(6) How to use all the fire fighting equipment.

(7) Where all the normal exits and emergency exits are, and where the assembly point is outside the building if there is an evacuation.

It is the head's responsibility to see that the fire logbook is kept up to date. The logbook should include details of any outbreak of fire and details of fire drills, tests on fire alarms and maintenance of fire equipment.

Fire precautions

The best way to fight fire is to prevent fires starting in the first place. Like all hazards, fire prevention depends upon identifying the risk, understanding it and devising and operating systems and procedures to reduce and eliminate the risk.

There are a number of basic fire safety rules for schools, many of which are no more than tidiness and good house keeping.

(1) Combustible materials, such as cardboard boxes and packaging materials, should not be kept about the school unless they are needed.

(2) Corridors and stairways and other entrances and exits should be kept clear and, in particular, kept clear of combustible materials. Stairways and corridors on escape routes should always be kept clear.

(3) Classroom displays and work displayed in corridors should be set up with care. Decorations can be a fire risk if they are hung near sources heat or hung from light fittings.

(4) Fire doors can save lives if there is a fire. They should always be kept free to close and never wedged open.

(5) Wastepaper bins should be made of metal or other noncombustible materials. They should be used and wastepaper should not be left lying around.

(6) Rubbish should not, in any event, be allowed to collect in hidden places, and particular attention needs to be paid to general tidiness and cleanliness around electrical appliances.

(7) There must be adequate ashtrays in smoking areas, and a proper

system, and for collecting waste from ashtrays separate from waste-paper bins.

(8) Stock rooms for stationery and other combustible materials should be kept securely locked when not being used. No smoking signs should be placed on doors to these rooms.

(9) Boiler rooms must be kept clean and clear and locked.

(10) Open fires (gas, electricity or solid fuel) must have a fixed fire guard, according to the appropriate British Standard.

(11) Electrical equipment must be used properly and kept in a safe working order. Electrical points should never be overloaded and wiring should be checked regularly. Electrical safety is discussed further on pp. 106−9.

(12) Some clothing and costumes for school plays and musicals can be highly inflammable. If there is no alternative but to use these, then they should never be placed close to any heat source.

As science work can present a special fire risk on account of the nature of the materials used in experiments, there must always be a safe system of work in operation. There must be proper supervision at all times, and staff should be familiar with safe practice. A number of fire safety precautions should be taken in science laboratories in addition to those already mentioned, and these include:

(1) Potentially dangerous experiments and demonstrations should not take place near a laboratory door because that could be the only way out.

(2) Combustible material, especially chemicals, should be kept in a secure place, never in store rooms or cupboards containing exposed electrical switchgear. All stores where highly flammable liquids are kept should be marked 'flammable liquids − no smoking − no naked lights'.

(3) Good housekeeping is essential in laboratories and rubbish and combustible waste should be cleared away regularly.

(4) Any gas taps should be checked before leaving the room, and if there is an isolating valve, it should be turned off.

(5) Open flames should be used only after checking that nearby materials are not inflammable. Flammable liquids should not be poured from one vessel into another or heated near to an open flame.

(6) Goggles or some other suitable eye protection must be worn whenever there is a risk to the eyes from spills or splashes or explosions.

(7) There can be a risk of explosions from substances which are themselves relatively stable. Pupils should be warned not to:
   (a) Mix combustibles with oxidizing agents.

(b) Add concentrated strong acids to chlorates or vice versa.
(c) Add water to concentrated strong acids when diluting those acids but, instead, to add the acid to the water.

Bomb scares

In recent years, many bomb attacks have been carried out indiscriminately on civilian, and terrorists continue to be active. Bomb threats and bomb hoaxes are becoming an increasing occurrence and schools need to be prepared. Any bomb threat, however it is received, must be taken seriously and dealt with urgently. There should be a named person in the school responsible for dealing with the situation initially, and a deputy in that person's absence. At all times, the safety of those present in school must be the paramount consideration, and ultimate responsibility rests with the head.

A number of factors should be borne in mind:

(1) A bomb threat is often issued over the telephone and if details are given, they should be recorded immediately.
(2) The police should be notified without delay if a telephone call is received, or if a suspicious parcel or packaged is spotted. No suspicious article should be touched.
(3) The school should be familiar with any relevant LEA regulations and these must, of course, be followed.
(4) The police may make the decision whether or not to evacuate, or they may leave it to the head. If there is an evacuation, then the fire evacuation procedure should be used.
(5) No search of the school buildings should start until the police have arrived. It may be that a search takes a considerable period of time, at the end of which a judgement still has to be made about whether it is safe to return to the building. If the police are unwilling to make this decision, then the judgement will ultimately rest with the head, who should certainly consult the LEA. Clearly the head will need to know how the search was carried out and any other information about the nature of the threat, such as whether any deadlines were given.
(6) If the head decides that it is not safe to declare the school safe to reenter, there will be an obligation to see that the school is properly dismissed. It may be that because of the ages, numbers of the children and the location of the school, it is not safe for the children to be sent home. One possible solution is for the children to be taken to a

school or schools close by. It may be that there are transport problems for some children and that, in the case of others, there is nobody at home or elsewhere to receive them. In these circumstances, one possible solution is for the children to be taken in temporarily by a school or schools close by, and it is the LEA's responsibility to make such arrangements.

10
SCHOOL TRANSPORT

Transport to school

Section 36 of the 1944 Education Act says that it is the parents' duty to see that each child of compulsory school age receives efficient full-time education by regular attendance to school or otherwise. Section 39 confirms that if a child fails to attend regularly at school, then the parents are guilty of a criminal offence. But the Section also contains some exceptions. In particular, a child is not deemed to have failed to attend regularly, if the parent can show that the school is not within walking distance from the child's home, and that no suitable arrangements have been made by the LEA to transport the child to and from school. The Section says that 'walking distance means in relation to a child who has not attained the age of eight years – two miles and in the case of any other child, three miles, measured by the nearest available route'.

The LEA's statutory responsibility is to make whatever arrangements for the provision of transport are necessary to facilitate the attendance of pupils at schools, and any transport provided in this way must be free of charge. To assist the LEA in making a decision about any particular request for free transport, the 1944 Act, as amended by the Education (No. 2) Act 1986, says that the LEA must have regard (among other things) to the pupil's age and the nature of the route or alternative routes that the pupil could reasonably be expected to take.

Two recent House of Lords decisions have considered this legislation. In 1987, in the case *Essex County Council v Rogers*, the court decided that an 'available' route must be a route along which a child accompanied as necessary can walk and can walk with reasonable safety. According to the court, such a route does not fail to qualify as 'available' because of dangers which would arise if the child were unaccompanied.

In that case, the parents of an eight-year-old girl were prosecuted for failing to send her to school. They argued that the only safe route to school was over three miles in distance, and although there was a shorter route, this involved the girl walking alone across a rough, unlit country track. The Court of Appeal held that this route could not be regarded as an available route, and decided that the parents had acted reasonably in not letting a child use it. The House of Lords decided differently, indicating that whether or not the nearest available route fell within the 1944 Act was purely arithmetical and need take no account of safety factors.

The House of Lords looked at this issue again in December 1988 in another case, *R v Devon County Council ex parte G*, which involved a nine-year-old pupil whose route to school was along an unlit country road, without a footpath. It was used by tractors, cattle wagons and milk tankers. The boy's mother was a housewife and his stepfather was unemployed. He had a four-year-old sister and an older brother who suffered from asthma and, for that reason, had free transport to and from school.

The argument put forward on behalf of the boy was that if the route, however short, was unsafe for an unaccompanied child, the LEA was obliged to provide free transport. In other words, the LEA was not entitled to take into account even the possibility of a child being accompanied, when deciding whether it should provide free transport. The LEA had stated that it did not accept that it would not be reasonably practical for one of the boy's parents to accompany him to school.

The parents' argument was rejected by the House of Lords, which said that in order to discharge the duty to secure the child's attendance at school, the parent had to do those things that were reasonably practicable, and that might include accompanying the child where it would be unsafe for it to go unaccompanied.

It seems that in neither of these cases was the safety of the child the paramount consideration. The courts took the view that if an LEA has formed the opinion that it was reasonably practical for a child to be accompanied, then it is entitled to take that factor into account when deciding whether or not to provide free transport to school.

It is, of course, all a question of cost. The Association of County Councils estimated that had the decision been in favour of the parents in the second House of Lords case, it could have cost rate−payers in England and Wales £90 million a year to provide free transport to satisfy the claims of parents in similar situations.

Transporting children

The safety of children when they are being transported, whether individually, in small or large groups, can sometimes be taken for granted and great care must be exercised to see that children do not travel in dangerous conditions.

Teachers' cars

Teachers use their cars at work for a whole range of reasons. As well as travelling to and from school and, perhaps, between school sites, a teacher may carry equipment and children to other schools, for extra-curricular activities or to sporting events. Teachers' cars are also used in an emergency to carry sick or injured children home or to the hospital.

A number of out-of-school activities, particularly sports fixtures at another school, simply could not take place without the goodwill of teachers who offer to carry pupils in their own cars.

A teacher can legally use his or her own car to carry passengers, so long as:

(1) The vehicle cannot carry more than eight passengers.
(2) Any money paid to the teacher for the journey is not more than normal running costs, and any arrangements about payment are made before the journey.
(3) Seatbelt legislation is complied with. The present position is as follows:
   (a) Front seats. It is the driver's responsibility to see that children under fourteen years old do not travel in the front seat of a car or minibus, unless they are wearing a seabelt or an approved child restraint. For passengers aged fourteen and over, that responsibility rests with the passengers.
   (b) Back seats. The relevant law is set out in the Motor Vehicles (Wearing of Seat Belts by Children in Rear Seats) Regulations 1989. As from 1 September 1989, if seat belts or child restraints are fitted in the rear of a car, the driver is legally responsible for seeing that children under fourteen years old use them. A child in the back seat does not have to be restrained if:
      (i)   All the available belts or restraints are being used or
      (ii) all the seats are occupied by adults who are restrained or
      (iii) the available seat belts or restraints are inappropriate to the

child's weight and can only be removed using tools. For children of four to fourteen years, an adult belt is 'appropriate'.

A teacher needs to be particularly careful to check that the car's insurance cover is adequate. If any payment is received, even if this is just a mileage allowance, the insurance cover could be affected. In any event, the teacher should make sure that there is insurance cover for business purposes because social, domestic and pleasure cover will not be enough when using cars in connection with school business. A number of insurance companies offer specific business cover for teachers, and it is advisable to read all policies carefully as they are legal contracts.

Personal business use cover for one teacher does not cover other teachers using the car in connection with their business and a special extended cover, with an additional premium, is available for other teachers' business use.

Parents' cars

In many schools, parents play an important part in transporting pupils to out-of-school activities. Teachers need to check that pupils are being carried in roadworthy vehicles and driven by competent drivers. These checks need not be extensive or exhaustive, provided that the teacher can be reasonably sure that there is neither an irresponsible driver nor a clearly unsuitable vehicle. Schools who ask parents to help with transport should point out to the parents that they are obliged to ensure that their own vehicles are roadworthy and adequately insured. Parents, like teachers, must check their vehicle insurance cover carefully.

So far as the actual travel arrangements are concerned, it is again the school's responsibility to make reasonable checks to see that the arrangements are safe. For example, it is not only dangerous for cars to be overloaded, but it will also invalidate insurance cover, which could be disastrous in the event of an accident.

Minibuses

Accident figures on our roads are horrific, and there have been regular reminders that children travelling in minibuses can be caught up in these tragedies.

Many LEAs issue their own detailed regulations about the use of minibuses and these have to be followed closely. Also, the Royal Society for the Prevention of Accidents (RoSPA) has produced a booklet *An introduction to Basic Minibus Driving*, which sets out routine precautions that should be taken before a minibus is taken on the road and while it is being uses. The booklet is aimed at those who may be experienced motorists, but are inexperienced in driving minibuses. The differences between driving a car and a minibus are significant and, as RoSPA points out, they are not only the obvious ones of size and weight:

> The mere fact of carrying a number of passengers, in some cases perhaps children or handicapped people, adds considerably to the driver's workload. It is therefore tremendously important both for the sake of the passengers and other road users that he or she makes adequate preparation for this new task'.

Many schools now have their own minibuses, which are used for short, (ibid., introduction), regular journeys and also for longer trips, both in this country and abroad. The regulations dealing with the construction, equipping and use of minibuses are extremely complicated, as they contain elements of European Community legislation as well as domestic law. In some cases, EEC Regulations are stricter than those of domestic law, one example being drivers' hours in respect of which EEC Regulations require tachographs to be fitted to monitor driving.

Education bodies operating vehicles adapted to carry eight to sixteen passengers can be exempted from public service vehicle licensing requirements, and conditions for exemption are set out in the Transport Act 1985. Drivers have to be over twenty-one years of age with a full driving licence, and the vehicle must comply with safety standards similar to those laid out in the Public Service Vehicle Regulations. The Department of Transport has produced two booklets, *Public Service Vehicles 385* and *Public Service Vehicles 375*, which deal with the relevant legislation at home and abroad respectively.

There are a number of regulations which lay down specification about the construction and fitting out of minibuses. These regulations deal with among other things, the number and position of doors, emergency exits, seating, ventilation, roof racks and internal equipment, including fire extinguishers and a first-aid box.

The law requires that all passenger vehicles built to carry no more than twelve passengers and minibuses with a gross weight of no more than 3,500 kg, must have seat belts and anchorage points for the driver's seat and one other front passenger seat. A passenger vehicle built to carry no more than eight passengers which was first used after 1 January 1987 must have seat belts and anchorage points for any forward-facing seats alongside the driver, and for at least two forward-facing rear seats immediately behind the driver's seat. The Secretary of State indicated at the end of 1989 that the Government intended to introduce regulations to require seat belts for all seats in new coaches and minibuses.

Preparation is essential before any journey and the driver should have a check list of items to inspect before starting out. This should include:

(1) Fuel engine oil and water.
(2) Tyre pressure and tyre condition; wheel nuts.
(3) Breaks and break liners.
(4) Lights, horn and indicators.
(5) Windscreen wipers and washers.
(6) Reflectors.
(7) The vehicle body and internal fittings.

As well as these regular inspections, the minibus should be serviced as required and, in addition to these mechanical checks, the driver should make other preparations. For example, the driver should check the route and the location of any roadworks. Information on road conditions can be obtained from regular travel bulletins on local radio and BBC radios 1, 2, and 4, BBC's Ceefax and ITV's Oracle and the AA Roadwatch.

Care is needed with luggage, particularly where bulky luggage is being carried. The minibus should never be overloaded or overcrowded and the driver's view should not obstructed. Entrances, exits and gangways should be clear of luggage or any other obstruction. It is important that the balance of the vehicle is maintained, especially when roofracks and/or trailers are attached.

LEA regulations will usually give guidance on supervision levels for minibuses. On short trips with older pupils, it may be safe for the driver to be the only adult with the group. If there are younger children on a longer journey, then there should be at least one adult in addition to the driver. On long journeys and trips abroad, there will need to be at least two drivers available. Pupils should know that they have to behave responsibly in a minibus. There must always be good order and discipline inside a minibus, so that the driver is neither distracted nor jostled.

Rest stops should be planned in advance so that nobody is required to drive for more than two or three hours without at least a fifteen minute break.

Particular attention should be paid planning and preparing a journey for children with special needs, so that routine matters do not cause unnecessary trouble or inconvenience. The possibility of having to make an emergency evacuation should always be kept in mind, so luggage should be kept secure and out of the way, so as not to be likely to block a passage way or exit.

The Department of Transport's Vehicle Standards and Engineering Division has produced a Code of Practice 'The Safety of Passengers in Wheelchairs on Buses', which offers advice to manufacturers and operators on the safe carriage of passengers in wheelchairs. The Code of Practice includes recommendations about the space needed for wheelchairs, their positioning, the size of doorway and gangways, restraints, lifts and ramps and general safety issues.

Buses

Children can travel to and from school either as fare paying passengers, or with a free bus pass on public service buses, or on buses run by a public service vehicle operator under contract with the LEA, or as a free passenger on an LEA operated bus. An LEA bus can also be used to carry fare paying passengers.

The LEA's obligation under Section 55 of the Education Act 1944 is to provide transport and also escort and accompany children where the LEA decides that this is necessary. The nature of this duty was considered in a 1967 case, *Jacques v Oxfordshire County Council*, where the court had to decide the question of liability for injuries to a fourteen-year-old boy travelling in a school bus provided by the LEA. The boy was hit in the eye by a paper or lead pellet, although there was no evidence that it had been flicked by another pupil. There was no adult supervisor on the bus, but a senior boy and senior girl had been appointed prefects to be in charge. There had never been an incident like this before, although things were sometimes thrown about or paper pellets were flicked. When this did happen, the prefects would normally put a stop to it and, on the whole, the standard of behaviour was good. The court decided that the LEA had discharged its duty to see that the bus was reasonably safe for the children as, in the absence of any evidence of particular disruption on this bus before the incident, it was reasonable to leave supervision to prefects.

Steps are being taken to make school buses more recognisable by other vehicles. In November 1989, the Secretary of State for Transport announced that he would shortly initiate a consultation procedure to devise a distinctive sign for school buses and, in advance of this, the DES is encouraging LEAs to introduce new signs on their buses on an experimental basis. In June 1990, it was proposed by the Minister for Road and Traffic that distinctive safety signs should be used on school buses. On the front and back of each bus, the silhouette of two children should be displayed. In addition to this, flashing amber warning lights will be introduced, which will be used when children are boarding or alighting from the vehicle.

A working party on school transport, set up under the auspices of RoSPA to examine the safety of school transport in the UK, reported its findings in 1990. The working party included representatives from relevant voluntary organizations and associations, from central and local government and from industry, as well as safety education experts. Among the recommendations made in the report were that there should be clearer statistics of road accidents involving school transport, drivers should be fully informed of potential dangers, such as when children are getting on and off buses, and the needs of disabled children should be properly taken into account.

The working party's report contains a Code of Good Practice for school transport, which is produced in conjunction with the DES and the Department of Transport.

Although schools and governors are not directly responsible for carrying pupils to and from school, the safety of pupils on school premises when there are buses present is a matter for the school. In larger schools in particular, there will be many buses arriving and leaving the school to carry pupils to and from home, and so there must be clear arrangements for the arrival, parking and departure of the buses, and pupils should be told to be as careful for their own safety as they would if they were on the streets.

Any misbehaviour by pupils waiting for a bus at school or on the bus travelling to and from school, should be dealt with under the school's disciplinary rules.

11
EDUCATION REFORM ACT 1988

Local management of schools

One of the major changes introduced by the Education Reform Act 1988 was local management of schools. The principle that underpins local management of schools is that major financial and managerial responsibilities are given to governing bodies, so that they and heads can plan how the school's money is used, having regard to the school's own needs and priorities. Local management is a radical change in the way that schools are run.

The Act says that all secondary and primary schools with 200 or more registered pupils must have their own delegated budget, and LEAs are free to extend delegation to small primary schools if they wish. LEAs had to submit their LMS schemes to the DES for approval by September 1989, and by spring 1990 over eighty schemes had been approved.

Although the governors will have far greater powers in employment matters, the LEA (except in aided schools where the governing body is already the employer) remains the employer and will therefore have primary responsibility for health and safety under the Health and Safety at Work etc Act 1974. However, as the governors take on greater responsibility for the school's finances, so they will have to make more decisions which involve health and safety considerations. The governors' main health and safety responsibilities will be:

(1) The purchase and maintenance of safety equipment, such as fire-fighting equipment and first-aid equipment.

(2) Nonstructural repairs and maintenance.
(3) Cleaning.

Day-to-day responsibilities will include:

(1) Monitoring the condition of nonstructural items in the school
    and authorizing any maintenance in accordance with its budget
    responsibility.
(2) Advising the LEA of structural defects that create a forseeable risk to
    the health, safety and welfare of staff, pupils and any visitors to the
    school.
(3) Discharging their specific responsibilities under the Health and Safety
    at Work etc Act 1974 in connection with the safe condition, storage
    and maintenance of all equipment at the school, and ensuring that the
    school premises, the means of access and exit, and any plant or
    equipment in the school are safe and without risk to health.
(4) Dealing with any other potential risk to health and safety, either by
    taking direct action themselves or by contacting the LEA.
(5) Drawing up any health and safety policies appropriate to the school,
    including safety rules, and seeing that those policies and rules are
    properly displayed and followed by staff and pupils.
(6) Ensuring that goods purchased from out of the school's budget conform
    with necessary safety standards, principally British standards, and
    that all equipment purchased is safely and properly installed. Provision
    for the purchase of equipment and materials for the school will be
    part of the governors' delegated budget. Section 36(vi) of the 1988
    Act exempts governors from liability for negligent action where such
    action is directly attributable to the spending of a school's delegated
    budget, provided that the governors have acted in good faith. In
    practice, governors will delegate responsibility for spending on equip-
    ment and materials to the head and other senior staff, but no doubt
    governors will be anxious to know that items that are purchased are
    manufactured to the appropriate standards and safe.

The British Educational Equipment Association represents over
150 educational suppliers with a combined turnover of around £220
million each year. In January 1990, the Association launched a Code
of Practice which each of its members had individually agreed to
adopt. The first item of the Code says 'our products are of a proper
quality, safe and suitable for educational use'. Products purchased
from a BEEA member are guaranteed to comply with current British
safety regulations, and the Code also says that all products will be
marked with full safety instructions and symbols. The Code contains

a commitment by the suppliers to describe and advertise equipment fully and accurately, so that schools can make informed choices. For example, where different types of test tube are being advertised, the sales literature will advise when nonheat resistant test tubes can be used and when heat resistant test tubes are needed. BEEA members will carry public liability insurance so if there is an accident involving any of their products, there will be appropriate cover in the event of a legal claim. A directory of the BEEA membership has been sent direct to all schools.

In an annex to the DES Circular 7/88, the DES sets out the division of responsibility between LEAs and governors for the maintenance of school buildings and schools, and this is reproduced in Appendix IV.

The LEA retains its obligation to produce a written health and safety policy, and should a governing body fail to comply with that policy then the LEA can arrange for the work to be carried out, and can charge the school for the work if the governors were at fault. The DES therefore recommends that LEAs should have accurate information on the condition of the school premises and equipment before delegation, so that any decision about whether or not to charge schools can be made on an informed basis.

The responsibilities of the head and staff for safety matters, both at common law and under the Health and Safety at Work etc Act 1974, are unaffected by delegation (see pp. 11–15).

Grant-maintained schools and city technology colleges

While the LEA delegates its responsibilities for schools under a local management scheme, but retains its responsibilities as employer and owner of school premises, the LEA has no involvement at all in grant-maintained schools and city technology colleges. In the case of both of these new institutions, the governors or trustees are the employer as well as the owner of school premises. They will, therefore, have full responsibility for all health and safety matters and will, for example, need to draw up a health and safety policy and see that this policy is implemented.

12
HEALTH AND WELFARE

First aid

Legislation and codes of practice

St John Ambulance has produced a manual of first aid advice for teachers called *Emergency Aid in School*. As the book's foreword says compellingly, just occasionally comes a moment dreaded by all of us who look after young people:

> instead of the usual minor grazes and bruises, we are faced with a severe accident. The child might be drowning or might be bleeding profusely, a staff member could have suffered a heart attack and we have to cope. It is a fearful responsibility and yet there are a few simple procedures that anyone can learn and which if applied correctly during the first minutes after an accident could mean the difference between life and death.

Outdoors, children often fall down and sometimes break a limb or fall unconscious. Inside a school there could be burns injuries or a child could be scalded. A child could have an electrical shock, or could be poisoned, or asphyxiated or have a fit.

Before 1981, the law on first aid at work was contained in a number of different pieces of legislation covering different situations. Then came the Health and Safety (First Aid) Regulations 1981 and, as the Regulations were made under the auspices of the Health and Safety at Work etc Act 1974, which places duties on the employer in respect of both employees and nonemployees at the workplace, one would assume that the Regulations would also take nonemployees into account. However, this is not so. The obligations under the Regulations and the Code of Practice attached to them only apply in relation to employees and not to nonemployees such as pupils. Regulation 3 places a great duty on the employer to provide 'such equipment and facilities (and also such numbers of "suitable persons") as are adequate and appropriate in the circumstances for enabling first aid to be rendered to employees if they are injured or become ill at work'. This duty is subject to 'the nature of the undertaking, the number of employees at work and the location of the establishment'.

The current Code of Practice, drawn up in 1990, says that the number of employees should not be the only factor in deciding about first aid provision and suggests that other factors may be more important. It advises that in low-risk situations, e.g., offices or libraries, an employer will in any case need one first aider for every fifty employees. The original Code of Practice had said that the number of employees was a significant factor, and where there are at least 150 employees on site there must be a qualified first aider. The Code of Practice confirms that the Regulations only place requirements on an employer in respect of employees while they are at work and that there is no requirement for an employer, when deciding about first aid provision to take into account nonemployees (e.g., pupils in schools, patients in hospital, customers in shops, etc.). It then adds 'Employers whose premises are regularly attended by such persons may however wish to consider making some provision for them.' It is crazy that the law considers it necessary to have at least one first aider where there are fifty adult employees at a work place, but considers it unnecessary to have a first aider in schools, where they may be hundreds of children, perhaps in old buildings and perhaps on split sites, unless there are a certain number of staff.

In workplaces where a first aider is not required, the Regulations call upon the employer to appoint an 'appointed person' who takes charge should there be a serious injury or major illness and is responsible for first-aid equipment on site.

The first aid in schools issue has been raised in both Houses of Parliament in recent years. In the House of Lords during the debate on the Education Bill 1986, Baroness Cox pointed out what we all know which is that children, especially when they are in large groups, are just as much at risk of being injured playing sport or working in workshops or kitchens as adults are at risk working in factories. Yet it can be pure chance whether teachers at any particular school have the necessary skills to deal with serious emergencies.

In 1988, the Professional Association of Teachers made two attempts to secure a statutory footing for first aid in schools. The Association initiated a Commons amendment to the Education Reform Bill, which stipulated that schools would have to meet minimum health and safety standards before they could be considered for a delegated budget. In particular, a school with 150 pupils or more on roll would have to have at least one qualified first aider. This amendment was defeated and a similar amendment proposed in the Lords was withdrawn, following the Government's undertaking to look into the matter. Nothing further happened.

There was further Parliamentary activity in 1989, including an early-day motion dealing with the provision of first aid in school, which was signed by 336 Members, more than 50 per cent of the House of Commons.

The Government's position was set out in the Standing Committee on the Education Reform Bill, where Wyn Roberts MP stated that LEAs should take into account health and safety when preparing their local management schemes, but that the Government would decline to give specific advice to LEAs about health and safety matters. He said:

> Previous Governments have not felt it necessary to describe such matters in detailed regulations. I believe that they were right in that. It is difficult to see how general guidance or regulations could prescribe the practical steps that would need to be taken in individual schools in the interests of health and safety. In practice, health and safety must be dealt with locally.

In February 1990, in an adjournment debate, the Government was again asked to legislate on first aid in schools. The Under-Secretary of State for Education and Science, Alan Howarth MP, acknowledged that this was a 'topic of the greatest interest and importance to us all', but gave no indication that the Government was prepared to legislate. He suggested that the Government considered that the common law doctrine of *in loco parentis* gave adequate protection to school children.

It is, of course, all a matter of money. But what is the cost of a young life? We know that schools are dangerous places, so why does the law not make first aid a priority? It is a complete paradox that at the same time that we are quite properly teaching our children the importance of good diet, personal hygiene and general health and fitness as ways of avoiding illness or disease, the most effective preventative measure of all, first aid, is in reality an optional extra at school. For as long as this situation continues, there will be the risk of children dying or being seriously injured when first aid could have saved a life or avoided serious injury. There is also the risk that in the absence of a properly trained first aider in an emergency, someone will make a genuine effort to give first aid or attend to a victim, only to take the wrong action and make things worse.

In 1989, St John Ambulance carried out a survey of schools in England

and Wales and received a response from over four thousand schools. Almost 40 per cent of those schools had no member of staff with a recognized first aid qualification, and one in five of the schools did not have a member of staff with even basic first-aid training. Almost half of the primary schools had no trained staff and 29 per cent of those schools had no first aid cover at all.

The results of the survey were set out regionally as well as by type of school. In Wales, 50 per cent of the schools surveyed had no trained first aider and 41 per cent had no cover at all. The best results came from Greater London, where 81 per cent of the schools had qualified first aiders.

Only 27 per cent of all the schools surveyed actually displayed lists of first aiders on the premises. Sixty-one per cent of primary schools had no kind of first-aid room and, in the south west, this figure was 85 per cent. Nationally, only just over half of the schools surveyed had a first-aid room.

Mr Robert Balchin, Director General of the St John Ambulance said when the survey was released, 'I have not the slightest doubt that lives could be saved if more teachers attended a short first aid course.'

Both the St John Ambulance and British Red Cross offer first aid training courses to the general public. St John Ambulance offers a four-day course on first aid at work for a statutory certificate lasting three years. There is a four-hour course in emergency aid for appointed persons, a sixteen-hour course on the essentials of first aid, a twenty-hours preliminary course on caring for the sick and a sixteen-hour course on child welfare.

The British Red Cross Society offers a four-day standard first aid course covering the full first aid syllabus. Successful students are awarded the Society's standard First Aid Certificate, which is valid for three years. There is also a one-day intensive occupational first aid course for those holding the standard First Aid Certificate, which covers the organization and practice of first aid at work and is again valid for three years. There is also an emergency aid course for appointed persons and a basic first aid course which deals with emergency procedures and practices in more detail than the emergency aid course.

Despite the lack of legal obligation, many LEAs are recognizing first aid as a priority. Those LEAs which recognize the absurdity of this gap in the law are, like the proposals put before Parliament, linking the requirement for a first aider with pupil numbers, not just teacher numbers. In these LEAs, first aiders will be provided with recognized first aid training and paid a premium in return for their responsibilities.

The DES and the Health and Safety Commission have made a number of statements about first aid provision in schools.

(1) In *First Aid in Educational Establishments*, the Health and Safety Commission's Education Service Advisory Committee says 'where possible it is sensible to combine first aid arrangements for employees and nonemployees. Such arrangements could also cover visitors to educational establishments', and later it adds, 'combined arrangements in general are welcomed by the Health and Safety Executive so long as they do not dilute the level of provision for employees'.

(2) So far as general first aid in schools is concerned, DES booklet *Safety at School: General Advice* says 'All teachers should have a simple working knowledge of first aid and it is important for them to be able to recognize when medical advice is necessary. It is also very desirable that some teachers on the staff of every school should have attended a course of training and taken a certificate in first aid issued by the British Red Cross or the St John Ambulance Brigade.'

(3) The DES advises in *Safety in Science Laboratories* that 'A first-aid kit should be kept readily available in every laboratory. Its contents should be checked frequently and at intervals re-approved by the Specialist in Community Medicine (Child Health). Both teacher and laboratory assistant should know how to use it.'

(4) In *Safety in Practical Studies*, the DES advises that teachers should have sufficient knowledge of first aid to offer assistance in the case of accidents that are likely to arise.

(5) DES Safety Bulletin No. 2 recommends that all schools, colleges and polytechnics should provide first-aid boxes equipped according to Health and Safety Executive guidance in every laboratory, gymnasium or sports hall, workshop and home economics or catering area.

(6) DES booklet *Safety in Outdoor Education* says 'leaders should have a working knowledge of first aid. Small accidents sometimes happen during outdoor activities and the actions of those around at the time can greatly affect the eventual outcome. It is therefore as well for all staff involved to possess an understanding of how to cope with the most common slight injuries and to develop an awareness of appropriate courses of action in emergencies.'

The Health and Safety Commission recommends that every educational establishment should prepare a written statement of its policy on first aid, covering both employees and nonemployees. This could be incorporated in the health and safety written policy statement, and should include the names and location of first aid personnel, the location of first aid facilities, special arrangements for dealing with accidents away from school premises or outside normal school hours, and arrangements for liaison with the ambulance service.

Close liaison with the local ambulance service is important so that ambulances are not delayed in reaching the scene of an emergency. If a school is close to a hospital accident and emergency department, then the school may be able to take advantage of this in its first aid arrangements. However, it should not be assumed that staff at an accident and emergency department will leave their posts to come to assist with an emergency in school.

It remains to be seen how governors will respond to the first aid issue when they have control of the financial management of schools, because provision for first-aid facilities and first-aid training will almost inevitably have to come from the school's own budget. In schools that opt out and take up grant-maintained status (see p. 137), the governors will assume total responsibility for first aid and first aid matters will rest entirely with them.

First aid responsibilities

The head has overall responsibility for seeing that:

(1) There is adequate first-aid equipment and supplies in the school and that these are properly maintained.

(2) There is at the very least one notice telling those in the school where first-aid equipment is kept, and the names and locations of any first aiders and the appointed person. All existing staff and all future staff should be informed and kept informed of these details. All staff should be informed of what the first aid arrangements and first aid facilities are, particularly the names and location of the first aiders. There will need to be a scheme of induction training for new members of staff, so that they have this information straight away.

(3) First aiders and appointed persons are clear about their respective roles and responsibilities and have written details, including details of precautions to be taken against the risk of infection (see p. 152).

(4) There is a written record of all first aid treatment provided at the school.

(5) There is immediate access to a telephone to call an ambulance in an emergency, and the ambulance access to the school premises is always maintained clear. The local ambulance service should be kept informed of where the school access is.

The first aider's responsibilities will include:

(1) In the event of an injury or illness that necessitates the calling of an ambulance, doctor or nurse, to provide help to preserve life and to minimize the consequences of the injury or illness, while waiting for the ambulance, doctor or nurse to arrive. This can include resuscitation, treatment of unconsciousness, or control of bleeding.
(2) To supervise an injured person and to ensure that he or she is only moved in a safe way.
(3) In cases where it not necessary to call an ambulance, doctor or nurse to administer first aid as appropriate.

There are other responsibilities which may rest upon the first aider, the head or the appointed person, depending upon the arrangements within each school. These include contacting the parents of a sick or injured child, either to collect that child, or to go to hospital with him or her. If such contact cannot be made or if the parent is unable to go to hospital, then somebody else would have to go to hospital instead.

It is normal practice for an LEA to arrange to indemnify a first aider against any legal action alleging negligence while carrying out the first aid responsibilities.

LEAs and schools need to have clear information on how to deal with accidents and illnesses. It is not unreasonable to ask all members of staff to deal with basic first aid situations, such as cuts and grazes, splinters, nose bleeds, burns and scolds, etc., but where there is any doubt about the prognosis or if the injury is more serious, the first aider should be called. If there is no first aider, the head or named member of staff should be called to make a decision about what to do. All staff should be clear about who makes the decision whether or not a parent should be contacted and asked to collect the child. Normally this decision would rest with the head or, in his or her absence, the deputy or one of the deputies. In larger schools, the head of year may also share this responsibility. The Pupils Registration (Amendment) Regulations 1988 require all schools to keep a record of at least one telephone number at which a parent can be contacted in an emergency.

Teachers administering first aid need to be aware that physical contact with a pupil can be misconstrued either by the pupil or by others. Indeed, it can be argued that contact with a child during first aid treatment without the parents' consent is assault. However, a teacher who acts reasonably and gives first aid in the approved manner should not feel at risk. If a teacher is in any doubt about his or her position, then whenever it is possible, it is wise to have another adult present while giving first aid treatment.

First-aid boxes

The Guidance Notes to the Health and Safety (First Aid) Regulations 1981 contain a list of recommended items in a first-aid box. The current requirements are:

A guidance card
20 individually wrapped sterile
adhesive dressings
20 sterile eye pads, with attachment
6 triangular bandages individually wrapped
6 safety pins
6 medium-sized, sterile unmedicated dressings, individually wrapped and approximately 10 × 8 cm in size
2 large, sterile unmedicated dressings, individually wrapped and approximately 13 × 9 cm in size
3 extra-large, sterile unmedicated dressings, individually wrapped and approximately 28 × 17.5 cm
10 individually-wrapped moist cleaning wipes

The Guidance Notes add that sterile water or sterile normal saline in disposable containers needs to be kept near the first-aid box where tap water is not available.

Medication

Teachers should be very careful before agreeing to administer medication to a child, although there will be situations where there is no alternative. If medication has to be given during the school hours and neither parent is available to do this, then it will be up to the school. Before agreeing to give medication in any particular case, the following points should be considered:

(1) The school should have information from a doctor, confirming that the child does need to take medicine during school hours and giving clear instructions about when the medication is to be taken and the dosage.
(2) The parents, not the child, should whenever possible, bring the medicine into school, and the medicine must be clearly labelled,

showing the contents, the dosage and the owner's name. Medicines should be kept in a secure place, so that there is no risk of them being stolen or tampered with.

(3) If a school has a welfare assistant or nurse, he or she can help with medication and, if not, a teacher should only be required to give medication once he or she has been fully briefed on what is required. There may be situations where certain details are particularly important. For example, when the medication is to be taken could be vital, and there could be serious consequences if the teacher forgot or was late administering a dose.

(4) Where medical knowledge is required, then a teacher should not be asked to give medication without the necessary training and, in any event, injections should only be given by a qualified doctor or nurse.

Aspirin

Some LEAs do not allow teachers to give out any tablets to pupils. Other LEAs do not allow paracetomol to be given to infant or junior pupils, but allow secondary pupils to be given paracetamol for minor complaints such as headaches, menstrual pains, toothaches, etc. The recommended dosage for secondary school pupils is one or two tablets just once during a single day, as only rarely is it necessary to repeat the dosage. In schools where tablets are kept, they should not be in the first-aid box. The member of staff responsible for tablets should keep a record of how many tablets have been given and to whom.

Head lice

Head lice infection is becoming more common, and anyone can catch head lice, even if he or she has perfectly clean hair. Children between the ages of four and six are the most vulnerable, and over the age of twelve, girls are more vulnerable than boys. Transmission of head lice takes place by head-to-head contact.

Eggs, which are called nits, are laid by adult lice and are stuck firmly to a single hair so that they cannot be moved easily. The best treatment for head lice is to use one of the lotions containing carbaryl or malathion or pyrethoid group substances. The lotion should be applied according to the manufacturer's or chemist's instructions. This treatment, may not be suitable for people with any skin problems or asthma sufferers.

Primary responsibility for dealing with head lice rests with the parents, and when a school discovers head lice, all parents should be notified and asked to check their children and treat them if necessary. At the same time, the Area Health Authority should be contacted.

Epilepsy

It is becoming increasingly common for teachers to have one or more children with epilepsy in their classes. Epilepsy is the second most common neurological disorder and it affects around 1 in 200 of the population. Seventy-five per cent of those affected have their first seizure before the age of twenty. The British Epilepsy Association is dedicated to the welfare of all people affected by epilepsy, and provides a range of appropriate services. The Association has produced a booklet, *Epilepsy: a guide for teachers* (revised in 1990), and an information package for schools, which includes teacher's notes, pupil's materials, a first aid poster and a book dealing with a small boy with epilepsy.

Epilepsy is not a disease or illness. People of all ages, backgrounds and levels of intelligence can be affected, and there may be no identifiable cause, particularly with young people.

There are three types of seizure, each of which is clearly described in the Association's booklet. Although each type of seizure looks different and can affect children in different ways, the cause is the same in each case, namely, a brief malfunction of the brain's biochemistry that self corrects after a short time.

The tonic-clonic seizure (also know as 'grand mal' or described as convulsion) is the most noticeable and dramatic type of fit. The child may make a strange cry, fall down suddenly and then the body will start to jerk convulsively and muscles first stiffen and then relax. There may be saliva round the mouth and the child may pass water. This type of fit can last for up to several minutes, and then the child will regain consciousness although he or she may be dazed or confused from anything up to a few minutes to several hours.

It can be frightening to watch this type of fit but despite what an onlooker may think, the fit is not harmful to a child, unless it is prolonged or the child is injured during the fit.

An absence seizure, which used to be called 'petit mal', is far less alarming and may even pass unnoticed, as there will be none of the outward signs of a tonic-clonic seizure. Although the child will lose consciousness for a short period, he or she may not realize this and may simply appear to be day dreaming.

Partial seizures, that is, seizures originating in one part of the brain, may be simple seizures involving the jerking of an arm or a leg or impaired smell or taste, or complex partial seizures, know as 'psychomotor' or 'temporal lobe' seizures, which may involve involuntary tic-like movements, plucking at clothes or lip-smacking periods, or unresponsiveness or aimless, dazed walking. Although the child will appear to be conscious, he or she will be confused and may be unable to speak or respond.

The British Epilepsy Association provides the following rules for a teacher who is faced with a child having a tonic-clonic seizure in class:

(1) Cushion the head with something soft (a folded jacket would do) but do not try to restrain convulsive movements.
(2) Do not try to put anything at all between the teeth.
(3) Do not give anything to drink.
(4) Loosen tight clothing around the neck, remembering that this could frighten a semi-conscious child and should be done with care.
(5) Do not call for an ambulance or doctor unless you suspect status epilepticus. (When a seizure shows no signs of stopping after a few minutes or if a series of seizures take place without the child properly regaining consciousness in between, this is called status epilepticus and immediate medical treatment will be necessary.)
(6) As soon as possible, turn the child on to his or her side in the semiprone (recovery/unconscious) position, to aid breathing and general recovery. Wipe away saliva from around the mouth.
(7) Be reassuring and supportive during the confused period which often follows this type of seizure. If rest is required, arrangements could be made for this purpose.
(8) If there has been incontinence, cover the child with a blanket to prevent embarrassment. Arrange to keep spare clothes at school if epilepsy is a regular occurrence.

The Association adds that it is not usually necessary for the child to be sent home following a seizure, but each child is different. If the teacher feels that the period of disorientation is prolonged, it might be wise to contact the parents. Ideally, a decision will be taken in consultation with the parents, when the child's condition is first discussed, and a procedure established.

In any event, the Association recommends that a teacher in charge of any children with epilepsy should know the answers to the following questions:

(1) What kind of seizure(s) do they usually have?
(2) What does it look like?
(3) How long does it usually last?
(4) What kind of first aid, if any, is required?

(5) How long a rest period do they typically need after a seizure?
(6) Are there special conditions or events known to trigger the seizures?
(7) How often do they take medication and is it necessary to take any in school?
(8) Are there any side effects?
(9) Have parents or the doctor requested any limitation on school activities?
(10) Do they have a warning (aura)?
(11) Do they have any other conditions?
(12) Do they have an understanding of their epilepsy and its treatment?

Children with epilepsy should be able to join in physical education and sports, except for such activities as climbing where a child could be injured during a seizure. There must be full consultation with the parents and medical advisers, and teachers must be aware of the condition so that whatever extra supervision is necessary can be provided.

The Association has produced a booklet *Swimming and Epilepsy*, which is mainly concerned with swimming in indoor public swimming pools. It contains advice about how swimming can be made safe for people with epilepsy and says that under controlled conditions, a fit in water should present only a minimal danger.

The Association confirms that the number of people who suffer from photosensitive epilepsy is very small, and a common cause is television. The risk of a pupil who has photosensitive epilepsy having a fit in front of a television can be reduced if the child is a sensible distance away from the screen (2.5 metres or more is recommended) and the room is well lit. If a television has to be adjusted or the channel changed, then this should be done by somebody apart from the pupil concerned.

Visual display units may present some risks to pupils with epilepsy and precautions set out on pp. 113–114 should be followed.

Infectious diseases

There are a number of infectious diseases that can spread within a school, including chicken pox, german measles, mumps and whooping cough. Although outbreaks of disease of epidemic proportions are rare, it is prudent for LEAs and schools to have agreed procedures to deal with any outbreak of an infectious disease, which will set out the steps to be taken by the head and also the school nurse or doctor, the school's medical officer, or the medical officer of environmental health as the case may be.

Most of the infectious diseases have known normal incubation periods, and the procedure will need to set out what those periods are in addition to the period of exclusion from school in each case. The exclusion periods should be regarded as minimum periods, as some children take longer to recover while others may be able to return to school.

Two infectious diseases that have become well-known in recent years are AIDS and hepatitis.

AIDS

'AIDS' is the acronym for Acquired Immunodeficiency Syndrome. AIDS is a disease caused by a virus infection known as Human Immuno-deficiency Virus (HIV). The body's natural defences against infection and certain cancers is defective and so the victim becomes vulnerable to many infections which the body would normally resist. Once an infection has developed as a result of this breakdown of defences, the infected person is said to have AIDS and will eventually die, because at present, despite a number of recent medical advances, there is no cure for AIDS and no preventive vaccine. But not everyone who becomes infected with the virus will necessarily develop AIDS, and many may even be unaware that they are infected unless they have a positive blood test. Anyone who is infected is believed to remain infected for life, and therefore a carrier for life capable of passing the infection to others.

The virus is thought to be passed on when blood, semen or vaginal fluids from an infected person pass directly into someone else's blood-stream, for example, during sexual intercourse or by intravenous drug misuse. So in practice, it is the sexually active, particularly those with many partners and drug misusers, who are most at risk.

Normal social and work contact with an infected person cannot spread the virus. There is no risk of infection through the air by coughing or sneezing, or from touch either directly or indirectly by handling objects touched by an infected person, or sharing washing, toilet or eating facilities.

In 1986, the DES and the Welsh Office jointly produced the booklet *Children at School and Problems related to AIDS*, and for Scotland there is the booklet AIDS – *Guidance for Educational Establishments in Scotland* from the Scottish Education Department. In 1987, the DES, Welsh Office, Scottish Office and Northern Ireland Office combined to produce 'AIDS – *Some Questions and Answers*, to help teachers in schools in dealing with questions about AIDS.

The DES gives advice in its booklet about particular school subjects or activities where risk may occur, and that advice which is reproduced with the permission of the Controller of Her Majesty's Stationery Office, is as follows:

Craft, design and technology	– normal safety precautions should be taken.
Home economics	– normal safety precautions should be taken.
Music lessons	– the sharing of wind instruments presents no risk. The usual hygienic practices should be observed.
Science subjects	– no HTLV-III/LAV [HIV] antibody positive person should give blood for class use.
Sport and outdoor pursuits	– (a) may be freely allowed provided there is no other medical condition which prevents the child participating.
	(b) Swimming pools should be chlorinated or suitably treated according to standard practice. Normal precautions should be taken.
	(c) Barefoot work presents no risk.
First Aid	– When teaching mouth-to-mouth resuscitation, it is sound, hygienic practice for children to use the specially-designed device incorporating a valve and mask. No cases of AIDS have arisen as a result of direct mouth-to-mouth resuscitation. In an emergency, direct mouth-to-mouth resuscitation should not therefore be withheld.

The DES also points out that there are some games and social practices which schools and heads should discourage to prevent the spread of infection, not only of HIV, but also other conditions such as hepatitis (infectious jaundice). These include:

(1) Blood brothers/sisters. Sometimes it is fashionable for children to confirm friendship by cutting or pricking the skin so that two or more children can become blood brothers or sisters with the mingling of blood.
(2) Ear piercing. Many girls and some boys have their ears pierced. Unless the ear piercing equipment is properly sterilized, there is a risk of infection.

(3) Tatooing. Similar considerations apply as for ear piercing.

The most common symptoms of AIDS and AIDS related conditions are:

(1) Swollen glands, especially in the neck and armpits.
(2) Profound fatigue, lasting for several weeks, and having no obvious cause.
(3) Unexpected weight loss.
(4) Fever and night sweats.
(5) Prolonged diarrhoea, with no obvious cause.
(6) Prolonged shortness of breath and a dry cough.
(7) Skin disease – pink or purple blotches appear on the skin, in the mouth or on the eyelids, looking a bit like a bruise or a blood blister.

Any of these symptoms can be associated with other illnesses and so a person who has one or more of these symptoms does not necessarily have AIDS or an AIDS related condition.

Precautions with infected children

The annex to *Children at School and Problems related to AIDS* gives advice on practical precautions and safeguards that can be taken so far as general hygiene is concerned, as well as advice on what to do if there is an accident causing bleeding. This is set out in full in Appendix III.

A number of precautions need to be taken to reduce the risk of the patient passing on other infections, apart from AIDS, to a first aider and these standard precautions are also effective against the AIDS virus. For example:

(1) First aiders should always cover any exposed cuts or abrasions they may have with a waterproof dressing before treating any casualty.
(2) Hands should be washed before and after applying dressings.
(3) Whenever blood, semen or other body fluids have to be mopped up, disposable plastic gloves and an apron should always be worn and paper towels used.
(4) Gloves, apron and paper towels should be put in plastic bags and safely disposed of after they have been used, ideally by burning.
(5) Mouthpieces are available for first aiders to use for mouth-to-mouth resuscitation, but they should only be used by properly trained persons. Mouth-to-mouth resuscitation need not be withheld in an emergency, even if there is no mouthpiece available. As already mentioned, no case of infection has been reported as a result of giving mouth-to-mouth resuscitation.

A sensitive question in relation to AIDS is that of confidentiality and privacy. If others in the school know about a child's infection with the virus, he or she could become isolated, yet there will be those in school who have to know about the child's condition to ensure proper care. The DES advises that the number of people, including teachers who know that a child is infected, should be 'rigourously confined' to those who need to know to ensure the child's well being.

Hepatitis A

The virus of Hepatitis A is disseminated in the faeces, and ingested by mouth in contaminated water and foodstuffs including meat, salad and shellfish. It is most common in warmer countries, especially where sanitary standards are low. People living in areas where Hepatitis A is endemic become immune to it, and those at greatest risk are travellers from areas where the virus in uncommon.

Symptoms include aches and pains and general malaise leading to nausea, abdominal pain and yellowing of the whites of the eyes (yellow jaundice).

Hepatitis B

Hepatitis B is one of a number of hepatitis viruses which cause liver infection, the first symptoms of which are general malaise and jaundice. The infection can be severely disabling and even fatal, but vaccines have been developed to prevent disease and also to treat any infection. Transmission of the infection is by infected blood to blood, or by infected body fluid to blood contact. The most common forms of transmission is through sexual activity and the use of infected needles to inject drugs.

Drug abuse

Misuse of drugs, particularly by children and young people, is a major problem and teachers must appreciate that all pupils can be at risk regardless of their age, sex or their family background. In 1989, the British Customs seized 331 kilos of heroin, 424 kilos of cocaine and 50,000 kilos of cannabis. An HMI report 'A Limited Survey of Health Education in ten Liverpool Primary Schools: May 2−4 1989', which was published in January 1990, found evidence of very young children being exposed to drug dealing. The report revealed that drugs were seen being sold from a car outside the nursery department of a primary school. In another school, discarded hypodermic needles and syringes were found in the playground. The report said 'Many children are reported as having a 'streetwise' knowledge of substances such as alcohol and drugs and of talking fluently about them without necessarily understanding their effects or the complex personal and social factors involved with their use.'

There are seven types of illegal drugs which are:

(1) Amphetamines ('purple hearts', 'speed'). This group of drugs acts as a stimulant and can be taken in tablet or powder form.
(2) Barbiturates. These are antidepressant drugs usually taken by mouth to reduce tension and make the user relaxed. A user can become dependent very quickly and withdrawal symptoms can vary.
(3) Benzodiazepines. These include tranquillizers such as valium and librium. They are usually taken by mouth and withdrawal symptoms can include insomnia and vomiting.
(4) LSD ('acid'). LSD stands for Lysergic Acid Diethylamide, which is a hallucinatory drug in the form of pills or small tablets.
(5) Cannabis ('hash', 'dope', 'pot', 'weed', 'grass') is used to produce relaxed feelings and various physical sensations. It has an intoxicating effect and is taken either by smoking dried cannabis leaves or, alternatively, plant resin mixed in with tobacco.
(6) Cocaine ('coke'). This is a powerful stimulant drug which gives a strong but temporary sense of euphoria. Users become dependent on the drug in order to maintain this feeling. It is normally taken by sniffing the white powder form of the drug. Withdrawal symptoms can be severe including depression and anxiety feelings. 'Crack' refers to the sound cocaine base makes when it is smoked. This gives a quicker and more intense high with the result that the consequent low is far deeper, and can only be alleviated by another high. There is currently great concern that crack is becoming increasingly popular and available to users.
(7) Heroin ('smack', 'H'). Heroin also creates rapid dependency and larger doses are constantly needed to keep up the relaxed and detached effect that inhalation, sniffing or injection produces. Again, withdrawal symptoms are severe and can include vomiting, feverishness and cramps. Injecting the drug creates the risk of infection with the HIV virus.

Drug abuse is normally a group activity, but it can be difficult for a teacher to detect. Hypodermic needles are one indication of drug abuse, but drug abuse can also be linked with other objects which could have an innocent explanation. For example, ordinary cardboard tubes are used for inhaling and matches are used to provide a flame for heating drugs. LSD is taken with sugar lumps.

Similarly, an individual's symptoms could also have an explanation apart from drug abuse. These include listlessness and loss of appetite, wearing sunglasses for no apparent reason, or attempting to cover up the smell of drugs by strong scent.

Most LEAs have written procedures for schools to follow if they are confronted with drug abuse, and in the booklet *Drug Misuse and the Young*, the DES reproduces the procedure drawn up by the Education Department of the Metropolitan Borough of Wirral. This procedure is intended to treat cases of confirmed repeated drug abuse consistently across the Authority's schools, to ensure that cases are handled in a way that recognizes the view that such pupils are seriously at risk, and to secure the benefit of the co-ordinated resources of the school concerned and the Authority. In addition to the Education Welfare Officer, LEAs will have Drug Education Co-ordinators with valuable expertise in these matters.

The Department of Employment has issued a booklet *Drug Misuse and the Workplace: A Guide for Employers*. This booklet which was produced in autumn 1989, offers guidance to employers in formulating policies to prevent drug misuse by employees at work, and the DES has instructed LEAs to circulate copies to schools. In June 1990, the Health and Safety Executive produced a booklet *Drug Abuse at Work: A Guide to Employers*, which also encourages employers to formulate policies to help an employee with a drug problem.

Solvent abuse

Under the Intoxicating Substance (Supply) Act 1985, it is an offence to knowingly supply a young person with any substance likely to be inhaled, and which causes intoxication. Possessing or sniffing solvents is, however, not illegal.

St George's Hospital Medical School, London, recently completed a 40 year study of all solvent abuse. In 1986 there were 93 deaths, 34 from butane gas refills, 21 from aerosols, 17 from cleaning and correcting fluids, 18 from glues with solvents and 1 unclassified death. Half of those who died were 17 years of age or younger and 18 per cent were girls.

A large number of household products which are all perfectly safe when used normally, can be used for 'sniffing'. These include glues, gas lighter fuel, nail polish remover, aerosols and typewriter correcting fluid. Sniffing is a very dangerous form of experimentation tried by young people of both sexes and all social classes.

Serious organic damage can be caused to those who have been abusing solvents for a long time, but the two most serious risks arise from accidents which occur as a result of intoxication, and from what are known as 'sudden sniffing deaths'. A solvent abuser becomes intoxicated very quickly as solvent vapours are absorbed into the blood via the lungs. The solvent affects the brain, which accounts for the 'high' feeling, and children can also appear drunk and suffer from hallucinations. Children have been involved in road accidents and have drowned while abusing solvents; others have suffocated with a plastic bag over their heads or suffocated on their own vomit.

Sudden sniffing deaths have arisen from sniffing aerosol solvents, and it appears that the reason for this is that the rhythm of the heart is affected and this leads to heart failure.

Symptoms of solvent abuse, which can also be brought about by other causes, include:

(1) Nausea.
(2) Change in moods and listlessness.
(3) Rashes around the mouth and nose.
(4) Pupil dilation.
(5) A fixed stare.
(6) Loss of concentration.
(7) Sudden violent behaviour.

Most schools have the benefit of written procedures on solvent abuse, which are similar to procedures dealing with drug abuse and set down the action that is taken when incidents occur or are suspected.

If a pupil is found sniffing or otherwise abusing solvents at school, emergency treatment will almost certainly be required. It will help the hospital receiving a pupil for emergency treatment if a sample of the solvent involved is taken to the hospital.

Alcohol

Many teachers will say that the problem of alcohol abuse by children is a greater problem than drug abuse and solvent abuse, because the raw material is much more readily and cheaply available, and also because excess drinking is in many places an acceptable social practice.

If a pupil is found drunk at school, the school's first duty is to that pupil's health and safety, and any necessary treatment should be given or emergency assistance sought as necessary. In all cases, parents should be informed of the incident, as is the case if a pupil is found in possession of alcohol at school.

In *Health Education from 5 to 16*, the DES advises that in health and personal and social education courses as well as in biology, pupils should be told about alcohol, its effects on the body and the consequences of excess alcohol, particularly in relation to road accidents.

In June 1989, the Department of Employment issued a booklet *Alcohol in the Workplace: a Guide for Employers*, which gives advice on how employers can establish procedures to stop alcohol abuse by employees at work. The DES has suggested to LEAs that they may wish to encourage heads to formulate such procedures in schools. In February 1989, the DES, the Home Office and the Departments of Health, Employment and Transport combined to produce a Circular entitled 'Alcohol Misusers', which contains advice on how drink problems can be dealt with locally using the expertise of local agencies.

Child abuse

All right-minded people are appalled at the mere thought of young children being subjected to sexual abuse. Child sexual abuse, according to the National Society for the Prevention of Cruelty to Children, is 'the involvement of children in sexual activities they do not truly comprehend, to which they are unable to give informed comment, or that violate the social taboos of family life'. But sexual abuse is only one element of child abuse which also includes physical injury, neglect, including emotional neglect, and continued ill treatment. DES Circular 4/88 'Working together for the protection of children from abuse: procedures within the education service' advises schools and LEAs on what to do if child abuse is suspected or identified. School staff are in a good position to detect signs of sexual abuse, physical abuse or physical neglect. Bruises, cuts or burns may be evident, and indicators of physical neglect include inadequate clothing, poor growth or regular complaints of being hungry. Excessive dependence or attention seeking may indicate emotional neglect. Sexual abuse may exhibit physical signs or cause a marked change in behaviour.

The DES advises that these signs 'can do no more than give rise to suspicion – they are not in themselves proof that abuse has occurred. But as part of their pastoral responsibilities teachers should be alert to all such signs.' Circular 4/88 recommends that all LEAs should have detailed procedures advising staff if child abuse is suspect. LEA procedures will include the following matters:

(1) Each school should have a designated member of staff who has overall responsibility for child abuse action.
(2) Should a teacher suspect child abuse, then the DES advises as follows:

'were teachers see signs which cause them concern, they may have the opportunity to seek information from the child, with tact and sympathy. If not, or if the child's responses do not dispel suspicion, teachers should immediately make their concern known to the senior member of staff with specific designated responsibility.' So far as the actual questioning is concerned, the Circular states that 'Care must be taken in interpreting children's responses to questions about indications of abuse. Abused children may have been told by the abuser what to say in response to questions, and may have been threatened. The abuser may be a close relative.'

(3) All cases of suspected abuse or nonaccidental injury should be reported to the designated member of staff who, in turn, will need to know who to contact. That person will normally be the head.

(4) A detailed record should be kept of all suspected incidents of child abuse or nonaccidental injury, and it is particularly important to give a clear description of the injuries or symptoms involved. The record, which should be confidential and secure, must be kept up to date so as to include notes of interviews and minutes of meetings.

(5) Nevertheless, information about particular cases or suspected cases should be confidential to the designated member of staff, the teacher who initially reported the matter and the head. This group, after consulting the LEA procedure, will need to decide whether to refer the matter through the LEA procedure straight away, or whether it is necessary to question the child concerned and/or seek information from the parents.

(6) If the matter is referred beyond the school, the LEA procedure will indicate that this will entail contacting a named member of the Social Services Department and informing a named education officer. It may also be necessary at that stage to inform the school's chairman of governors.

It is very important that there is interagency co-operation for the protection of children from abuse, and this is highlighted in the DHSS booklet '*Working together*'. One area in which co-operation is necessary is the Social Services' role in supplying schools with details of children known to be on the Child Protection Register. Child Protection Committees have been set up by Social Service Departments and Circular 4/88 recommends that an LEA representative and a teacher should be on the Committee. The Circular also recommends that LEAs should designate a senior officer as having LEA wide responsibility for co-ordinating child abuse policy, and action which will include liaising with the Social Services Department and other agencies.

Smoking at work

Could it be said that this is a burning issue. It is certainly an issue that is attracting a considerable amount of publicity, and an area where the Health and Safety Executive has undertaken a great deal of work. The Executive has produced a booklet called *Passive Smoking at Work*, which discusses the risks of the exposure of nonsmokers to tobacco smoke at work. Also the Health Education Authority has published a booklet *Smoking at Policies at Work*, giving detailed guidance on drawing up and implementing smoking policies at work. It includes case histories of workplaces where the problem has been successfully tackled.

Over the years, we have become increasingly aware of the serious health risks that smokers face, and there is now additional concern over the possible effects of breathing in other people's tobacco smoke. At work, there are situations where people have to spend long periods of time close to smokers. In schools, this would mainly happen in the staff room, either at break time or during staff meetings. Smoke from another person's cigarette has been called 'sidestream' smoke. This includes smoke from cigars and pipe tobacco as well as from cigarettes.

This is another safety issue where there is a legal backcloth in the shape of statutory law and common law. The Health and Safety at Work etc Act 1974 requires the employer to provide and maintain a working environment for employees that is so far as is reasonably practicable, safe and without risk to health, and the employer's common law duty of care imposes a similar obligation.

A number of practical steps can be taken to protect nonsmokers. What is and what is not practicable and what is and what is not appropriate, will depend on the particular circumstances of each workplace, but whatever action is taken, there should be full consultation with those concerned, so that nobody can say that they were not given the opportunity of contributing to the debate.

There could be a total ban on smoking or smoking could be restricted to certain times of day. Alternatively, smoking could be banned in certain rooms. If this does not happen and, for example, smoking remains permissible in staff rooms, it may be that improving ventilation or devising other ways of removing smoke from the environment as quickly as possible would improve things. A number of heads take the view that it is best to let the staff decide for themselves whether there should be smoking and, if so, where and when this is most wise.

Before there could be a complete ban on smoking in schools on health and safety grounds alone, there would need to be clear medical evidence to suggest that employees were being harmed by sidestream smoke at work, and this evidence would have to be brought to the school's attention. It is now accepted that such a health risk may exist, both as regards relatively minor health problems such as chestiness, coughing, general discomfort and irritation, as well as major health problems. There has been recent research into the possible connection between passive smoking and lung cancer, and the fourth report of the Independent Scientific Committee on Smoking and Health concluded in 1988 that there was a 'small increase' in risk (a 10 to 30 per cent increase) of lung cancer from exposure to environmental tobacco smoke.

In November 1989, the Department of Health, the DES and the Health Education Authority launched a five-year national campaign aimed at reducing teenage smoking. One of the objectives set out at the start of this campaign was to 'seek support for the elimination of smoking from all educational establishments for the age range four to nineteen', and the aim was stated as being 'to work towards the voluntary elimination of smoking on a twenty-four hour basis from educational establishments serving the age range four to nineteen and on out of premises activities involving pupils from the same, by consultation and agreement with staff'.

Meetings began at the start of 1990 to look into the feasibility of guidelines for schools implementing written policy statements on smoking.

Some councils have already made moves to ban smoking in the workplace. Strathclyde Regional Council banned smoking in all its work premises occupied by two or more persons with effect from 1 September 1989. Work areas are exempt from this restriction only if all the employees on site vote to allow smoking. Once a work place has been designated as a no smoking area, then persistent and deliberate failure to abide by that decision will be regarded as a breach of the Council's disciplinary procedures.

There have been cases before Industrial Tribunals dealing with smoking bans at work. In 1984, a firm of insurance brokers from Birmingham moved offices and imposed a nonsmoking regime at the new premises. One employee who had been with the firm for two years, claimed that she had in effect been dismissed, because the employers had been in fundamental breach of her contract. The Industrial Tribunal accepted this argument and said that the employers had acted unreasonably, because they had failed to consult staff before making the change and they had failed to consider practical alternatives to a total ban on smoking. In 1987, an employee resigned after his employers announced that there would be a ban on smoking. He saw the proposed ban as being an ultimatum − either give up smoking or be dismissed. But in that case the Industrial Tribunal rejected the claim and, in particular, declined to imply a right to smoke in the employee's contract, because in its view there was an equal right for employees who did not smoke not to be placed in an environment with those who do. The Tribunal also found that on the facts, there had been adequate consultation before the ban was announced.

In August 1990, the Social Security Commissioner decided that Joan Clay, a Social Security Officer from Bedfordshire, was entitled to make a claim for disablement benefit on account of illness caused by passive smoking at work, which was classified as an industrial accident. Miss Clay, who was very sensitive to cigarette smoke on account of bronchial asthma, suffered painful injury to her lungs as well as nausea, headaches and extreme breathlessness on six occasions between 1982 and 1986, after inhaling her colleagues' tobacco smoke. It took her up to four days to recover on each occasion. The Social Security Commissioner has been careful to say that this is a decision based upon special facts and that it is not a precedent for others to make similar claims on account of passive smoking, but it remains to be seen whether or not this will open the floodgates. So far as Miss Clay's own workplace is concerned, there is now a tobacco ban at her office, and a room has been set aside for the 100 smokers in the building.

13
VIOLENCE AT WORK

In recent years, some extensive research has highlighted the problem of violence being threatened and inflicted on people going about their normal work. The Health and Safety Commission set up a steering committee on violence to staff, which commissioned a report by the Tavistock Institute of Human Relations. The Report 'Preventing Violence to Staff', published in 1988, contains nine detailed case studies, one of which deals with an Education Authority. Certain groups of employees have been identified as being particularly vulnerable to attacks at work, which can range from minor incidents to very serious ones. Concern has focused on social workers, staff in the health services and public services, and staff who have direct contact with the public in situations that can quickly become tense and then out of control. For example, in 1987, the Association of Directors of Social Service produced a paper setting out guidelines and recommendations to employers on violence against employees and, in the same year, the Health Services Advisory Committee of the Health and Safety Commission produced a report on violence to staff in the health services.

The problem of assaults on teachers in school by pupils, parents and, in some cases, complete strangers, has increased alarmingly and should not be ignored. In 1988, the Professional Association of Teachers in conjunction with the Daily Express carried out a survey of 1,500 teachers, 32 per cent of whom said that they had been attacked at work by pupils at some stage in their careers. Five per cent had been assaulted by parents.

The situation is a legal one. The Health and Safety at Work etc Act 1974, imposes a general obligation on the employer to ensure so far as is reasonably practicable, the health, safety and welfare at work of all employees. In particular, there is an obligation under the Act to provide and maintain a working environment for all employees that is so far as is reasonably practicable, safe and without risks to health. As well as this, there is the employer's common law duty of care for the safety of employees. In the context of employment law, an employee who resigns on account of the employer's failure to provide reasonable precautions for his or her safety, can consider pursuing a claim for constructive dismissal.

The important phrase is, of course, 'so far as is reasonably practicable'. LEAs are not expected to take such stringent precautions that there is no possibility at all of any physical attack on a teacher. That would be impossible and, in any event, it would create an impossible teaching situation in school. The legal obligation is to respond to this risk of violence, where it can be reasonably anticipated, unless it can be said that the risk is no more than a mere possibility and therefore so small that it can be safely ignored. So LEAs should first identify the nature and extent of the risk, and then devise means of providing teachers with a safe workplace and a safe system of work.

The law provides teachers with some degree of protection against attack from outside the school. Section 40 of the Local Government (Miscellaneous Provisions) Act 1982 says that it is a criminal offence for any person to come on to educational premises without lawful cause and to cause a nuisance, a disturbance or an annoyance to anyone who is lawfully on the premises. This is aimed at deterring those who would come into schools intent on causing trouble, and the offence is committed not when there has been an attack, but when a nuisance or a disturbance is created. At that point, the police can intervene. Many LEAs have used this legislation to send warning letters to parents who have been involved in a disturbance at school. A parent or parents may either be banned from the school or, alternatively, told to secure the head's prior agreement before coming into school.

So far as assaults by pupils are concerned, it is often difficult to see what could have been done to prevent an unprovoked and unexpected attack on a teacher. Nevertheless, schools need to show that they have proper rules and an adequate disciplinary procedure for pupils which operates effectively. If a pupil is physically violent in class, but no sanction is imposed by the school and the pupil repeats an attack, then the LEA could be legally vulnerable, because the second incident could not be called unexpected.

If a teacher is attacked, then one of the criminal offences set out in the Offences Against The Person Act 1861 will have been committed. These offences include assaults causing grievous bodily harm and actual bodily harm, and there is also common assault. Investigations into an alleged assault are carried out by the police, but decisions about whether or not to prosecute are now made by the Crown Prosecution Service. A child under ten is deemed incapable of committing a criminal act.

Criminal courts are able to make compensation orders for personal injury caused by a criminal offence, and also an injured teacher can also make a claim for compensation from the Criminal Injuries Compensation Scheme, operated by the Criminal Injuries Compensation Board. The Board pays compensation for personal injuries caused by a crime of violence, which was reported to the police or alternatively, not reported, but for a good reason. Minor injuries are excluded from the scheme in that the injuries must warrant compensation of at least £750, but an application is free and there are no legal formalities involved.

Early in 1988, a Committee of Inquiry, chaired by Lord Elton, was set up to investigate discipline in schools and to recommend action. In 1989 the Committee produced a 290 page report 'Discipline in Schools', containing a number of recommendations for action by central government, LEAs, heads, teachers and parents. One of the recommendations was that there should be a national register of all violent incidents in schools, so as to keep an up-to-date and accurate record of the size of the problem. Also, teacher training should include training aimed at reducing discipline problems and, in response to this particular recommendation, the DES announced that initial teacher training would include training in managing pupil behaviour and that LEA grant schemes for in-service training of teachers in 1990/91 would provide funding. On the issue of practical support for teachers who have been attacked, the Report said that staff 'must be confident that all violence against them will be taken seriously and that they will be supported by their employers. This support may need to be personal, for example through legal advice or counselling.' The Report also recommended that chief officers of police should take staff morale into account when deciding whether or not to refer a case of physical attack to the Crown Prosecution Service, and that the CPS should take the same factor into account in deciding whether or nor to prosecute. The Report made a number of recommendations about school rules:

(1) 'Heads and teachers should, in consultation with governors, develop whole school behaviour policies which are clearly understood by pupils, parents and other school staff.'
(2) 'Schools should ensure that their rules are derived from the principles underlying their behaviour policies and are consistent with them.'

(3) 'Schools should strike a healthy balance between rewards and punishments. Both should be clearly specified.'

(4) 'Pupils should learn from experience to expect fair and consistently applied punishments for bad behaviour which make the distinction between serious and minor offences apparent.'

(5) 'Heads and teachers should ensure that rules are applied consistently by all members of staff, but that there is flexibility in the use of punishments to take account of individual circumstances.'

(6) 'Heads and teachers should avoid the punishment of whole groups.'

(7) 'Heads and teachers should avoid punishment which humiliate pupils.'

HM Inspectorate has produced a number of written reports under the title 'Education Observed'. The fifth booklet in the series is *Good Behaviour and Discipline in Schools*, and was published by the DES in 1987. It sets down a number of principles of good practice in achieving and maintaining high standards of behaviour and discipline.

There should be clear policies throughout the school based on clear and defensible principles and setting the acceptable boundaries for behaviour. They should be clear both to pupils and to parents, and firmly and consistently applied. The aim of such a policy should be to develop a positive climate throughout the school based on what the report calls 'a quiet yet firm insistence on a high standard of behaviour at all times'. The ethos of the school should be cemented in the quality of relationships at all levels between staff, staff and pupils, and the pupils themselves. Such relationships, says the report, should be characterized by 'mutual respect, by a willingness to listen and understand and by a positive view of teachers as professionals and pupils as learners'.

A new national system was set up in the summer of 1990 to monitor pupils' expulsion from the maintained schools in England, and a similar system was set up in Wales at the same time. The DES requires information from schools and LEAs about every permanent exclusion of a pupil. Although the pupil will not be identified, the DES will want to know about the pupil's personal details and previous history at the school, as well the incidents leading up to and causing the expulsion. The DES will also keep a record of whether or not the pupil has special educational needs. The scheme will last for two years, at the end of which the DES will assess the information and decide whether the existing statutory arrangements for exclusions, which are set out in the Education (No. 2) Act 1986, are adequate. In November 1990 the Health and Safety Commission Education Service Advisory Committee produced its own practical guidance, in *Violence to Staff in the Education Sector*.

14
SAFETY EDUCATION

Accidents are the commonest cause of death among toddlers and other children. Three children are killed every day by accidents and, each year, one child in every five (about 2.5 million) attends an accident and emergency department as a result of an accident. Between the ages of ten and fifteen, nearly half of all deaths are due to accidents.

In 1987, over 2,300 children between the ages of five and nine were killed or seriously injured on British roads, and that is four times the adult rate. The cost of road accidents in 1987, including NHS costs, damage to property and vehicles, police and insurance costs, lost output and a notional figure for pain, grief and suffering was £4,990 million.

Although there are many accidents that are caused either wholly or partly by defective premises, faulty equipment or environmental conditions, the biggest single cause of accidents is human error. Schools therefore have a most important role to play in safety education of young people because their youth, inexperience and propensity to act without considering safety makes them particularly vulnerable. Safety education should encourage children to become masters of their environment and not victims of it, and clearly with so many deaths and injuries in accidents each year, it is essential that safety awareness and a proper attitude towards safety is developed at a young age.

The National Curriculum includes elements of safety, for example, in science, but safety education must also be a cross curricular item, so that safety can be dealt with in the course of teaching subjects both within and outside the National Curriculum. As well as actual teaching, a school's attitude to health and safety and the priority that is given to health and safety will rub off on the children. This can start at an early age. For example, reception children will be told what the school rules are and why those rules exist. Most rules are to do with safety. Instructions to children not to run around inside or in the playground, and not to tamper with anything hot or electrical, are teaching them to be careful for their own safety and the safety of others. The general school ethos is an integral part of safety education. Self discipline leads to responsible behaviour and to children considering the implications of what they do, both for themselves and others. Personal safety cannot be taught just by providing children with information, literature, or even educational videos, because personal safety is an attitude of mind and children must be shown that safety is an integral part of their everyday lives.

Schools are under great pressure to deliver the curriculum effectively, yet the time available to do this seems to be diminishing, because of other pressures on teachers' time. It is easy for safety in education to be put aside under this pressure.

Themes for safety in education can include road safety, safety in the home and safety in the environment. Schools can involve outside agencies such as the police, the local fire officer, road safety officers and any parents with the relevant knowledge or experience. Visiting speakers can also include school lollipop ladies, bus drivers and anyone else with a particular expertise in safety. It may be that the location of the school demands that particular attention is given to a particular aspect of safety. The school may be on a busy main road with children arriving by car, bus, on bicycles and by foot. Alternatively, the school may be close to a railway line, which children have to cross using a footbridge. In these circumstances, a visit by the railway safety office will be particularly helpful.

There is a wide range of safety education material available to schools, including both literature and video resources. RoSPA does a great deal to promote good practice in safety education, and runs an annual competition for the RoSPA award of good practice in safety education. The Society also produces a wide variety of information and resource packs for teachers on a wide variety of safety issues. Information about the good practice in safety education award and teaching resources are available from the safety education department at RoSPA. One of RoSPA's recent safety education programmes is 'Streets Ahead', which is a series of four modules, dealing with communication, movement, rules and risks. For each activity, the appropriate national curriculum attainment targets have been indicated for the course subjects of English, mathematics and science, so that this safety education programme can work within the National Curriculum.

The Child Accident Prevention Trust, which was set up as an advisory body to investigate all aspects of accident prevention of children's safety, has produced a number of papers, publications and fact sheets about different risks to children and preventative strategies. A recent Child Accident Prevention Trust publication is *Basic principles of child accident prevention: a guide to action*.

In some schools there will be a safety committee of senior pupils, and the committee's functions would include introducing topics for assembly, producing safety information for the school and designing safety displays and other visual presentations.

Road safety

A survey by the Automobile Association Foundation in 1990 revealed that children are more at fault than drivers when involved in a road accident. According to the survey report called 'Urban Accidents: Why Do They Happen?', less than half the drivers and motorcyclists involved in accidents were at fault, as against 81 per cent of child pedestrians. More than half of the children in the survey admitted not taking proper care before crossing the road, with 67 per cent failing to look properly.

In 1989, the Department of Transport produced a road safety video called *Street Sense*, which is aimed at fifteen to eighteen year olds. It portrays four trips by a pop group, during which potential and actual accidents occur as a result of various drivers failing to observe basic road safety rules. The video is available from CFL Vision, PO Box 35, Wetherby, West Yorkshire LS23 7EX, at a cost of £9.99.

In 1989, the Department of Transport undertook a major road safety education project and the School of Education at Reading University has been given a contract to do further work which it will complete in 1992. The DES and RoSPA are also involved in the project which will use Hertfordshire and Sheffield as trial areas. A draft consultative document was produced in April 1989, which introduced the subject as follows:

> In its broadest context, road safety education is much more than the acquisition of knowledge and skills. It is the process of developing those safe attitudes and patterns of behaviour which will enable young people to cope with traffic and remain safe throughout their lives. As such, it should involve experimental learning to help children to develop the concepts and understanding that are needed to deal with a complex and ever changing road environment.
>
> The principles essential to safe road usage also have a relevance to many other activities and a place within a wider context of behaviour and morality. Road safety education, therefore, is not only vital in the fight to reduce road accidents, but plays an important part in the total educational process.

The DES in its safety series booklet *Safety in Schools: General Advice*, introduces road safety as follows:

> Traffic is a hazard all children have to cope with. What is required is a responsible and effective partnership between parents, teachers and the road safety organizations to develop the necessary knowledge, skills and attitudes in children which will enable them to use the roads safely, as pedestrians or cyclists and so to minimize the risks to others as well as to themselves.

In 1989, the County Road Safety Officers Association produced a version of the Highway Code specifically for children called *A Highway Code for Young Road Users*. Copies have been sent direct to schools and are also available from local safety offices. There are sections dealing with walking, cycling, riding in cars, and using buses, and the booklet also deals with road signs, traffic lights, signals and animals on the road. There is also a very helpful section that explains to children the meaning of some of the words used in the booklet.

In the summer 1990 a three-year campaign called 'Safety on the Move' was launched jointly by the DES and the Department of Transport, aimed at reducing the number of child deaths and injuries in road accidents. A target was set to save 150 child deaths and over 2,000 serious injuries each year by the end of the century.

Part of the campaign's attention is directed at developing better road safety education and integrating road safety into the National Curriculum. There is also a pre-school project and a £1.8 million publicity campaign, which includes making parents more aware of the importance of road safety training for children.

First aid

First aid is an enormously beneficial skill to teach in schools. The St John Ambulance has set up a first aid programme for schools which is called the 'Three Cross Award Scheme', and in the five years since its inception, more than 100,000 certificates have been issued to children learning emergency aid skills.

The One Cross award is achieved when a child can dial 999 and give proper instructions to the emergency services, knows how to make an accident victim comfortable, can make sure the victim can breathe and knows what not to do. The Two Cross is awarded once the child has learnt how to help a person who cannot breathe and how to treat choking and a heart attack. A child who can deal with emergencies such as burns, bleeding and poisons is awarded the Three Cross.

There is a Three Cross video available to help teachers teach first aid, and many teaching schemes include first aid as part of health education, citizenship or as part of a wider project as well as within the National Curriculum.

A number of schools have successfully approached local businesses for sponsorship or donations towards the costs of the Three Cross scheme.

Fire safety

Fire safety is another important area of safety education and the Home Office has produced a fire safety education package for nine to thirteen year olds which is called 'Firewise'. It consists of a guide, project sheets, a map of a fictional town, and a computer disk with a data base which can be used with BBC computers and contains details of all the fires that have occurred in the fictional town over ten years and includes projects using a town map. The package is free of charge to all schools in England and Wales, and is available from Firewise, Fire Prevention Literature, CO1 Stores, 184 Shepherds Bush Road, London W6 7MP.

Abduction

Stranger danger is becoming an important part of safety education. Children need to be told that it is never a good idea to talk to a stranger, and if a stranger approaches them, he or she should be ignored. Younger children in particular would need to be reassured that an adult will not be angry with them for refusing to talk to a stranger, and they should never keep it a secret if they have talked to a stranger. There are a number of leaflets and information sheets available which help teachers educate children about the dangers of talking to strangers.

15
SPECIAL NEEDS

Children with special needs, whether physical or mental, will require a different form of education for safety. A pupil with a physical disability who is in a wheelchair will face vastly different problems and hazards at home, at school and on the roads. The same will apply to pupils with sensory impairments, or emotional, behavioural or learning difficulties. Safety education will be adapted for those needs so that the programme and the rate of progress suits the particular pupil concerned.

In January 1988, there were 138,067 children with special educational needs, which is just over 2 per cent of the school population. Of these children, 36,000 were at ordinary schools, either in ordinary classes or in special classes or units. After the Education Act 1944, the education of children with disabilities was largely provided by special schools until the Education (Handicapped) Act 1970 brought all children, whatever their handicap, within the scope of the 1944 Act. Then, the Secretary of State for Education and Science, the Rt Hon. Margaret Thatcher MP announced the convening of a committee of inquiry under the chairmanship of Mrs Mary Warnock, to review education provision for children and young people handicapped by disability of body or mind. The committee's report 'Special Educational Needs — Report of the Committee of Inquiry into the Education of Handicapped Children and Young People' was published in May 1978.

A major theme of the Warnock Report, which was subsequently set out in the Education Act 1981, was that there should be no educational distinction between 'ordinary' and 'handicapped' or between 'remedial' education in mainstream schools, and 'special' education in special schools.

It also recommended that pupils currently in special schools should be integrated into ordinary schools.

The Education Act 1981 defined a child with special education needs as a child having a learning difficulty which requires special educational provision to be made. A child has learning difficulties if he or she has significantly greater difficulties in learning than the majority of children of the same age, or has disabilities preventing or hindering the child from making use of educational facilities of a kind generally provided in schools within the LEA for children of that age.

Special education provision is education additional to, or different from, the education provision made generally by the LEA for children of that age. LEAs are obliged to have regard for the need to ensure that special education provision is made for pupils who are identified as needing it. The LEA must ensure that children for whom statements are made are educated in ordinary schools, provided that such education is compatible with their receiving the special education they need, the provision of efficient education for the other children at the school and the efficient use of resources.

Mainstream schools

Schools with special needs children can expect to have advice and support available from agencies within the LEA, the health authority and social services. Educational psychologists, advisory teachers and school medical officers will provide this function. Within the school there may be a co-ordinator of special educational needs who has an advisory function in relation to the head and staff.

The inclusion of pupils with special needs in classroom and out-of-school activities will require teachers to review their preparation for these activities and their supervision while the activities are taking place. While the educational and social value of these children being involved as full members of the classroom community is unquestioned, this integration has to be achieved safely. Children with special needs will be unaccustomed to situations and surroundings that are familiar to the other children. Also children with special needs cannot be assumed to display initiative and an awareness that they need to look after their own safety, to the same extent that other children may do in the same circumstances.

Mainstream schools will not be able to make major changes to provide special facilities for a small number of pupils, so initial choice of school will be restricted to single storey buildings with existing escape routes and other facilities that can be adapted for use by disabled pupils. In these schools, it will be particularly important that passage ways are kept clear, so that wheelchairs can pass along them and, indeed, the passage ways will need to be checked, to see that they are wide enough to accommodate wheelchairs. If a wheelchair became stuck in a corridor in an emergency, then the consequences could be disastrous.

Special schools

Children with severe learning difficulties in special schools are able to achieve a remarkably wide range of educational activities. For example, children can be taught cookery and other home skills, to do art work, CDT and also sporting activities, both indoor and outdoor.

Some children with special needs can have a greater physique and more strength than their contemporaries, yet in many situations, teachers are concerned about injuring a child when they are attempting to restrain them. The normal procedure for restraining a child with special needs is for the teacher to face the child, putting his or her arms around the child to stop them moving and also holding down their hands. The teacher's legs need to be apart to stop the child kicking them and it may be that the teacher needs to have his or her head to one side to stop the child head butting.

DES Circular No. 23/89 'Special schools for pupils with emotional and behavioural difficulties' contains guidance about educational provision for pupils with emotional and behavioural difficulties in special schools. The guidance takes account of the findings and recommendations in the HMI survey of national provision for pupils with emotional/behavioural difficulties in Maintained Special Schools and Units during the period 1983–1988 which contains recommendations about meeting the educational and emotional care needs for their pupils. One of the DES recommendations concerns staffing and in-service training. The Circular says 'LEA support services will have a valuable part to play in providing in-service training for all those working with emotionally and behaviourally disturbed pupils. This training for both schools and individual staff should be organized and planned on a regular basis.'

In December 1989, in the House of Commons, the Secretary of State was asked the provision of in-service teacher training on disability awareness. Mr Alan Howarth MP answered as follows:

> No information is collected centrally on the extent of awareness training on disability. The Government provide substantial support, through the LEA training grants scheme, for training to meet special educational needs, which include certain disabilities. Five categories of training in respect of special

educational needs are currently designated as national priorities, eligible for support at the higher rate of grant under the scheme. In the current financial year, grant is available to support expenditure of £6.6 million in these areas. In addition, authorities are free to draw on the grant available to them under the scheme at the lower rate, in support of further expenditure at their discretion on training on aspects of disability.

In Circular 11/90 (December 1990) *Staffing for pupils with Special Educational Needs*, the DES advises on relevant factors in staffing levels, and suggests a model for calculating staffing levels for pupils in each band of learning difficulty.

School buildings

Pupils with special educational needs will need special facilities in schools, and there may be ways that the school has to be designed or adapted to accommodate their needs. DES Design Note 18 'Access for the physically disabled to educational buildings', contains design guidance to improve access to educational premises for disabled people. The Design Note deals with a number of issues:

(1) Parking facilities. When Pupils arrive at or leave school in coaches, minibuses or cars, then they will need to be close to the school building and sheltered while they are being loaded and unloaded. There will need to be adequate lighting and slip-resistant surfaces.

(2) Access approaches to schools should be level and ramps should be used where necessary.

(3) Doors and doorways. These should be wide enough to allow wheelchairs to go through them comfortably. Doors should have suitable handles at a convenient height and raised thresholds or doormats should be avoided, because they can cause difficulties. So as to allow a wheelchair user to open the door, there should be sufficient wall space adjacent to the door handles. If there are swing doors, then the door closures should be correctly tensioned.

(4) Internal levels. Short or narrow flights of stairs from one internal level to another can pose tremendous problems for disabled pupils, which cannot always be solved by a ramp, because that would invariably be too narrow or steep. Lifts are a quick and convenient way of travelling from one level to another.

(5) Sanitary facilities. At school, disabled pupils will need additional toilets for wheelchair users of either sex with appropriate doors, fittings and support rails. Wash basins and taps will need to be such

that they can be used comfortably by disabled children and, in order to maintain standards of hygiene, there must be adequate waste disposal arrangements.

(6) Means of escape. There must be adequate arrangements for emergency escape for disabled pupils and multistorey buildings pose the greatest problems, because lifts should not be used in the event of fire. There are alternative ways of securing an emergency escape, such as external ramps to ground level, link bridges on the same level to adjoining blocks, or lobbies adjacent to stairways which are fire resistant for at least half an hour. Alternatively, a school may create fire zones in upper floors, so that if a fire breaks out at one zone, it can be confined within it for long enough to allow pupils to be moved to an adjacent zone out of danger. If there was no escape route from their zone, then the pupils have to be kept there until rescued, which could be a frightening experience. Alternatively, nonambulant pupils can be excluded from all parts of the building other than the ground floor.

The DES in the booklet 'Safety at School: General Advice', suggests that general safety precautions should apply even more forcefully to special needs children and it also identifies particular areas when special attention is needed.

It is important to have regular fire drills involving special needs children so as to ascertain how much extra time is needed to evacuate children with difficulties.

The DES also highlights the importance of emergency lighting in key positions and the vital importance of non-slip floors. Corridors should be clear of obstructions and ramps should be available for the use by wheelchairs.

Physical education

Children with special needs can gain enormous benefits, both educationally and socially, from PE and sport. Regular physical education is an essential part of the development of children with special needs, including children in wheelchairs. As well as encouraging physical development, physical education is the ideal opportunity for a child to reach his or her full potential, and this is particularly important as children with handicaps can often have serious confidence problems. There will need to be specific regulations and procedures to allow them to follow these activities safely.

The British Association of Advisers and Lecturers in Physical Education has produced a very helpful book *Physical Education for Children with*

Special Educational Needs in Mainstream Education. This contains safety advice as well as information about the common handicapping conditions and their implications for physical education, and it gives practical advice to teachers for each sport and leisure activity. Included with the book is a computer disk for use with any BBC micro or master computer, which contains further information on this subject.

Supervision arrangements are particularly important and if possible the numbers of pupils in any group should be modified to take account of any child with a particular special need. In any case, the teacher in charge should be aware of all the children's strengths and weaknesses, which include any health problems or physical restrictions or disabilities. Teachers and others in charge of special needs children need to remember that hazards can be accentuated for a person with a sensory impairment or a disability, and someone with a mental handicap or a learning difficulty finds it difficult to understand the meaning of danger.

Teachers have to bear in mind that children with special needs will probably not be able to use apparatus without it being adapted. When adapting apparatus, teachers should make sure that the apparatus remains stable and that it is safe to use before the activities start. There are a number of basic precautions that need to be taken:

(1) The teacher in charge needs to have enough information about the nature of the child's special need. If there is a clear instruction about a child's involvement in a particular activity, then that must be followed, regardless of what the child may say. This was illustrated in a the case of *Moore v Hampshire County Council*, discussed on p. 55.

(2) Proper communication between the teacher and the child is particularly important. The teacher needs to be sure that the child understands what is being asked of him or her, although there will inevitably be cases where the teacher cannot be absolutely sure that the child has understood instructions and advice sufficiently clearly. In these situations, the teacher will benefit from any special support that may be available from a colleague or from strategies that have been designed to deal with such situations. A simple strategy is to adjust the speed of the teaching process to take account of the child's ability.

(3) The question of physical support for a child with special needs is important, and the teacher will need to exercise sound judgement about when such support can be safely withdrawn.

(4) Particular care may be needed with some special needs children before and after the activity itself. Extra supervision may be necessary

when they are using showers, when they are washing and when they are getting dressed and undressed.

Swimming

When special needs children are swimming, adequate supervision and proper communication between supervisors and the children are especially important to ensure that children in water are safe. Supervisors should never assume that children are safe in the water, even those who are wearing swimming aids.

LEAs may, in their own safety regulations, specify minimum life saving qualifications for supervisors. The regulations will also set down supervision ratios and the amount of supervision needed in any particular case will depend on the number of special needs children in the group, what handicaps they have involved, how old the children are and what facilities are available. The regulations may also specify the maximum depth of pools for special needs children.

APPENDIX I: LIST OF HEALTH AND SAFETY EXECUTIVE LOCAL OFFICES

Area name and number	Address	Telephone number	Local authorities
01 South West	Inter City House Mitchel Lane Victoria Street Bristol BS1 6AN	0272 290681	Avon, Cornwall, Devon, Gloucestershire, Somerset, Isles of Scilly
02 South	Priestley House Priestley Road Basingstoke RG24 9NW	0256 473181	Berkshire, Dorset, Hampshire, Isle of Wight, Wiltshire
03 South East	3 East Grinstead House London Road West Sussex RH19 1RR	0342 26922	Kent, Surrey, East Sussex, West Sussex
04 London North	Maritime House 1 Linton Road Barking Essex IG11 8HF	081 594 5522	Barking and Dagenham, Barnet, Brent, Camden, Ealing, Enfield, Hackney, Haringey, Harrow,
	Chancel House Neasden Lane London NW10 2UD	081 459 8855	Islington Newham, Redbridge, Tower Hamlets, Waltham Forest

05	London South	1 Long Lane London SE1 4PG	081 407 8911	Bexley, Bromley, City of London, Croydon, Greenwich, Hammersmith and Fulham, Hillingdon, Hounslow, Kensington and Chelsea, Kingston, Lambeth, Lewisham, Merton, Richmond, Southwark, Sutton, Wandsworth, Westminster
06	East Anglia	39 Baddow Road Chelmsford Essex CM2 OHL	0245 84661	Essex, Norfolk, Suffolk
07	Northern Home Counties	14 Cardiff Road Luton Beds LU1 1PP	0582 34121	Bedfordshire, Buckinghamshire, Cambridgeshire, Hertfordshire
08	East Midlands	Belgrave House 1 Greyfriars Northampton NN1 2BS	0604 21233	Leicestershire, Northants, Oxford, Warwicks
09	West Midlands	McLaren Building 2 Masshouse Circus Queensway Birmingham B4 7NP	021 200 2299	West Midlands
10	Wales	Brunel House 2 Fitzalan Road Cardiff CF2 1SH	0222 497777	Clwyd, Dyfed, Gwent, Gwynedd, Mid Glamorgan, Powys, South Glamorgan, West Glamorgan
11	Marches	The Marches House Midway Newcastle under Lyme Staffs ST5 1DT	0782 717181	Hereford and Worcester, Shropshire, Staffs

12	North Midlands	Birbeck House Trinity Square Nottingham NG1 4AU	0602 470712	Derbys, Lincs, Notts
13	South Yorkshire	Sovereign House 40 Silver Street Sheffield S1 2ES	0742 739081	Humberside, South Yorkshire
14	West and North Yorkshire	8 St Pauls Street Leeds LS1 2LE	0532 446191	North Yorkshire, West Yorkshire
15	Greater Manchester	Quay House Quay Street Manchester M3 3JB	061 831 7111	Greater Manchester
16	Merseyside	The Triad Stanley Road Bootle L20 3PG	051 922 7211	Cheshire, Merseyside
17	North West	Victoria House Ormskirk Road Preston PR1 1HH	0772 59321	Cumbria, Lancs
18	North East	Arden House Regent Centre Gosforth Newcastle upon Tyne NE3 3JM	091 284 8448	Cleveland, Durham, Northumberland, Tyne and Wear
19	Scotland East	Belford House 59 Belford Road Edinburgh EH4 3UE	031 225 13113	Borders, Central, Fife, Grampian, Highland, Lothian, Tayside, island areas of Orkney and Shetland
20	Scotland	314 Vincent Street Glasgow G3 8XG	041 204 2646	Dumfries and Galloway, Strathclyde, the Western Isles

APPENDIX II: MODEL COSHH ASSESSMENT

Produced by The Professional Association of Teachers.

Department: Date:

Location: Assessor:

Task:

1. Who carries out the task and how much time per month is spent on the task?

Name: Job: Hours/month:

2. Describe the task

3. List the substances and include appropriate hazard data sheets

Trade name	Substance	Quantity used per month	Occupational exposure limit	Nature of hazard

Comments on the nature of the hazard:

4. Observations

Storage of materials:

Transportation:

Handling and use:

Packing:

Disposal:

5. Identify and categorize sources of exposure

6. Estimate duration of exposure and concentration

7. What controls are in use? How often are they tested and what maintenance is carried out?

8. Has any monitoring/health surveillance been carried out? If so, specify

9. Conclusions about the risks

a. risks significant
b. risks high
c. risks controlled now but could become higher in the future
d. uncertain about the risks, nature of the hazards known
e. cannot decide about the risks

10. Recommendations

11. Date of review:

12. Signature of assessor ....
 Date ....

COSHH Regulations

Introducing COSHH (1988)
HSE (IND(G)65)

COSHH: Guidance for Schools (1989)
HMSO
ISBN 0 11 885511 5

COSHH Assessments: a step by step guide to assessments and the skills needed for it (1988)
HMSO
ISBN 0 11 885470 4

Hazard and Risk Explained (1988)
HSE (IND(G)67)

Introducing Assessment (a Simplified Guide for Employers) (1988)
HSE (IND(G)64)

APPENDIX III: HTLV-III/LAV INFECTION CONTROL

HTLV-III/LAV Infection control guidelines for local education authorities, schools and health staff, set out in *Children at School and problems related to* AIDS and reproduced with the permission of the Controller of Her Majesty's Stationery Office.

This guidance applies to HTLV-III/LAV infected children.

1. Personal hygiene.
1.1 Razors, toothbrushes or other implements which could become contaminated with blood must not be shared.
1.2 Minor cuts, open or weeping skin lesions and abrasions should be covered with waterproof or other suitable dressings.
1.3 Sanitary towels must be burnt in an incinerator or the procedure for disposal of infected waste followed (see below)
1.4 Tampons may be flushed down the toilet.
2. Accidents involving external bleeding.
2.1 Normal first aid procedures should be followed, which should include the use of disposable gloves where possible.
2.2 Wash the wound immediately and copiously with soap and water. Apply a suitable dressing and pressure pad if needed.
2.3 As soon as possible seek medical advice.
2.4 Splashes of blood from the HTLV-III/LAV antibody positive child on to another child.
    • Splashes of blood on the skin should be washed off immediately with soap and water.
    • Splashes of blood into the eyes or mouth should be washed out immediately with copious amounts of water.
2.5 After accidents resulting in bleeding, contaminated surfaces, e.g. tables or furniture, should be cleaned liberally with household bleach, freshly diluted 1:10 in water. Such solutions must not come into contact with the skin.
NB. Bleach can corrode metal and burn holes in fabrics if used for too long or in the wrong concentration, and must never be used on skin.

2.6 Complete an accident form in the usual manner.
3.   General hygiene.
3.1 Cleaning:
   • Normal cleaning methods should be used. No special disinfectants are necessary for either the bath or toilet.
   • Use disposable cloths.
   • Use separate cloths for kitchen, for bathroom, and for toilet.
3.2 Spillages of blood and vomit should be cleared up as quickly as possible. Ordinary household bleach freshly diluted 1:10 in water (preferably hot) should be gently poured over the spill and covered with paper towels. (See warning in paragraph 2.5.)
3.3 If practical the diluted bleach should be left for 30 minutes before being wiped up with disposable paper towels. (See warning in paragraph 2.5.) Disposable gloves and apron should be worn.
3.4 Individual paper towels may be discarded down the toilet. However, if many are used, it is prefereable to treat them as infected waste. Gloves and aprons should be discarded as infected waste. (See paragraph 5.2.)
3.5 Clothes and linen that are stained with blood or semen should be washed in a washing machine at 95 degrees centigrade for 10 minutes or boiled before handwashing.
3.6 Crockery and cutlery can be cleaned by handwashing with hot soapy water or in a dishwasher or dish steriliser.
4.   Staff precautions.
     As a general policy, if staff giving physical care to infected children have cuts and abrasions, these should be covered with waterproof or other suitable dressings.
5.   Waste disposal.
5.1 Urine and faeces should be eliminated or discarded into the toilet in the normal manner. Potties should be washed and dried with paper towels after use. Disinfectant is not necessary.
5.2 Soiled waste, i.e. nappies and pads, should be burnt. If this cannot be done in the school, the rubbish including protective disposable gloves or aprons should be 'double bagged' in yellow plastic bags and effectively secured. Arrangements should be made with the responsible local authority for collection of this waste for incineration.
5.3 Non-infected waste is discarded into bin liners or dustbins. This should be collected and disposed of in the usual manner by the local authority cleansing department.
5.4 When work is completed wash and dry your hands.
6.   Uniformed youth organisations, clubs and discos.
     There is no risk in HTLV-III/LAV antibody positive children attending such groups or social activities. These children may attend and partake in all such gatherings freely.
7.   School and public libraries.
     Libraries may be used in the normal way.

APPENDIX IV: MODEL DIVISION OF MAINTENANCE RESPONSIBILITIES

The model division of maintenance responsibilities for the school building between LEAs and schools, as set out in DES Circular 7/88 and reproduced with the permission of the Controller of Her Majesty's Stationery Office.

LEA responsibility	School responsibility
A. STRUCTURE	
Foundations	
Structural frames	
Floor structures (including ground floor slabs)	Repair or replacement of floor finishes
Roof structures (including weather-proof coverings and insulation)	Repair of ceiling finishes
Skylights, rooflights and verandahs	Minor repairs and repairs of glazing
Rainwater goods	Clearing out gutters and downpipes
Staircase and landing structures (including handrails and balustrades)	Repair of finishes and coverings
External walls and surfaces (including insulation)	Repair of exposed internal finishes
Internal walls, partitions and glazed screens	Repair of surface finishes and glazing
Windows and fittings (including window walls)	Minor repairs, adjustment and glazing
Doors and fittings	Minor repairs, adjustment and glazing

LEA responsibility	School responsibility
Ceiling structures (including suspension systems)	Ceiling tiles/finishes and minor plaster repairs Glazing: to include all glazing throughout as indicated above
Timber preservation	

B. DECORATION

All external decoration	All internal decoration: including cleaning and preparation

C. WATER AND DRAINAGE SERVICES

Internal water supply services (including pumps, pipes, tanks and insulation)

Replacement of water supply including sanitary equipment	Minor repair and adjustment including taps and other fittings.
Waste and soil drainage services	Cleaning of pipes and maintenance of traps, wire guards, etc.

D. ELECTRICAL SERVICES

Servicing, repair and replacement of general electrical installations including switchgear, cables and conduits up to and including switches, sockets and other outlets	Replacing lamps, tubes and plugs
All external lighting, including columns, floodlights and road lighting	
Steel chimneys	
Alarm, emergency and time systems (except for any systems purchased at school cost)	Reset of alarms and fire detection systems; minor repairs to clocks and bells; maintenance of any systems purchased at school cost
Fan convectors and other fixed space and water heating equipment; fixed ventilation units	Portable heating and ventilation equipment; general cleaning; maintenance and replacement of fittings on all items Kitchen equipment: servicing and repair of fixed cooking equipment including ovens, ranges, fryers, boilers, steamers, grills and mixers. Heated trolleys, refrigerators, cold rooms, fixed water boilers and sterilizing sink heaters

LEA responsibility   School responsibility

Laundry equipment: servicing and repair of washing machines, tumble driers, spin driers, extractors and irons (excluding drainage systems)

Lifts, hoists, barriers and electric door motors and controls

Specialist external equipment e.g. earthing, lightning conductors

Standby generators

Temporary accommodation: all power supply and wiring

E. MECHANICAL SERVICES

Servicing, repair and replacement of mechanical installations and plant including:

Boilers, including automatic controls and electrics

Ancillary boiler equipment: pumps and tanks

Heating and domestic hot water distribution systems, including replacement of radiators and other heat emitters, taps and shower fittings

Minor repairs and adjustments to heat emitters, taps and shower fittings

Gas distribution systems

Fixed air-conditioning and ventilation equipment

Direct oil and gas fired heater units

Sewage pumps and chambers

Kitchen equipment: servicing and repair of gas cooking equipment including motors and burners, etc.

Swimming pools: including filtration plant, pumps, pipes and boilers

Chemical dosing, cleaning and minor maintenance

Fire fighting equipment: extinguishers, fire blankets and fixed hoses

Fume cupboards, including extractor fans and ductwork

LEA responsibility	School responsibility

F. FURNITURE AND FITTINGS

Internal joinery fixtures: including cupboards, shelves, display boards, fixed benches and other internal seating with its coverings

Gymnasium equipment: repairs of all fixed sports and gymnasium equipment and markings

Supply, fixing and maintenance of all internal signs, blinds, curtain tracks, etc.

Fires and fireplaces

G. EXTERNAL WORKS

Demolition of buildings and clearance of sites; sealing of services

Major repairs to hard-paved areas including roads, playgrounds, car parks and courts	Minor repairs to hard paved areas
Perimeter and retaining walls; perimeter fencing and gates	Minor repairs to walls, fencing and gates
Major external fixtures	Minor external fixtures eg signs and notices
Mature trees	Upkeep of grounds: maintenance of grounds, playing fields, amenities land, landscaped areas and boundary hedges (except mature trees)
Mains drainage including traps, gullies and manholes	Cleaning unblocking drainage systems
	Refuse containers and bins
	Pest control
Gas, electric, water and heating mains	
Maintenance of ancillary including garages and huts, constructed at LEA cost	Maintenance of ancillary buildings constructed at school cost

H. MISCELLANEOUS

Asbestos removal or treatment

External maintenance on temporary buildings	Internal maintenance on temporary buildings; all glazing repairs

APPENDIX V: USEFUL ASSOCIATIONS AND PUBLICATIONS

Health and Safety Executive Publications

The HSE's library and information service produces a free education subject catalogue which lists all legislation, guidance, leaflets and reports relevant to education. This is available from any of the HSE public enquiry points. As well as this, the Health and Safety Commission's Education Service Advisory Committee has published a bibliograph relating to health and safety in educational establishments and entitled *Health and Safety in Education*. It costs £6.00.

Health and Safety Public Enquiry Points

There are three public enquiry points based in HSE's Library and Information Services at London, Sheffield and Bootle, which are open between 10.00 a.m. and 3.00 p.m. each week day. The fourth enquiry point is available on Prestel, open twenty-four hours a day.

Health and Safety Executive
Library and Information Services
Broad Lane
Sheffield S3 7HQ
Tel: 0742 752539
Telex: 54556

Health and Safety Executive
Library and Information Services
St Hugh's House
Stanley Precinct
Trinity Road
Bootle
Merseyside L20 3QY
Tel: 051 951 4381
Telex: 628235

Health and Safety Executive
Library and Information Services
Baynards House
1 Chepstow Place
Westbourne Grove
London W2 4TF
Tel: 071 221 0870
Telex: 25683

Health and Safety Executive Publications

The Health and Safety at Work Act 1974

The Act Outlined (1975)
HSE (HSC 2)

Essentials of Health and Safety at Work (1990)
HMSO
ISBN 0 11 885445 3

A Guide to the HSW Act (1983)
HMSO (HS(R)6)
ISBN 0 11 883710 9

Health and Safety at Work etc Act 1974: Advice to Employees (1975) HSE
(HSC 5)

The Health and Safety at Work Act 1974: Advice for Employers (1975) HSE
(HSC 3)

Health and Safety at Work etc Act 1974: Your Obligations to Non-Employees
(1985) HSE (HSC 11)

Protecting Your Health at Work (1988)
HSE (IND(G)62)

Regulations, Approved Codes of Practice and Guidance Literature (1976)
HSE (HSC 7)

*Securing Compliance with Health and Safety Legislation at Work: How it is Done
and How it Affects You* (1983)
HSE (IND(G)14)

Writing Your *Health and Safety Policy Statement: How to Prepare a Safety Policy
Statement for a Small Business* (1986)
HMSO
ISBN 0 11 883882 2

Asbestos

Alternatives to Asbestos Products: a Review (1986)
HMSO
ISBN 0 11 883812 1

Asbestos and You: Working with Asbestos (1985)
HSE (IND(G)17)

Effects on Health of Exposure to Asbestos (1985)
HMSO
ISBN 0 11 883803 2

Drugs

Drug Abuse at Work: a Guide to Employers (1990)
HSE
IND(C)91L

First Aid

First Aid at Work (1981)
HMSO (HS(R)11)
ISBN 0 11 8834460

First Aid at Work (Approved Code of Practice) (1990)
HMSO
ISBN 0 11 8855360

First Aid at Work: General First Aid Guidance for First Aid Boxes (1987)
HMSO (IND(G)4)
ISBN 0 11 8839586

First Aid in Educational Establishments (1985)
HMSO
ISBN 0 11 883837 7

First Aid Provision in Small Work Places: Your Questions Answered (1985)
HSE (IND(G)3)

First Aid Needs in your Workplace (1990)
HSE IND(G) 3(L)

Farms

Accidents to Children (poster) (1987)
HSE (AS20)

Farm Safety for Kids (poster) (1987)
HSE

Preventing Accidents to Children in Agriculture. Approved Codes of Practice and Guidance Notes (1988)
HMSO
ISBN 0 11 8839977

School Visits to Farms (1989)
HSE (IND(G)70)

Gas and Electricity

Electrical Safety in Schools (1983)
HMSO
ISBN 0 11 883567 X

Electricity at Work Regulations 1989: Memorandum of Guidance (1989)
HMSO (HS(R)25)
ISBN 0 11 883963 Z

Flexible Leads, Plugs, Sockets etc. (1985)
HMSO
ISBN 0 11 883519 X

The Gas Regulations: For Everybody's Safety (1985)
HSE (IND(G)24)

Protection against Electric Shock (1984)
HMSO
ISBN 0 11 883583 1

The Safe Use of Portable Electrical Apparatus (1983)
HMSO
ISBN 0 11 8835637

Noise

Introducing the Noise at Work Regulations (1989)
HSE
IND(G)75(G)

Noise at Work: Guidance on Regulations (1989 and 1990)
HMSO
ISBN 0 11 885123 and 0 11 885430 5

100 Practical Applications of Noise Reduction Methods (1983)
HMSO
ISBN 0 11 88369 9

Practical Subjects and Science

Categorization of Pathogens according to Hazard and Categories of Containment
  (1984)
HMSO
ISBN 0 11 883761 3

Do You Work with Chemicals and Other Materials in Educational Establishments?
  (1986)
HSC (IAC/L19)

A Guide to the Safety Science Regulations 1980 (1981)
HMSO (HS(R)7)
ISBN 0 11 883415 0

A Guide to Woodworking Machines Regulations 1974 (1981)
HMSO (HS(R)9)
ISBN 0 11 883437 1

Safety in the use of Abrasive Wheels (1984)
HMSO (HS(G)17)
ISBN 0 11 883739 7

Safety in the use of Woodworking Machines (1970)
HMSO (HSW41)
ISBN 0 11 880837 0

Welding (1978)
HMSO
ISBN 0 11 8831844

Reporting Accidents

A Guide to the Reporting of Injuries, Diseases and Dangerous Occurences Regulations 1985 (1986)
HMSO
ISBN 0 11 883858 X

Reporting an Injury or a Dangerous Occurence (1986)
HSE (HSE 11)

Report that Accident (1988)
HSE21

Safety Representatives

Safety Representatives and Safety Committees (1977)
HMSO
ISBN 0 11 8803352

Time off for the Training of Safety Representatives (1976)
HSE (HSC 9)

Visual Display Units

Health Effects of VDUs: Bibliography (1984)
HMSO
ISBN 0 7176 01943

Human Factors Aspects of Visual Display Units' Operation (1980)
HSE Research Paper 10

Visual Display Units (1983)
HMSO
ISBN 0 11 883685 4

Working with VDUs (1986)
HSE (IND(G)36)

Violence at Work

Preventing Violence to Staff (1988)
HMSO
ISBN 0 11 8854674

Violence to Staff (1989)
HSE (IND(G)69)

Violence to Staff in the Education Sector (1990)
HMSO, ISBN 0 11 8855581

Miscellaneous

Passive Smoking at Work (1988)
HSE (IND(G)63)

Manual Handling and Lifting: an Information and Literature Review with Special Reference to the Back (1985)
HMSO
ISBN 0 11 883778 8

Mind How You Go! (1984)
HSE (IND(G)2)

Safety in Swimming Pools (1988)
HSC and Sports Council
ISBN 0 90 657783 7

A Short Guide to the Employer's Liability (Compulsory Insurance) Act 1969 (1985)
HSC (HSE 4)

Watch Your Step: Prevention of Slipping, Tripping and Falling Accidents at Work (1985)
HMSO
ISBN 0 11 8837182 6

Health and Safety Executive Guidance Notes

The HSE Guidance Notes are available from HMSO and include the following:

Guidance Note GS5 Entry into Confined Spaces
Guidance Note GS8 Articles and Substances for Use at Work
Guidance Note GS10 Roof Work: Prevention of Falls
Guidance Note GS23 Electrical Safety in Schools
Guidance Note GS29/1 Health and Safety in Demolition Work
Guidance Note GS31 Safe Use of Ladders, Step Ladders or Trestles
Guidance Note C52 The Storage of Highly Flammable Liquids
Guidance Note CS4 The Keeping of Liquified Petroleum Gas in Cylinders and Similar Containers
Guidance Note EH36 Work with Asbestos Cement
Guidance Note EH37 Work with Asbestos Insulating Board
Guidance Note PM32 Safe Use of Portable Electrical Apparatus
Guidance Note PM38 Selection and use of Electric Hand Lamps

ESAC and Education Service National Interest Group Literature

The Education Service Advisory Committee (ESAC) and HSE's Education Service National Interest Group have produced the following literature, available from Maritime House, I Linton Road, Barking, ESSEX IG11 8HF.

ESAC

Safety policies in the education sector
First aid in educational establishments
Storage and use of highly flammable liquids in educational establishments
Guidance on a voluntary scheme for the collection, collation and analysis of injury, disease and dangerous occurence data in the education sector
Do you work with chemicals and other materials in educational establishments?
Guidance to cleaning staff who clean laboratories in educational establishments
Guidance on provision of a safe system of work for the unattended operation of experimental apparatus outside normal working hours in educational establishments
Temporary use of liquified petroleum gas heaters in schools
Health and safety in education: A source book of reference material
Building contracts undertaken on education premises: strategies for the health and safety of staff and pupils
Centrifuge warning label
Health and safety of catering staff in educational establishments
Fumes in solid fuel boiler rooms at educational establishments
COSHH − Guidance for Schools
ISBN 0 11 885511 5

Education Service National Interest Group

Investigated school science accidents in educational premises April 1986 − June 1987
Woodworking machine accidents in educational premises
July 1984 − May 1986
Laboratory accidents in higher education
Investigated electrical accidents in educational premises September 1984 − September 1989
Health and Safety Executive Safety Film Catalogue
The HSE published in 1989 a second edition of its resource catalogue which lists films, videos and tapes/slides available in the United Kingdom
The catalogue *Audiovisual Resources in Occupational Health and Safety* is available at £6.50
ISBN 07176 03342

DES Circulars and Administrative Memoranda

Copies of circulars and administrative memoranda can be obtained free of charge from the Printing and Stationary Unit of the DES, Honeypot Lane, Stanmore, Middlesex HA7 1AZ.

Administrative memoranda

2/65   Poisonous substances in pencils and other allied materials used in schools
2/68   Physical education apparatus in schools and colleges
3/70   Carcinogenic aromatic amnines in schools and other educational establishments

7/70 Use of lasers in schools and other educational establishments
2/76 Use of ionising radiation in educational establishments
6/76 The laboratory use of dangerous pathogens
2/86 Children at school and problems related to AIDS
3/86 The use of asbestos in educational establishments
1/89 Animals and plants in schools: legal aspects

Circulars

7/74 Guide to the Education (Work Experience) Act 1973
4/88 Working together for the protection of children from abuse: procedures within the education service
7/88 Education Reform Act (1988): local management of schools
11/88 Admission of pupils to county and voluntary schools
4/89 Alcohol abuse
23/89 Special schools for pupils with emotional and behavioural difficulties
11/90 Staffing for pupils with special educational needs

Scottish Education Department Circulars and Memoranda

Circulars and memoranda from the Scottish Education Department are available from 43 Jeffrey Street, Edinburgh EH1 1DN.

Memoranda

13/62 Fire precautions − storage of bottled gas containers
3/62, 3/65 Use of inflammable materials in homecraft classes
39/66 Hazards of experimenting with explosives
6/68 Inhalation of asbestos dust − preventative measures
22/70 Schools
8/74 High pressure oxygen (manifold) systems

Circulars

555 The Education Service and Nuclear Attack
766 Use of Lasers in Schools, Colleges of Education and Further Education Establishments
689 Ionising Radiations in Schools, Colleges of Education and Further Education Establishments
825 Use of Carcinogenic Substances in Educational Establishments
848 Safety in Outdoor Pursuits
1113 Use of Asbestos in Educational Establishments
1125 Treatment and Quality of Swimming Pool Water
1166 Procedures for the Use of Ionising Radiation in Educational Establishments

DES Building Bulletins and Design Notes

Building bulletins are available from HMSO bookshops and other large bookshops. Out of print bulletins are available free (subject to limited availability) from:

Architects and Building Group
Department of Education and Science
Room 7/38
Elizabeth House
York Road
London SE1 7PH
Tel: 071 934 9521

DES BB7	Fire and the design of schools
DES BB28	Playing fields and hard surface areas
DES BB31	Secondary school design: workshop crafts
DES BB35	New problems in school design: middle schools
DES BB38	School furniture dimensions: standing and reaching
DES BB39	Designing for science: Oxford School Development Project
DES BB50	Furniture and equipment: working heights and zones for practical activities
DES BB52	School furniture: standing and sitting postures
DES BB55	Energy conservation in educational buildings
DES BB67	Crime prevention in schools: practical guidance

Design Note 17. Guidelines for environmental design and fuel conservation in educational buildings
Design Note 18. Access for disabled people to educational buildings
Design Note 29. Fume cupboards in schools
Design Note 40. Maintenance and renewal in educational buildings – needs and priorities

Department of Education and Science – Safety Series booklets: available through HMSO and other large bookshops.

No. 1 Safety in Outdoor Education
No. 2 Safety in Science Laboratories
No. 3 Safety in Practical Studies
No. 4 Safety in Physical Education
No. 5 Safety in Further Education
No. 6 Safety at School: General Advice

Other DES Publications

Standards in Education 1988/89: The Annual Report of HM Senior Chief Inspector of Schools in January 1990

A limited survey of health education in 10 Liverpool Primary Schools May 2–4 1989

Education Observed 5 – Good Behaviour and Discipline in Schools
ISBN 085522 200 X

Curriculum Matters (an HMI Series)

Number 5 Home Economics from 5–16
ISBN 0 11 270580 4

Number 6 Health Education from 5−16
ISBN 0 11 270592 8

Number 9 Craft design and technology from 5−16
ISBN 0 11 270642 8

Number 14 Personal and Social Education from 5−16
ISBN 0 11 270679 7

Number 16 Physical Education from 5−16
ISBN 0 11 270684 3

Discipline in Schools (The Elton Report) (1990)
HMSO
ISBN 0 11 2706657

Microbiology: An HMI guide for schools and non-advanced further education
  (1985)
HMSO
ISBN 0 11 2705782

General Addresses

Association of Advisers in Craft Design and Technology
124 Kidmore Road
Caversham
Reading
Berks RG4 7NB
Tel: 0734 470615

Association for Science Education
College Lane
Hatfield
Hertfordshire AL10 9AA
Tel: 07072 67411

British Educational Equipment Association
20 Beaufort Court
Admirals Way
London E14 9XL
Tel: 071 537 4997

British Epilepsy Association
Anstey House
40 Hanover Square
Leeds LS3 1BE
Tel: 0532 439393
(Epilepsy helpline 0435 089599; all calls charged at local rates)

British Red Cross Society
9 Grosvenor Crescent
London SW1X 7EJ
Tel: 071 235 5454

(For further information about the British Red Cross, contact the nearest Red Cross County Branch Headquarters. The address can be found in the telephone directory under 'B' for British or 'R' for Red Cross. Alternatively, contact the Head Office.)

British Safety Council
62 Chancellors Road
London W6 9RS
Tel: 081 741 1231

British Veterinary Association
7 Mansfield Street
London W1M OAT

Central Council of Physical Recreation
Francis House
Francis Street
London SW1P
Tel: 071 828 3163

Child Accident Prevention Trust
28 Portland Place
London W6 9RS
Tel: 071 636 2545

Consortium of LEAs for the Provision of Science Services (CLEAPS)
Brunel University
Uxbridge
Middlesex UB8 3PH
Tel: 0895 51446

Criminal Injuries Compensation Board
Whittington House
19–30 Chenies Street
London WC1 7EJ
Tel: 071 636 2812

Criminal Injuries Compensation Board (Scotland)
Blythswood House
200 West Regent Street
Glasgow G1
Tel: 041 221 0945

Fire Protection Association
140 Aldergate Street
London EC1A 4HX
Tel: 071 606 3757

Health and Safety Commission
Regina House
259–269 Old Marylebone Road
London NW1 5RR
Tel: 071 723 1262

Health Education Authority
Hamilton House
Mabledon Place
London WC1H 9TX
Tel: 071 387 9528

Institute of Biology
20 Queensberry Place
London SW7 2DZ
Tel: 071 581 8387

Institute of Ceramics
Shelton House
Stoke Road
Shelton
Stoke-on-Trent ST4 2DR
Tel: 0782 202116

The Institute for the Study of Drug Dependence (ISDD)
1 Hatton Place
Hatton Gardens
London EC1N 8ND
Tel: 071 430 1991

The Laboratory Animals Centre
Woodmansterne Road
Carshalton
Surrey SM5 4EF

National Back Pain Association
31–33 Park Road
Teddington
Middlesex TW11 0AB
Tel: 081 977 5474

National Playing Fields Association
25 Ovington Square
London SW3 1LQ
Tel: 071 584 6445

(Scotland)
20 Queen Street
Edinburgh EH2 1JX
Tel: 031 225 4307

Re–Solv
The Society for the Prevention of Solvent Abuse
St Mary's Chambers
19 Station Road
Stone
Staffordshire ST15 8JP
Tel: 0785 817885

Royal Society of Chemistry
Burlington House
Piccadilly
London W1V 0BN
Tel: 071 437 8656

Royal Society for the Prevention of Accidents
Cannon House
The Priory
Queensway
Birmingham B4 6BS
Tel: 021 233 2461

Royal Society for the Prevention of Cruelty to Animals
The Causeway
Horsham
West Sussex RH12 1HG
Tel: 0403 64181

St Andrews Ambulance Association
48 Milton Street
Glasgow G4 0HR
Tel: 041 332 4031

St John Ambulance Association
1 Grosvenor Crescent
London SW1X 7EF
Tel: 071 235 5231

(For further information about the St John Ambulance Association, contact the
  nearest County Branch Headquarters or Head Office.

Safety and First Aid
59 Hill Street
Liverpool L8 5SA
Tel: 051 708 0397

The Standing Conference on Drug Abuse
1 Hatton Place
Hatton Gardens EC1N 8ND
Tel: 071 430 1991

The Teachers Advisory Council on Alcohol and Drug Education (TACADE)
1 Hulme Place
The Crescent
Salford
Manchester M5 4QA
Tel: 061 745 8925

Physical Education and Sport

The British Association of Advisers and Lecturers in Physical Education has
  produced a number of booklets dealing with different aspects of physical
  education

Safe Practice in Physical Education (1990)
(available from White Line Press, 60 Bradford Road, Stanningley, Leeds LS28 6EF)

Health – Focused Physical Education
White Line Press

Gymnastics in the Secondary School
White Line Press (a video is also available)

Physical Education for Children with Special Needs in Mainstream Education
White Line Press (book plus disk)

Teaching and Learning Strategies in Physical Education
White Line Press

Teacher Effectiveness in Physical Education
available from:

Studies in Education Limited
100 Driffield Road
Nafferton
East Yorkshire YO25 0JL

Attainment in Physical Education
Studies in Education Limited

The Bulletin of Physical Education (quarterly publication)
Studies in Education Limited

There are many other useful information sheets and booklets available from national sports bodies:

The Sports Council

Sports Council Headquarters
16 Upper Woburn Place
London WC1H 0QP
Tel: 071 388 1277

Northern Region
Aykley Heads
Durham DH1 5UU
Tel: 091 384 9595

North West Region
Astley House
Quay Street
Manchester M3 4AE
Tel: 061 834 0338

Yorkshire and Humberside Region
Coronet House
Queen Street
Leeds LS1 4PW
Tel: 0532 436443

Greater London and South East Region
20 Box 480
Crystal Palace NSC
London SE19 2BQ
Tel: 081 778 8600

Southern Region
51A Church Street
Caversham
Reading
Berks RG4 8AX
Tel: 0734 483311

East Midlands Region
Grove House
Bridgford Road
West Bridgford
Nottingham NG2 6AP
Tel: 0602 821887/822586

West Midlands Region
Metropolitan House
1 Hagley Road
Five Ways
Birmingham B16 8TT
Tel: 021454 3808

Eastern Region
26/8 Bromham Road
Bedford MK40 2QP
Tel: 0234 45222

South Western Region
Ashlands House
Ashlands
Crewkerne
Somerset TA18 7LQ
Tel: 0460 73491

Sports Council for Wales
National Sports Centre for Wales
Sophia Gardens
Cardiff CF1 9SW
Tel: 0222 397571

Scottish Sports Council
Caledonia House
South Gyle
Edinburgh EH12 9DQ
Tel: 031 317 7200

Sports Council for Northern Ireland
2a Upper Malone Road
Belfast BT9 5LA
Tel: 0232 381222

Sports Bodies

Amateur Athletic Association
3 Duchess Place
Hagley Road
Birmingham B16 8NM
Tel: 021 456 4050

Amateur Swimming Association
Harold Fern House
Derby Square
Loughborough LE11 0AL
Tel: 0509 230431

Badminton Association of England
National Badminton Centre
Bradwell Road
Loughton Lodge
Milton Keynes
Bucks MK8 9LA
Tel: 0908 318685

British Association of Advisors and Lecturers in Physical Education
3 Nelson House
6 The Beacon
Exmouth
Devon EX8 2AG

British Association of Caving
Instructors
Coronet House
Queen Street
Leeds LS1 4PW

British Canoe Union
Adbotton Lane
West Bridgford
Nottingham NG2 5AS
Tel: 0602 821100

The British Horse Society
The British Equestrian Centre
Stoneleigh
Kenilworth
Warwickshire CV8 2LR
Tel: 0203 52241

British Mountaineering Council
Crawford House
Precinct Centre
Booth Street East
Manchester M13 9RZ
Tel: 061 273 5835

British Orienteering Federation
Riversdale
Dale Road North
Darley Dale
Matlock
Derbyshire DE2 2HX
Tel: 0629 734042

British Schools Canoeing Association
Flexel House
45–57 High Street
Addlestone
Weybridge
Surrey KT15 1JU
Tel: 0932 41341

British Ski Federation
Brocades House
Pyrford Road
West Byfleet
Surrey KT14 6RA
Tel: 0932 336488

British Sub Aqua Club
16 Upper Woburn
London WC1H 0QW
Tel: 071 837 9302

Mountain Walking Leadership Training Board
Crawford House
Precinct Centre
Booth Street East
Manchester M13 9RZ
Tel: 061 273 5839

National Caving Association
Vallefort Road
Stoke
Plymouth PL1 5PH

Rugby Football Union
Rugby Road
Twickenham
London TW1 1DZ
Tel: 081 892 8161

Scottish Mountain Leader Training Board
Caledonia House
South Gyle
Edinburgh EH12 9DQ
Tel: 031 317 7200

Swimming Teachers' Association
Anchor House
Bird Street
Walsall WS2 8HZ
Tel: 0922 645097

School Trips

There are a number of organizations that can help those organizing a school trip:

British Waterway Board
Melbury House
Melbury Terrace
London
NW1 6JY
Tel: 071 262 6711

Central Bureau for Educational Visits and Exchanges
Seymour Mews House
Seymour Mews
London W1H 9PE
Tel: 071 486 5101

The Council for Environmental Education
School of Education
University of Reading
London Road
Reading
Berks RG1 5AQ

Field Studies Council
Information Office
Preston Montford
Montford Bridge
Shrewsbury S74 1HW
Tel: 0743 850674

Medical Advisory Service for Travellers Abroad
London School of Hygiene and Tropical Medicine
Keppel Street
London WC1E 7HT
Tel: 071 631 4408

National Association for Outdoor Education
50 Highview Avenue
Grays
Essex RM17 6RU

National Association for Outdoor Education (Scotland)
57 Melville Street
Edinburgh EH3 7HL

National Youth Bureau
17—23 Albion Street
Leicester LE1 6GD
Tel: 0533 471200

PGL Schools Adventure
Adventure House
Station Street
Ross-on-Wye
Herefordshire HR9 7AH
Tel: 0989 764202

The Ramblers Association
1—5 Wandsworth Road
London SW8 2XX
Tel: 071 582 6878

The Royal Life Safety Society
Mounbatten House
Studley
Warwickshire B80 7NN
Tel: 052 785 3943

The School Journey Association of London
48 Cavendish Road
Clapham South
London SW12 0DG
Tel: 081 673 4899

Youth Hostels Association
Trevelyan House
8 St Stephen's Hill
St Albans
Hertfordshire A11 2DV
Tel: 0727 55215

Youth Hostels Association of Scotland
7 Glebe Crescent
Sterling
FK8 2JA
0786 72821

Youth Hostels Association of Northern Ireland
56 Bradbury Place
Belfast 7
Tel: 0232 224733

General Bibliography

Accidents

Basic Principles of Child Accident Prevention: A Guide to Action
Child Accident Prevention Trust
ISBN 1872071 007

AIDS

AIDS
Department of Employment
Aids: a guide to the law
Terrence Higgins Enterprises
52—54 Grays Inn Road
London WC1X 8JU

*AIDS — some questions and answers: facts for teachers, lecturers and youth
    workers*
Department of Education and Science

AIDS and Employment
Department of Employment and Health and Safety Executive

Children at school and problems related to AIDS
Department of Education and Science

AIDS: Guidance for Educational Establishments in Scotland
Scottish Education Department

Some facts about AIDS
Health Education Council

Alcohol, drug and solvent abuse

Alcohol in the workplace: a guide for employers
Department of Employment

Drug misuse and the workplace: a guide for employers
Department of Health and Social Security

Drug misuse: a basic briefing
Department of Health and Social Security

Drug misuse and the young: a guide for teachers and youth workers
DES Welsh Office

Prevention — Report of the Advisory Council on the Misuse of Drugs
Home Office
ISBN 0 11 340744 7

Young People and Drugs
Teachers Advisory Council on Alcohol and Drug Education
ISBN 0 950 6350 49

Drugs: what every caring parent should know
Institute of the Study for Drug Dependence

What to do about glue sniffing
Health Education Council

Information for children and parents
National Campaign against Solvent Abuse

Dealing with solvent misuse
Teachers Advisory Council on Alcohol and Drug Education

Child Abuse

*Working together: a guide to inter-agency co-operation for the protection of children
from abuse*
HMSO
ISBN 0 11 3211546

Fire Safety

*Fire Precautions Act 1971: guide for fire precautions in existing places of work that
require a fire certificate 1989*
HMSO
ISBN 0 11 3409060
Home Office/Scottish Home and Health Department

*Fire Precautions Act 1971: guide for fire precautions in existing places of work that
do not require a fire certificate*
HMSO
ISBN 0 11 340904 4

Fire Safety at Work 1989
HMSO
ISBN 0 11 340905 1
Home Office/Scottish Home and Health Department

First Aid

Emergency Aid in Schools
St John Ambulance Association

Essentials of First Aid
St John Ambulance Association
(also available from St John Ambulance is the Association's Three Cross Award
video)

First Aid Manual: Emergency Procedures for Everyone at Home or at Leisure
St John Ambulance Association
St Andrews Ambulance Association and the British Red Cross

Minor Illness: How to Treat it in the House
Health Education Authority

Motorists' First Aid
British Red Cross

Pocket First Aid
British Red Cross Society

Practical First Aid
British Red Cross Society

Road Safety

Code of Practice: The safety of passengers in wheelchairs on buses
Department of Transport Vehicle Standards and Engineering Division

The Highway Code: a Guide for Young Road Users
Local Road Safety Offices

An Introduction to Basic Mini-bus Driving
Royal Society for the Prevention of Accidents

Passenger Transport provided by Voluntary Groups
Department of Transport

School Trips

Medical Treatment During Visits Abroad
Leaflet SA 30
DHSS

Notice to Travellers – Health Protection
Leaflet SA35
DHSS

Out and About: A Teacher's Guide to Safe Practice Out of School
ISBN 0 416 07762 5
School Curriculum Development Committee

Outdoor Education, Safety and Good Practice in Guidelines for Teachers
Duke of Edinburgh's Award Office
5 Prince of Wales Terrace
Kensington
London
W8 5PG

School Travel and Exchange
Central Bureau of Educational Visits and Exchanges

The School Travel Organisers UK Handbook
Hobsons Publishing plc
18 Stackley Street
London WC2B 5LR

Science

Be Safe – Some Aspects of Safety in Science and Technology for Primary Schools
ISBN 0 86357 081 X
Association for Science Education

Guide to Safe Practices in Chemical Laboratories
ISBN 0 85186 4791
The Royal Society of Chemistry

Hazardous Chemicals – a Manual for School and Colleges
ISBN 0 05 003204 6
Scottish Schools Science Equipment Research Centre (SSSERC)

Hazards in the Chemical Laboratory
ISBN 0 85186 489 9
The Royal Society of Chemistry

Safeguards in the School Laboratory
ISBN 086357 0836
Association for Science Education

Safety in Biological Fieldwork: Guidance Notes for Codes of Practice
Institute of Biology

Safety in Biological Laboratories
ISBN 0 971 90833 9
Institute of Biology

Safety Manual
University of Manchester Institute of Science and Technology
PO Box 88
Manchester M60 1QD

Topics in Safety
ISBN 0 902786 87 3
Association for Science Education

Teachers' Unions

Each of the teachers' unions has produced health and safety literature for its own members, which in some cases is also available to nonmembers.

Assistant Masters and Mistresses Association
7 Northumberland Street
London WC2N 5DA
Tel: 071 930 6441

The Educational Institute of Scotland
46 Moray Place
Edinburgh EH36 6BH
Tel: 031 225 6244

National Association of Head Teachers
1 Heath Square
Boltro Road
Haywards Heath
West Sussex RH16 1BL
Tel: 0444 458133

National Association of Schoolteachers/Union of Women Teachers
Hillscourt Education Centre
Rose Hill
Rednall
Birmingham B45 8RS
Tel: 021 453 6150

National Union of Teachers
Hamilton House
Mabledon Place
London WC1H 9BD
Tel: 071 388 6191

Professional, Association of Teachers
2 St James' Court
Friar Gate
Derby DE1 1BT
Tel: 0332 372337
and

22 Rutland Street
Edinburgh
Scotland EH1 2AN
Tel: 031 229 7868

Secondary Heads Association
130 Regent Road
Leicester LE1 7PG
Tel: 0533 471797

Scottish Secondary Teachers Association
15 Dundas Street
Edinburgh EH3 6QG
Tel: 031 556 5919

British Standards

The British Standards Institution (BSI) produces standards and provides testing and quality assurance services for British industry in order that industry can meet the quality needs of the market place. The Head Office is at 2 Park Street, London W1A 2BS (Telephone: 071 629 9001).

The BSI's work on standards is financed by industry and a government grant as well as the sales of the standards themselves. In 1987/88 the total BSI turnover was £33 million. It is a member of the International Organization for Standardization (ISO) and the International Electrochemical Commission (IEC). More than 10,000 BSI publications are produced each year, including seventy new or revised standards, drawn up by bodies with a particular interest in the subject, such as manufacturers, users, research organizations, government departments or consumers. All standards are available for public comment before they are published.

The BSI catalogue, which is available for reference at most public libraries, contains details of all current British standards and others BSI publications. The catalogue is updated regularly by a sales bulletin. Telephone and postal enquiries should be directed to BSI's Sales Department, Linford Wood, Milton Keynes MK14 6LE (Telephone: 0908 320066). Details of subscriber membership of BSI are available from the Subscriptions Department. There is a discount of up to 50 per cent on British Standards for subscribers.

Relevant British Standards include:

BS415   Specification for safety requirements for mains operated electronic and related apparatus for household and similar general use
BS476   Fire tests on building materials and structures
BS638   Arc welding power sources, equipment and accessories

BS1542   Equipment for eye, face and neck protection against irradiation arising during welding and similar operations

BS1892   Specifications for gymnasium equipment
(Part 1 contains specifications of general requirements and Part 2 deals with particular apparatus, including wall bars, window ladders, ropes, boxes, bucks, trampolines and weight training equipment.)

BS2092   Specification for industrial eye protectors

BS2769   Portable electric motor operated tools

BS3456   Specification for safety of household electrical appliances

Part 101 general requirements

Part 102 section 102.15 appliances for heating water

Part 102 section 102.24 refrigerators and food freezers

Part 102 section 102.25 appliances for heating food by means of microwave energy

BS3999   Methods of ensuring the performance of household electrical appliances

BS4163   Recommendations for health and safety in workshops of schools and colleges

BS4402   Specification for safety requirements for laboratory centrifuges

BS5175   Specifications for safety of commercial electrical appliances using microwave energy for heating foodstuffs

BS5274   Specification for fire hose reels (water) before fixed installations

BS5306   Fire extinguishing installations and equipment on premises
(Part 0 is a guide to the selection of installed systems and other fire equipment. Part 1 deals with hydrant systems, hose reels and foam inlets. Part 2 covers sprinkler systems. Part 3 is a code of practice for the selection installation and maintenance of portable fire extinguishers. Part 4 deals with carbon dioxide systems. Part 5 deals with halon systems. Part 6 deals with foam systems. Part 7 deals with powder systems.)

BS5378   Safety signs and colours

BS5395   Code of practice for stairs

BS5423   Specification for portable fire extinguishers

BS5499   Fire safety signs, notices and graphic symbols

BS5588   Fire precautions in the design and construction of buildings (including a code of practice for means of escape for disabled people)

BS5665   Safety of toys code

BS5696   Play equipment intended for permanent installation outdoors

BS5726   Specification for microbiological safety cabinets

BS5873   Educational Furniture

BS6575   Specification for fire blankets

BS7272   Specification for safety caps for writing and marking instruments

BS7188   Methods of testing for impact absorbing surfaces

DD80   Laboratory Fume Cupboards

PP7303   Electrical and electronic graphical symbols for schools and colleges

PP7308   Engineering drawing practice for schools and colleges

PP7310   Anthropometics: an introduction for schools and colleges

CP209 part 1, care and maintenance of floor surfaces: wooden flooring

Special Needs

Association for all Speech Impaired Children
347 Central Markets
Smithfields
London EC1A 9NH
Tel: 071 236 6487

British Deaf Association
38 Victoria Place
Carlisle CA1 1HU
Tel: 0228 48844

British Diabetic Association
10 Queen Anne Street
London W1
Tel: 071 323 1531

British Epilepsy Association
Anstey House
40 Hanover Square
Leeds LS3 1BE
Tel: 0532 439393
(Epilepsy helpline 0532 439383; all calls charged at local rates)

British Sports Association for the Disabled
Mary Glen Haig Suite
34 Osnaburgh Street
London NW1 3ND
Tel: 071 383 7277

Centre for Studies of Integration in Education
The Spastics Society
16 Fitzroy Square
London W1P 5HQ
Tel: 071 387 9571

Cystic Fibrosis
Cystic Fibrosis Research Trust
5 Blyth Road
Bromley
Kent BR1 3RS
Tel: 081 464 7211

Disabled Living Foundation
380–384 Harrow Road
London W9 2HU
Tel: 071 289 6111

Down's Children's Association
12/13 Clapham Common South Side
London SW4
Tel: 071 720 0008

Handicapped Adventure Playground Association
Fulham Place
Bishops Avenue
London SW6 6EA
Tel: 071 736 4443

Handicapped Persons Research Unit
1 Coach Unit
1 Coach Lane
Coach Lane Campus
Newcastle-upon-Tyne NE7 7TW
Tel: 091 266 4061

Haemophilia Society
123 Westminster Bridge Road
London SE1
Tel: 071 928 2020

MENCAP
123 Golden Lane
London EC1Y 0RT
Tel: 071 253 9433

Muscular Dystrophy Group of Great Britain
Nattrass House
35 Macaulay Road
Clapham
London SW4 0QP
Tel: 071 720 8055

Multiple Sclerosis Society
25 Effie Road
London SW6
Tel: 071 736 6267

National Association for Remedial Education
2 Lichfield Road
Stafford ST17 4JX
Tel: 0785 46872

National Autistic Society
276 Willesden Lane
London NW2 5RB
Tel: 081 451 1114

National Council for Special Education
1 Wood Street
Stratford-upon-Avon CV37 6JE
Tel: 0789 205332

National Deaf Children's Society
45 Hereford Road
London W2
Tel: 071 229 9272

National Eczema Society
Tavistock House East
Tavistock Square
London WC1H 9SR
Tel: 071 388 4097

Partially Sighted Society
Queens Road
Doncaster DN1 2NX
Tel: 0302 323132

Riding for the Disabled Association
Avenue R
National Agricultural Centre
Kenilworth
Warwickshire
Tel: 0203 696510

Royal Association for Disablement and Rehabilitation (RADAR)
25 Mortimer Street
London W1N 8AB
Tel: 071 637 5400

Royal National Institute for the Blind
224 Great Portland Street
London W1N 6AA
Tel: 071 388 1266

Royal National Institute for the Deaf
105 Gower Street
London WC1E 6AH
Tel: 071 387 8079

SENSE (National Deaf-Blind and Rubella Association)
311 Gray's Inn Road
London WC1X 8PT
Tel: 071 636 5020

SKILL (National Bureau for Students with Disabilities)
336 Brixton Road
London SW9 7AA
Tel: 071 274 0565

Spastic Society
12 Park Crescent
London W1N 4EQ
Tel: 071 636 5020

Voluntary Council for Handicapped Children
8 Wakely Street
Islington
London EC1V 7QE
Tel: 071 278 9441

Bibliography

Active Games for Children with Movement Problems (1987)
A. Brown
Paul Chapman
London

Outdoor Pursuits for Disabled People (1981)
N. Croucher
Disabled Living Foundation London

PE for the Physically Handicapped
DES London

Physical Education for Children with Special Needs in Mainstream Education
British Association of Advisers and Lecturers in Physical Education (BAALPE)

Physical Education for Special Needs (1979)
L. Groves
Cambridge University Press
Cambridge

Sports and Recreation Provision for Disabled People (1984)
N. Thompson
Disabled Living Foundation
London

Swimming and Epilepsy (1987)
British Epilepsy Association

Wheelchair Proficiency Award Scheme
Safety Education Department
RoSPA

CASES

LEGISLATION

INDEX